FRAUD—THE COMPANY LAW BACKGROUND

FRAUD—THE COMPANY LAW BACKGROUND

FRAUD LAW—BOOK THREE

Sally Ramage

iUniverse, Inc.
New York Lincoln Shanghai

FRAUD—THE COMPANY LAW BACKGROUND

FRAUD LAW—BOOK THREE

Copyright © 2006 by Sally Ramage

All rights reserved. No part of this book may be used or reproduced by any means, graphic, electronic, or mechanical, including photocopying, recording, taping or by any information storage retrieval system without the written permission of the publisher except in the case of brief quotations embodied in critical articles and reviews.

iUniverse books may be ordered through booksellers or by contacting:

iUniverse
2021 Pine Lake Road, Suite 100
Lincoln, NE 68512
www.iuniverse.com
1-800-Authors (1-800-288-4677)

This book is not intended as a source of advice to any person. The author does not accept any responsibility for anything that any person does or does not do as a result of reading this book. The law in this book is the United Kingdom law as at 2005.

ISBN-13: 978-0-595-38135-7 (pbk)
ISBN-13: 978-0-595-82503-5 (ebk)
ISBN-10: 0-595-38135-9 (pbk)
ISBN-10: 0-595-82503-6 (ebk)

Printed in the United States of America

Dedication

Dedicated to all the fraud investigators I have had the privilege to be with at conferences and seminars., sharing their experiences and trade secrets. They are a special people with integrity and patience. This book is also dedicated to those whose encouragement means so much to me—to Roderick Ramage for all his help and to Dr Alex Costa, Principal Counsel, IFC Legal Department—IFC is the International Finance Corporation, the private investment arm of the World Bank. Dr Costa wrote to me after reading some of my work and has been an enormous source of advice and encouragement to me. I am at once humbled that my work has caught the attention of someone so knowledgeable and I am also determined to write these books in plain English for everybody to understand.

As a young person, my interest and dedication was directed to pure mathematics and I taught myself advanced level mathematics by reading the books and following the syllabus from the External Board of London University. I used to buy algebra books with my pocket money; I loved maths so much. I have always wished to remain an academic and law did not interest me until I faced injustice, dishonesty and deceit. It is a bad, bad world we live in. The saying "Great oaks from little acorns grow" applies to bad things as well as good things; it is why I am dedicated to writing in the way I do, so that someone, somewhere, might be stirred on to do the right thing. Like a long distance runner, I pass on my baton to the next person. Read it, understand it and run with it!

Sally Ramage

Table of Contents (outline)

Table of Contents (detailed) ix
Table of Statutes xv
Table of Cases xvii
Preface To Book Three—Fraud Law xxi

1—Introduction and Overview 1
2—Formation and Constitution 16
3—Share Capital 55
4—Meetings 79
5—Directors, Secretary and Powers of Companies and Officers 106
6—Borrowings, Securities and Debentures 129
7—Administration, Winding Up and Striking Off 142
8—Reconstruction, Merger, Acquisitions, Disposals 156
9—Crime 177
10—Partnerships 192
11—Revision—Law Cases 208
12—More Revision 225
13—Ready-Made Companies 237

Appendix 1—The Carr Case 239
Appendix 2—Assets and Share Acquisitions 249
Appendix 3—the Cushnie case 253
Appendix 4—United Kingdom: Document Destruction in Business 257
Appendix 5—Directors' Pensions 261
Appendix 6—Limited Liability Partnerships Act 2000 267
Appendix 7—the Guinness Case 281
Appendix 8—Business Names Act 1985 287
Appendix 9—Company Law Reform Bill 293
Appendix 10—Buchler and another v Talbot and others (the Leyland Daf case) 297
Appendix 14—Disqualification of Directors 299
Appendix 11—Culpability of Professionals 313
Appendix 12—Directors' Misrepresentation 315
Appendix 13—Directors Use of Company Funds 319
Appendix 14—Disqualification of Directors 321

Appendix 15—Professionals as Fraudsters 323
Appendix 16—Solicitors' Fraud in Probate Cases 325
Appendix 17—More Solicitors as Fraudsters 327
Appendix 18—Stop Press 329

Table of Contents (detailed)

Table of Contents (outline) vii
Table of Statutes xv
Table of Cases xvii
Preface To Book Three—Fraud Law xxi

1—Introduction and Overview 1
    1 Contracts—nature 2
    2 Contracts—characteristics 3
    3 Legal structure—sole trader, partnership, company 4
    4 Legal structure—Natural persons 5
    5 Legal structure—Registered Companies 6
    6 Who's who in a registered company? 7
    7 Who does what in a registered company? 8
    8 How are companies formed? 9
    9 M & A of A 10
    10 How a company operates 11
    11 Directors—definitions 12
    12 Directors—capacity to bind company 13
    13 Directors—personal liability 14
    14 Dissolution 15

2—Formation and Constitution 16
    1 Promoters 17
    2 Promoters powers & obligations—3rd parties 18
    3 promoters—personal gain 19
    4 Documents to register a company 20
    5 effect of registration 21
    6 effect of M of A of Association 22
    7 Articles of association 23
    8 Contents of articles of association 24
    9 Change of M & A of Association 25
    10 Which version of Table A 26
    11 Names 27
    12 Change and use of name 28
    13 Ready-made companies 29
    specimen formation agreement 30
    Table B-A private company limited by shares 35
    MEMORANDUM OF ASSOCIATION 35
    A NOVATION AGREEMENT 52

3—Share Capital 55
    1 What is capital? 56
    2 A company's capital 57
    3 Corporate organisation chart 58
    4 Shares and ordinary shares 59
    5 Preference shares 60
    6 Glossary—capital and shares 61
    7 Issue of shares—allotment, start 63
    8 Issue of shares—allotment, continued 64
    9 Increases in capital 65
    10 Other changes of capital—except reduction 66
    11 Reduction of capital 67
    12 Purchase of own shares—main 68
    13 Purchase of own shares and redemption—other 69
    14 Financial assistance 70
    15 Financial assistance—continued 71
    16 Class rights 72
    17 Dividends—what permitted? 73
    18 Dividends—how? 74
    19 Transfers of shares 75
    20 Illustrations of changes in capital 76

4—Meetings 79
    1 Introduction 80
    2 Shareholders' meetings 81
    3 Annual general meeting 82
    4 extraordinary general meetings & resolutions 83
    5 Elective resolutions 84
    6 special notice 85
    7 short notice & written resolutions 86
    8 Procedure—1 87
    9 Procedure—2 88
    10 Directors' meetings—standard 89
    11 Directors' meetings—alternatives 90
    Notice of annual general meeting1 91
    Notice of extraordinary general meeting13 94
    Basic form of members' written resolution19 96
    Meetings, Notice and Resolutions 98
    Company law: how many votes do you need? 101
    Test Yourself. 104

5—Directors, Secretary and Powers of Companies and Officers 106
    1 Who does what in a registered company? 107
    2 Directors and secretary—what and why? 108
    3 Appointment of directors 109

- 4 Retirement by rotation and removal 110
- 5 Removal by members—registration 111
- 6 Small print detail 112
- 7 Division and exercise of power 113
- 8 What can the company do? Ultra vires 114
- 9 Authority of directors 115
- 10 Directors' duties 116
- 11 Director's interest in shares 117
- 12 Dealings between director and company 118
- 13 Disqualification and personal liability 119
- Duties of Company Secretary 120
- Minutes of first meeting of directors after incorporation 121
- Test Yourself 125
- Test Yourself some more… 127

6—Borrowings, Securities and Debentures 129
- 1 Sources of capital (reminder from classes 2 & 1) 130
- 2 What do the parties want? 131
- 3 Loans—characteristics 132
- 4 Security—characteristics 133
- 5 Typical debenture 134
- 6 Multiple lenders 135
- 7 Power to borrow and mortgage 136
- 8 Companies Act requirements 137
- 9 Preference under Insolvency Act 1986 138
- 10 Avoidance under Insolvency Act 1986 139
- 11 Enforcement of charges 140
- Test Yourself 141

7—Administration, Winding Up and Striking Off 142
- 1 Overview 143
- 2 Receivership 144
- 3 Administration & floating charges 145
- 4 Appointment of administrator 146
- 5 Purpose, duration and effect of administration 147
- 6 Administrative receivers qualification and duties 148
- 7 Voluntary arrangements 149
- 8 Members' voluntary winding up 150
- 9 Creditors' voluntary liquidation 151
- 10 Liquidation by the court 152
- 11 Liquidation procedures 153
- 12 Dissolution and striking off 154
- Test Yourself 155

8—Reconstruction, Merger, Acquisitions, Disposals 156
- 1 What and why? 157

    2 How? 158
    3 Subsidiaries and divisions 159
    4 Part owned subsidiaries 160
    5 Shareholder leaving—Table A unaltered 161
    6 Shareholder leaving—special articles 162
    7 Sale of or by private company 163
    8 Sale of shares in private company 164
    9 Sale of business in private company 165
    10 Offer for shares—"takeovers" 166
    Specimen clause in share sale agreement setting out what is to be done on completion ... 167
    Business Sale Agreement—short form (eg) between connected companies: no warranties ... 169
    Warranties by sellers of shares or assets 175
    Test Yourself 176

9—Crime 177
    1 Reminder—How many votes? 178
    2 The Rule in Foss v Harbottle ([Fo1843] 2 Hare 461) 179
    3 Fraud on minority (company) 180
    4 Fraud on minority (individual) 181
    5 "Oppression of minority" 182
    6 Quasi partnership 183
    7 More examples—prejudicial conduct 184
    8 More examples—valuation 185
    9 Some statutory offences 186
    10 Crimes—whose mind? 187
    11 Crime—controlling minds 188
    12 Theft from company 189
    13 Corporate manslaughter 190
    Test Yourself 191

10—Partnerships 192
    1 Legal structure—sole trader, partnership, company 193
    2 Legal structure—natural persons 194
    3 Agency—meaning 195
    4 Agency—authority, enforcement &c 196
    5 Partnership—characteristics 197
    6 Partners and 3rd parties 198
    7 Partners—terms with each other 199
    8 Partnership names 200
    9 Small print 201
    10 Termination—grounds 202
    11 Termination—consequences 203
    12 Limited Partnerships 204
    13 Limited Liability Partnerships—introduction 205
    14 LLPs—formation and regulation 206

Test Yourself	207
11—Revision—Law Cases	**208**
Separate Legal Personality	208
Separate Legal Personality	209
Separate Legal Personality	209
Lifting The Veil of Incorporation	210
Promoters—definition	211
Promoters—personal profit	211
Promoters' contracts	211
Articles of association—contract between members	212
Memorandum of association—objects—*ultra vires* or outside the terms of business	213
Memorandum of association—Multiple Separate Objects	213
Memorandum of Association—Ancillary to Business	214
Memorandum of Association—Borrowing not an Object	214
Articles of association—Effect on earlier contract	215
Company's name—passing off	215
Class Rights—whether varied	216
Class Rights—rights to individual	216
Class Rights—shareholders' agreement	217
Directors—remuneration, unlawful distribution	217
Role of Chairman	218
Members' Resolutions—deemed to be passed	218
Members' Resolutions without meeting	219
Directors—Balance of power with General Meeting	219
Directors—Removal—Weighted Voting	220
Directors Contract over 5 years	220
Directors' powers—Managing Director's remuneration	221
Directors—unauthorised remuneration	221
Directors—level of skill	222
Director—level of skill—reliance on others	222
Directors' Duties—Conflict of Duty and Interest	223
Directors' Duties—Best Interests of Company, not themselves	223
Directors—account for profit	224
Director—disqualification	224
12—More Revision	**225**
Shares—nature of	225
Liquidation—fraudulent trading	225
Fraudulent trading—meaning	226
Director's duty of skill	226
Fraudulent trading—company secretary not liable	227
Wrongful trading—meaning	227
Wrongful trading—disregard to CA requirements	227
Debenture—nature of	228

Debenture—nature of—example 228
Debenture—floating charge—nature of 228
Retention of title 229
Debenture—date of registration 229
Debenture—registration out of time 230
Debenture—automatic crystallisation of floating charge 230
The rule in Foss v Harbottle 231
Foss v Harbottle exception—benefit of company 231
Winding up—just and equitable 232
Winding up—prejudicial conduct (dividends not increased) 233
Winding up—price for shares 233
Criminal liability—criminal liability—brain or nerve centre 234
Criminal liability—an employee who acts for the company 235
Civil liability—actual fault or privity 235
Shareholder's theft from company 236
13—Ready-Made Companies 237

Appendix 1—The Carr Case 239
Appendix 2—Assets and Share Acquisitions 249
Appendix 3—the Cushnie case 253
Appendix 4—United Kingdom: Document Destruction in Business 257
Appendix 5—Directors' Pensions 261
Appendix 6—Limited Liability Partnerships Act 2000 267
Appendix 7—the Guinness Case 281
Appendix 8—Business Names Act 1985 287
Appendix 9—Company Law Reform Bill 293
Appendix 10—Buchler and another v Talbot and others (the Leyland Daf case) 297
Appendix 14—Disqualification of Directors 299
Appendix 11—Culpability of Professionals 313
Appendix 12—Directors' Misrepresentation 315
Appendix 13—Directors Use of Company Funds 319
Appendix 14—Disqualification of Directors 321
Appendix 15—Professionals as Fraudsters 323
Appendix 16—Solicitors' Fraud in Probate Cases 325
Appendix 17—More Solicitors as Fraudsters 327
Appendix 18—Stop Press 329

Table of Statutes

Companies Act 1862	326
Companies Act 1883	321, 326, 329
Preferential Payments in Bankruptcy Act 1888	321, 326, 329
Partnership Act 1890	8, 204
Stamp Act 1891	286
Merchant Shipping Act 1894	243
Limited Partnerships Act 1907	8, 204, 214, 283
Companies (Consolidation) Act 1908	324
New Zealand Workers Compensation Act 1922	220
Trustee Act 1925	273, 304
Companies Act 1929	335
Finance Act 1930	183
Companies Act 1948	103, 302, 324, 331, 334
Theft Act 1968	196, 199, 249
Attachment of Earnings Act 1971	270
Local Government Act 1972	290, 311
Mental Health Act 1983	50
Business Names Act 1985	196, 210, 305
Companies Act 1985	7, 27, 39, 81, 82, 103, 110, 125, 135, 186, 196, 203, 229, 295, 298, 305, 332, 335, 345
Financial Services Act 1986	261
Companies Act 1989	89, 196
Chargeable Gains Act 1992	283

Social Security Contributions and Benefits Act 1992	286
Pension Schemes Act 1993	271
Local Government etc (Scotland) Act 1994	290
Companies Act 1995	12, 23
Pensions Act 1995	270
Employment Rights Act 1996	176
Contracts (Rights of Third Parties) Act 1999	21, 34, 57
Financial Services and Markets Act 2000	68, 293
Limited Liability Partnerships Act 2000	8, 204, 215, 276, 277
Enterprise Act 2002	153, 320
Company Law Reform Bill 2005	1, 312

Table of Cases

Aberdeen Railway Co v Blaikie Bros (1854) 2Eq Rep 1281, [1843-60] All ER Rep 249, HL	232
Aluminium Industrie Vaassen BV v Romalpa Aluminium Ltd [1976] 2 All ER 52, CA	237
Ashbury Railway Carriage & Iron Co Ltd v Riche [1875] LR 7 HL 653	222
Attorney General's Ref (No.2 of 1982) [1984] QB 624	244
Barings plc (No 5), Re, [2000] 1 BCLC 523, CA	233
Barleycorn Enterprises Ltd, Re, Mathias and Davies (a firm) v Down [1970] 2 All ER 155	1, 148, 317, 324
BAT v McCabe	267
Bell Houses Ltd v City Wall Properties Ltd [1966] 2 All ER 674, CA	223
Bird Precision Bellows Ltd, Re, [1986] Ch 658, [1985] All ER 523, CA	195, 241
Bradbury v English Sewing Cotton Co Ltd [1923] AC 744, [1923] All ER Rep 427, HL	234
Brightlife Ltd, Re, [1987] Ch 200, [1986] 3 All ER 673	238, 324
British India Steam Navigation Co v IRC (1881) 7 QBD 165	237
Brocklesby v Armitage & Guest (a firm) [2001] a All ER 172, CA	268
Brown v British Abrasive Wheel Co. [1919] 1 Ch 290	191
Bushell v Faith [1970] AC 1099, [1970 1 All ER 53, HL	229
Cane v Jones [1980] 1 All ER 533	228
Clemens v Clemens Bros Ltd [1976] 2 All ER 268	191
Cook v Deeks [1916] 1 AC 554, [1916-17] All ER Rep 286, PC	189
Cotman v Brougham [1918] AC 514, HL	223
Craven Ellis v Canons Ltd [1936] 2 KB, CA	229
Cumbrian Newspapers Group Ltd v Cumberland and Westmorland Herald Newspaper and Printing Co Ltd [1986] Ch1, [1986] 2 All ER 816	225
Daniels v Daniels [1978] Ch D 406	190

Case	Page
DHN Food Distributors Ltd v Tower Hamlets London Borough Council [1976] 1 WLR 852, CA	220
Director General of Fair Trading v Pioneer Concrete (UK) Ltd and Another (In Re Supply of Ready Mixed Concrete (No 2)) (1995) HL [1995] 1 AC 456	197, 243
Director of Public Prosecutions v Kent & Sussex Contractors Ltd [1944] IRLC 310, CA	198
DKG Contractors Ltd, Re, [1990] BCC 903	236
Dorchester Finance Co Ltd v Stebbings (1977) [1989] BCLC 498	231
Douglas and others v Hello ! Ltd and others (No 3) [2005] 4 All ER 128	267
Duomatic Ltd, Re, [1969] 2 Ch 365, [1969] 1 All ER 161	227, 229
Ebrahimi v Westbourne Galleries [1973] 3 AC 360	193, 240
Eric Holmes (Property) Ltd, Re, [1965] 2 All ER 333	238
Exxon Corp v Exxon Insurance Consultants International Ltd [1982] 1 Ch 119, [1981] 3 All ER 241, CA	224
Foss v Harbottle [1843] 2 Hare 461	189, 239, 240
Gluckstein v Barnes [1900] AC 240, HL	221
Guinness plc v Saunders [1990] 2 AC 663, [1990] 1 All ER 652	230, 268, 295
Halt Garage (1964) Ltd, Re, [1982] 3 All ER 1016	226
Harman v BML Group Ltd, [1994] 2 BCLC 674, CA	226
Heron International Ltd v Lord Grade and Associated Communications Corpn plc [1983] BCLC 244, CA	232
Industrial Development Consultants Ltd v Cooley [1972] 2 All ER 162	233
Infabrics Ltd v Jaytex Ltd [1982] AC 1, [1981] a All ER 1057	268
Introductions Ltd, Re, Introductions Ltd v National Provincial Bank Ltd [1970] Ch 199, [1969] 1 All ER 887, CA	223
Jefferson Ltd v Bhetcha [1979] 1 WLR 898	252, 257
John v Rees and others [1969] 2 All ER 274	227
Landauer v Comins & Co (1991) Times, 7 August	268
Lee v Lee's Air Farming ltd [1961] AC 12, [1960] 3 All ER 420, PC	220
Lennard's Carrying Co. Ltd v Asiatic Petroleum Company [1915] AC 705, [1914-15] All ER Rep 280, HL	198, 243
Levy v Abercorris Slate and Slab Co [1887] 37 ChD 260, [1886-90] All ER Rep 509	236

Case	Page
Leyland Daf Ltd, Re, Buchler and another v Talbot and another and others [2004] UKHL 9, [2004] BCLC 281	1, 148, 317
Lighting World Limited, Re, Jibrail v Secretary of State (Jacob J, 20.11.97 unreported)	252, 257
Loftus (deceased), Re, Green and others v Gaul and others [2005] 2 All ER 700	268
Logicrose v Southend United Football Club Ltd [1988] 1 WLR 1265, (1988) Times, 5 November	268
Macaura v Northern Assurance Co [1925] AC 619, [1925] All ER Rep 51, HL	219
Maidstone Buildings Provisions Ltd, Re, [1971] 3 All ER 363	235
Norman v Theodore Goddard (a firm) [1991] BCLC 1028	231, 235
O'Neill and another v Phillips and others [1999] 2 All ER 961, HL	194
P & O European Ferries (Dover) Ltd [1991] 93 Cr App Rep 72	200
Patrick & Lyon Ltd, Re, [1933] Cg 786, [1933] All ER Rep 590	234
Phonogram Ltd v Lane [1982] QB 938, CA	221
Produce Marketing Consortium Ltd (No 2), Re, [1989] BCLC 520	236
Quin & Axtens Ltd v Salmon [1909] AC 442, HL	228
R v Appleyard [1985] 81 Cr App Rep, CA	199
R v British Steel plc [1994] IRLR 310, CA	200
R v Cushnie and another 2005] EWCA Crim 962	262
R v F Howe & Son (Engineering) Ltd [1999] 2 All ER 249 (Great Western Trains – Southall crash)	200
R v Kirkup, Mitchell, Mason and Chapman [2004]	341
R v Panel on Takeovers and Mergers, ex p Fayed [1992] BCLC 938	251
Rayfield v Hands [1958] 2 All ER 194	221
Salomon v Salomon & Co Ltd [1897] AC 33, HL	219, 220
Sam Weller Ltd, Re, [1990] Ch 682	194, 241
Secretary of State v Crane [2001] 2 BCLC 222	251, 251
Southern Foundries (1926) Ltd v Shirlaw [1940] AC 701, [1940] 2 All ER 445, HL	224
Stein v Blake [1998] CA	240
Telomatic, Re, [1994]	238
Tesco Supermarkets Ltd v Nattrass [1972] AC 153	197, 199, 242, 244

TransTec plc, Re, Secretary of State for Trade and Industry v Carr and others, [2005] EWHC 1723 (Ch)	247
Versailles Trade Finance Ltd v Clough [2001] EWCA Civ 1509	252, 262
Virdi v Abbey Leisure Ltd [1990] BCLR 342, CA	195
Wallersteiner v Moir (No.2) [1975] 1 All ER 849, CA	190
Whaley Bridge Calico Printing Co v Green [1880] 5 QBD 109	221
White v Bristol Aeroplane Ltd [1953] Ch 65, [1953] a All ER 40, CA	225
William Leitch Brothers, Re, (No 1) [1931] AC 99, [1930] All ER Rep 754, HL	234
Wright and another v Atlas Wright (Europe) Ltd [1999] 2 BCLC 301, CA	229
Yorkshire Woolcombers Association Ltd, Re, Houldsworth v Yorkshire Woolcombers Association Ltd, [1903] 2 Ch 284, CA	237

Preface To Book Three—Fraud Law

UNDERSTANDING CORPORATE FRAUD by Sally Ramage

Feedback from readers of Books One and Two of this set, *Serious Fraud & Current Issues* and *Fraud and The Serious Fraud Office* made me realise that any person reading and learning about laws and strategies to combat fraud needs this Book Three, *Understanding Corporate Fraud*, in order to grasp where the fraud is taking place and what the United Kingdom's Companies Act has to say about it.

Whenever a serious corporate fraud is discovered and prosecuted, there usually follows liquidation and bankruptcy. It is as well to understand how these laws kick in well before the criminal charges are brought against the fraudsters.

Book Three—Fraud Law consists of 13 chapters which are straightforward bare bones company law. A sound basic grounding in company law gives the understanding of where to look if one suspects foul play. Finally, a set of appendices relevant to several chapters are included so as not to distract the flow of the basic company law ground rules.

Even in the legal profession, the knowledge about law relating to serious financial fraud is mostly non-existent. The ignorance is profound. It is the only stimulus for writing this set of books, urgent and vitally necessary, as water is to a man who has survived a volcano and who has not had a drop of water for seven days. He will die soon without a little water. So it is in global serious financial fraud. This Book Three concentrates on United Kingdom law as at November 2005.

We live in an age of specialization, which is both a good and a bad thing. Now that organised crime is apparent in unthinkable areas as well as in finance, steel, oil, people trafficking and drugs, there is a desperate need for all-round knowledge as well as experts in order to decipher the strategies used by organised crime, strategies that are beyond belief. To fight fraud successfully, one must think "outside the box".

The latest buzz in the financial world is *securitization*, a most complex subject; but it has sent the bankruptcy experts reeling and has upset all the carefully laid theories about bankruptcy. On 3rd November the UK's Department of Trade and Industry announced the company law bill. The Company Law Reform Bill contains sweeping changes to simplify and improve company law. Clause 868 of the Bill will reverse the House of Lords' decision in <u>Buchler and another v Talbot and another and others [2004] UKHL 91.</u> This is the famous "Leyland Daf Ltd" Case, which overturned the Barleycorn case precedent in respect of the meaning of "priority" and "preference". This Bill, if passed, will again enable liquidators to be free to investigate thoroughly, knowing that their full fees will be met. In legal words, assets of a company subject to a floating charge will be available to fund the general expenses of liquidation. After this Act is passed, secondary legislation will be passed to allow the liquidator and the floating charge holder to agree the quantum of general liquidation expenses. The practical reality of how such an agreement will be set out legally has not been sorted yet, although this is the reality in practice already, at present. Whether this will reveal the complexities of securitized debts is not known. Whether this will have the power to unravel such securitizations is not known. But whatever happens, a sound grasp of company law is absolutely necessary in order to combat serious financial fraud, because the cunning of the fraudster is unstoppable. CORPORATE FRAUD IS A CRIME.

The legal phrase *caveat emptor* or *buyer beware* is as pertinent today as in ages past. Law is divorced from morality and *caveat emptor* is the disclaimer. Today one can buy hedge funds online and lose all one's savings in one fell stroke of a computer keystroke. It is legal to buy hedge funds in this way, yet hardly anyone, including many finance professionals, understand what hedge funds are. *The Times Newspaper* on 21 November 2005 states in an article titled "Investors advised to stay out of hedge funds":

> *"The most authoritative academic study into the burgeoning hedge fund industry [in the UK] has advised individual investors to shun or minimise their exposure…"*

It is high risk but it is legal, like online gambling. In America, the Securities Exchange Commission's Annual Report each year shows that most frauds are in this area and perpetrated by broker-dealers and investment advisors, on-line and otherwise. It is to be noted that only the USA had capital adequacy legislation for banks and the rest of the world's is more recent. Because the USA's Enron is well publicised, it does not mean that there is no such large-scale fraud elsewhere. There must be many more Parmalats and Enrons in other developed countries; how the law's financial culture deals with them is the difference between their publication or not.

As I have said before, "There is nothing new under the sun"—and I am thereby repeating an old saying. We have had wrongful trading and fraudulent trading for ages. In 1706, Daniel Defoe said in the *Reveiw,* March 1706, [sic]:

> *"If breaking early, and stopping in time, is the way to prevent numerous and fatal bankrupts; an Act, TO Encourage Men to stop in time and be Honest, must be Entitled, to all the Preventive Quality, the other pretends to; when men know, that if they stop in time, they will be well Treated, that on a fair Surrender, they shall be us'd like Honest Men, and Pitty'd as Men of Misfortune; they have, then no Temptation no Excuse to run to all manner of Lengths."*

Three hundred years later, the former Director of the Serious Fraud Office, Rosalind Wright, also said much the same, that many serious corporate frauds are committed by professionals who think they will trade themselves out of trouble but, like a persistent gambler, become deeper and deeper embedded in the fraud that began with lofty ideals, such as keeping the workforce, instead of putting their hands up in surrender. But we must not forget the Parmalat types who blatantly sign off false accounts to line their own pockets with millions even billions of pounds, US dollars or Euros.

Finally, a huge thank you goes to Roderick Ramage for his kind permission to use some of his precedents. I am very grateful to be able to include them in this book. An equally huge thank you goes to my dear friend, Dr Alexandre Costa, a World Bank Senior Legal Consultant, Principal Counsel, IFC-International Finance—Chase Manhattan Bank. As I bounce my findings around those on the same wave-length as myself, people in the high echelons of the legal sphere as well as ordinary non-legal folk, law students and the uneducated, I know that we are closer to cracking corporate fraud—and writing simple books like these are a start. Let the lay person understand the law, please—this is my aim.

Even as the Police everywhere rely heavily on the help of the public, the financial authorities should rely on the public and the public can be simply informed without taking anything away from the essence of the law.

Company Law

1—Introduction and Overview

Contents

1 Contracts—nature
2 Contracts—characteristics
3 Legal structure—sole trader, partnership or corporation
4 Legal structure—natural persons
5 Legal structure—registered companies
6 Who is whom in a company?
7 Who does what in a company?
8 How are companies formed?
9 Memorandum and articles of association
10 How does a company operate?
11 Directors—definitions
12 Directors—capacity to bind company
13 Directors—personal liability
14 Dissolution

1 Contracts—nature

What is it?		civil legal obligation
		between two or more parties
How formed	1	conduct
	or	
	2	verbal
Verbal contacts	1	oral
	or	
	2	written
Written contracts	1	simple
	or	
	2	deed
Deed		must say so
	and	
		witness

2   Contracts—characteristics

three essentials   1   offer & acceptance

    2   consideration

    3   intention to create legal relations

exception   deeds

    1   no consideration

    2   limitation 12 not 6 years

variation   unilateral   impossible

unless   expressly provided for in the contract

so   by agreement ie new contract

3   Legal structure—sole trader, partnership, company

two basic categories	natural persons
	legal persons

natural persons	sole traders
	partnerships

legal persons	corporations sole
	corporation aggregate

normally — Companies Act 1985

possibilities:

public	private
limited liability	unlimited liability
quoted	unquoted
shares	guarantee

in commercial reality — company limited by shares "ltd" or "plc"

4   Legal structure—Natural persons

natural persons		main characteristics
	1	not a legal person
	2	no independent legal existence
	3	no legal personality
	4	not registered
	5	totality of the rights and duties of individual partners
	6	unlimited liability

ie   sole trader   or   partnership

the two questions
- "Who are the parties?"
- "What is the contract?"

Partnership Act 1890
Limited Partnerships Act 1907
Limited Liability Partnerships Act 2000

5 Legal structure—Registered Companies

Registered companies		some characteristics
Legal personality		Legal person
		independent of its member(s)
Shares		one of one penny
		to millions
		owned by shareholder(s)
Limited liability		liability limited to unpaid capital
Name	include	Limited or Ltd
	or	Public Limited Company or plc
		(almost) free choice
		changeable
Registered number	the loadstone	unique and unchangeable

6 Who's who in a registered company?

The main parties in a company

1	company
2	shareholders (members)
3	directors (members of the board)

Other parties

4	company secretary
5	auditor
6	third parties / the public
7	employees

7 Who does what in a registered company?

Directors	
	manage the company
	answerable to the company
	may work for it but not necessarily
	risk of personal liability, but normally none

Members	
	provide the capital
	owners (of the company, not the business)
	entitled to profits
	normally no liability
	appoint the directors
	no powers of management

Employees	
	work
	but (in theory) not manage

8 How are companies formed?

three essential documents	1	memorandum of association
	2	notice on form 10 1 directors 2 secretary 3 registered office
	3	declaration on form 12 compliance with the requirements of the Companies Act 1995
extra		articles of association
M & A of A		Memorandum and Articles of Association

9 M & A of A

	Memorandum of Association
1	Name of the company
2	that the company is public (if relevant)
2, 3	Country of the Registered Office
3, 4	objects
4, 5	that the liability of the members is limited (if relevant)
5, 6	Authorised Capital

	Articles of Association
eg	Issue of Shares
and	Classes of shares
ie	Transfers of shares
	General meetings and Votes
	Appointment and removal of Directors
	Directors' meetings and votes
	Dividends

NB — Table A

10 How a company operates

Meetings and resolutions

Members' meetings

| Annual General Meeting (agm) |
| Extraordinary General Meeting (egm) |

Members' Resolutions

| Ordinary |
| 14 days notice |
| Simple Majority ie 50% + 1 vote |

| Extraordinary |
| 14 days notice |
| Majority of 75% |

| Special |
| 21 days notice |
| Majority of 75% |

Directors' meetings

| Reasonable Notice |

Directors' resolutions

| simple majority |

Nb

| short notice |
| written resolutions |

11 Directors—definitions

NB | only one board of directors | no supervisory board

Statutory meaning — Director within the Companies Act (registered at Companies House)

Everyday meaning — Manager, chief, leader, eg research director, marketing director etc

Responsibility — only to the company

ie — all the shareholders (present and future)

no — personal interest / interest of any particular member or majority of members

to repeat — only to the company

exception 1 — interests of employees on cessation or transfer of business or on winding up

exception 2 — interests of creditors if unequivocal likelihood of insolvency or inanity to pay debts

12 Directors—capacity to bind company

capability to bind the company

theoretically and in general	only the whole board

exception 1	managing directors

exception 2	expressly authorised

exception 3	implied power

ostensible and actual authority

actual	(as above)	bind the company

ostensible authority		binds the company against 3rd parties

but	between the director and the company	action for lack of authority

but	between director and 3rd parties	perhaps risk of liability

13 Directors—personal liability

Personal liability of Directors and Liabilities

- fraud

- incorrect company name
  - incorrect description
  - no Ltd or Plc

- unauthorised transactions
  - if no ostensible or actual authority

- in liquidation
  - fraudulent trading
  - wrongful trading

MORAL — for directors as well as 3rd parties

- whether doubtful or careful
  - eg
    - express authority
    - decision of the board

14 Dissolution

The end of a company

either — winding up

or — striking off

winding up — 1 compulsory

or

2 voluntary

voluntary — 1 members

or

2 creditors

or

3 administrator

2—Formation and Constitution

Contents

1 Promoters
2 Promoters powers & obligations
3 Promoters persona gain
4 Documents to register a company
5 Effect of registration
6 Effect of M & A of A
7 Articles of association
8 Contents of articles of association
9 Changes of M & A of A
10 Which version of Table A
11 Names
12 Change and use of name
13 Ready-made companies

formation agreement

Table B (memorandum of association)

Table A

articles of association

novation agreement

paper

1   Promoters

NB — | corporate legal personality |

therefore — | pre-incorporation nothing |

but — | you want to set thing up, start, prepare |

so — | "Promoters" |

eg — | plan the business

find shareholders

find directors

buy property

make contracts

form the company |

2 Promoters powers & obligations—3rd parties

pre-incorporation

company	others
none	contract

who?

> C19 professional company promoters
> Now prospective shareholders

after incorporation

> fiduciary
>
> no profit on sale
>
> no secret profit
>
> contracts not binding on company

NB 1	do not contract
NB 2	novation
NB 2	Contracts (Rights of Third Parties) Act 1999

3 promoters—personal gain

fiduciary   ie

> less than a trustee
>
> may make profit if disclosed

eg

> sells own property to company

if not disclosed to company and

bought before start of promotion

> C may rescind
> if C keeps property
> no profit but damages

but if

bought after

> C may rescind
> if C keeps property
> & recover profit

4 Documents to register a company

three essential documents

ss 1, 10(1)	1	memorandum of association
s 10	2	notice on form 10 1 directors 2 secretary 3 registered office
s 11	3	declaration on form 12 compliance with the requirements of the Companies Act 1995

extra

Ss 7, 8, 10(1)	articles of association
s 117	PLC cannot do business without certificate (£50k allotted ¼ paid)
M & A of A	memorandum and articles of association

5 effect of registration

duties of Registrar

s 12(1)   if | satisfied that all the requirements of the Act have been complied with |

s 12(2)   must | register the memorandum and association (if any) |

s 13 (1),(2) | give a certificate that the company is incorporated |

S 711 | publish in London Gazette |

effect of incorporation

s 13(3) | subscribers to memorandum and all others who become members are a body corporate |

s 13(4) | that body capable of exercising functions with liability limited |

s 13(5) | persons named on form 10 are its first officers |

6 effect of M of A of Association

the M & A of A

s 14 — bind — **the company and its members**

(ie present and future)

s 14 — as if — **as if they had been signed [and sealed] by each member**

(ie as a deed)

s 14 — **and contained covenants by each member to observe their provisions**

except

s 16 — **member not bound by alteration if increases liability unless agrees in writing**

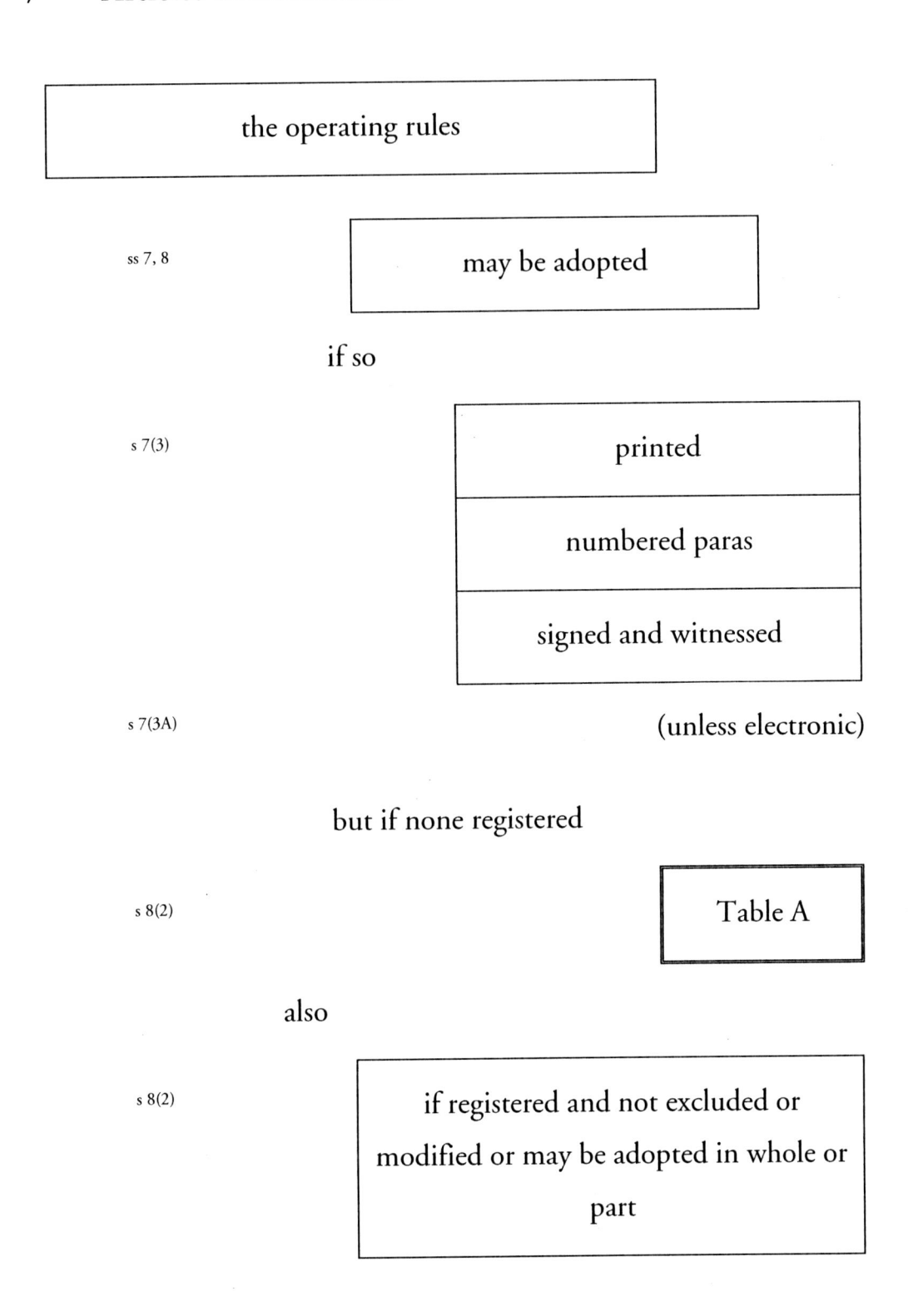

7 Articles of association

	the operating rules

ss 7, 8

	may be adopted

if so

s 7(3)

printed
numbered paras
signed and witnessed

s 7(3A) (unless electronic)

but if none registered

s 8(2)

Table A

also

s 8(2)

if registered and not excluded or modified or may be adopted in whole or part

8 Contents of articles of association

used to be scheduled to Companies Acts 1854 to 1948

now as prescribed

Companies (Tables A to F) Regulations 1985, SI 1985/805

As amended by

Companies (Tables A to F) (Amendment) Regulations 1985, SI 1985/1052

Companies Act 1985 (Electronic Communications) Order 2000, SI 2000/3373

list of contents headings

- share capital
- share certificates
- lien
- calls on shares and forfeiture
- transfer of shares
- transmission of shares
- alteration of share capital
- purchase of own shares
- general meetings
- notice of general meetings
- proceedings at general meetings
- votes of members
- number of directors
- alternate directors
- powers of directors
- delegation of directors' powers
- appointment and retirement of directors
- disqualification and removal of directors
- remuneration of directors
- directors' expenses
- directors' appointments and interests
- directors' gratuities and pensions
- proceedings of directors
- secretary
- minutes
- the seal
- dividends
- accounts
- capitalisation of profits
- notices
- winding up
- indemnity

9 Change of M & A of Association

(ss 4, 17)	memo	cannot be altered
s 4	except	objects
s 17		could be in arts
s 9	articles	special resolution
ss 5, 6	procedure	objection to change of objects
s 18		registration
ss 18, 19, 20		copies as altered
s 3A	NB why bother?	objects can be any trade or business

10 Which version of Table A

seven versions from 1856 to 1985

| previous version | 1948 |

seven amendments

| present version | 1985 |

two amendments

so which one?

s 8(2)

> the one in force at date of company's registration

s 9

exceptions

| special resolution |
| service of notices |

s 370(2)

SI 1985/805

NB also Tables B to F

11 Names

s 2(1)	Stated in memorandum	
Ss 25, 26	must end with "Ltd" etc	see below
ss 30,31	(unless exempt)	
s 26	prohibited	same as another
		criminal
		offensive
		Government
SI 1981/1685		as prescribed

the endings

Limited (Ltd) or Public Limited Company or (PLC)
Cyfyngedig (CYF) or Cwmni Cyfyngedig Cyhoeddus (CCC)

12 Change and use of name

S 28(1)	may change by	special resolution
s 28(2),(3)	must change	too alike
		misleading info
S 28(6)	registrar must	register new name
		issue altered certificate
S 28(6)	effective	date of certificate
s 34	offence & fine	use of "Ltd" etc if not limited
s 348	display etc	place of business
s 349		correspondence
ss 350, 36A		seal (if any)
s 351	particulars	correspondence

13 Ready-made companies

already has	1	certificate of incorporation
	2	name
	3	M & A of A
ss 288	4	"statutory books"
s 288	5	director(s)
s 288	6	secretary
s 287	7	registered office
s 22	8	member(s)
ss 88, 183 — query		shares allotted?

must change	5, 6, 7, 8
may change	2, 3
problems	whether shares allotted
	whether traded

specimen formation agreement

THIS FORMATION AGREEMENT made in year 2005

between

A   (*name*) of (*address*) ("Mr A");

B   (*name*) ("Mr B") of (*address*) ("Mr B");

C   (*name*) of (*address* ("Ms C");

D   (*name*) of (*address*) ("Mr D");

E   (*name*) of (*address*) ("Ms E");

F   (*name*) of (*address*) ("Ms F") and

G   (*name*) of (*address*) ("Mr G").

definitions

1   In this agreement the following terms shall have the following meanings.

"Business"	means the business of (*describe*) now carried on by Mr A and Mr B in partnership and intended to be carried on by the Company.
"Company"	means (*name*) Ltd, which is a company intended to be registered in England and Wales.
"Deceased"	means the first of the parties to die.
"Effective Notice"	means written notice served by the Personal Representatives on the Survivor or by the Survivor on the Personal Representatives during the lifetime of the Survivor and on or before whichever is the later of the expiry of
	– (*number*) months after the Deceased's death, or
	– (*number*) months after the grant of representation to the Deceased's estate.
"Personal Representatives"	means the Deceased's personal representatives.
"Sale Agreement"	means an agreement dated intended to be made in agreed terms between Mr A, Mr B and the Company for the sale to the Company of the Business.

"Sale Shares"	means all of the shares in the Company's capital registered in the Deceased's name at the date of his or her death.
"Survivor"	means the survivor of the parties after the Deceased's death.
"in agreed terms"	in relation to any document means in the form of the draft annexed to this agreement or as agreed in writing between the parties.
"3rd Parties Act"	means the Contracts (Rights of Third Parties) Act 1999.
"comply with"	includes "observe and perform".
"parties"	means the parties to this agreement.

formation of company

2.1 [The parties (*or*) Mr A] shall procure the incorporation of the Company.

2.2 The Company shall be called "(*name*) Ltd" if that name is available for registration or by such other available name as is agreed between the parties or in default of agreement as Mr A selects.

2.3 The Company's memorandum and articles shall be in agreed terms and shall be subscribed by the parties or their respective nominees each of whom shall agree in the memorandum to take one share of £1 in the Company's capital.

directorships etc

3 Each of the parties shall procure that:

(a) they are appointed the sole first directors of the Company and that ("Mr B") is appointed its first secretary;

(b) while any of them is a member of the Company he or she shall not be removed from office as director or secretary of the Company;

(c) Mr A shall be the Company's chairman [so long as he remains a director of the Company (*or*) until the close of the first annual general meeting whereupon the ("Mr B") shall be chairman and from then on each of them shall be the Company's chairman in alternate years starting at the close of each annual general meeting]; and

(d) so long as any of the parties is entitled to remain a director of the Company in accordance with this clause the maximum number of directors of the Company shall not exceed [seven].

Share Capital

4.1 The Company's authorised share capital shall be £[.....] ([.....] *pounds*) divided into (*number*) £1 shares.

4.2 Immediately on the incorporation of the Company each of the parties shall deliver to the Company an application for the allotment to him or her for cash at par of (*number*) ordinary £1 shares in the Company's capital and a cheque for the amount payable.

(*or*)

4.2 Immediately on the incorporation of the Company each of the parties shall deliver to the Company an application for the allotment to him or her for cash at par of the number of shares shown opposite his or her name in the following table and a cheque for the amount also shown in the table.

Name	number of shares	amount payable
Mr A	(*number*)	£[.....] ([.....] *pounds*)
Mr B	(*number*)	£[.....] ([.....] *pounds*)
Ms C	(*number*)	£[.....] ([.....] *pounds*)
Mr D	(*number*)	£[.....] ([.....] *pounds*)
Ms E	(*number*)	£[.....] ([.....] *pounds*)
Ms F	(*number*)	£[.....] ([.....] *pounds*)
Mr G	(*number*)	£[.....] ([.....] *pounds*)

4.3 The Company shall make simultaneous allotments of the shares to be allotted to the parties respectively in accordance with clause (4.2).

Loans

5.1 Immediately on the incorporation of the Company Mr A shall advance to the Company £(.....) ((.....) pounds) in cash (and Mr B shall advance to the Company £(.....) ((.....) pounds) in part consideration for the sale of the Business pursuant to the Sale Agreements.

5.2 The Company shall issue to the maker of each advance within (*number*) days of today a debenture in agreed terms.

Sale agreement

6.1 The applications for shares and making of the advances shall be conditional on Mr A, Mr B and the Company entering into the Sale Agreement within (*number*) weeks of the incorporation of the Company but shall be otherwise unconditional.

6.2 As soon as each of the parties has applied to the Company for shares and paid the subscription money for them in accordance with clause 4.2, Mr A and Mr B and the Company shall enter into the Sale Agreement.

Service agreements

7.1 As soon as is reasonably practicable after incorporation of the Company the parties shall procure that the Company offers to Mr A, Mr B, Ms E, Ms F and Mr G a service agreement in agreed terms for their services as executive directors of the Company under and offers to Ms C and Mr D contract in agreed terms for their services as non-executive directors.

7.2 Each of the parties undertakes to execute the respective agreement offered under clause 7.1.

Share sale on death

8 On the death of the first to die of the parties the Personal Representatives may by an Effective Notice require the Survivor to buy or be required by the Survivor to sell the Sale Shares to the Survivor in either case free from encumbrances. The provisions in the Company's articles of association shall apply mutatis mutandis to any sale of shares under this clause.

Performance of obligations

9 Each of the parties shall do everything for the time being in his or her power to procure that anything intended or needed to be done under this agreement by a person who is not a party to it is done promptly by that person.

Costs

10 The Company shall bear the reasonable costs fees and expenses of respectively (*name*) & Co of (*address*) (solicitors) and (*name*) & Co of (*address*) (accountants) relating to the preparation of this agreement, the formation of the Company and the sale of the business to the Company.

Notices

11.1 Any notice given under this deed shall be in writing and may be served

- personally,

- by registered or recorded delivery mail,

- by facsimile or other electronic transmission (confirmed by post), or

- by any other means which any party specifies by notice to the others.

11.2 Each party's address for the service of notice shall be (his) above mentioned address or such other address as (he) specifies by notice to the others.

11.3 A notice shall be deemed to have been served:

- if it was served in person, at the time of service,

- if it was served by post, 48 hours after it was posted, and

- if it was served by facsimile or other electronic transmission, at the time of transmission.

11.4 It shall be sufficient to prove that the notice was left, or that the envelope containing the notice was properly addressed and posted, or that the applicable means of telecommunication was addressed and dispatched and dispatch of the transmission was confirmed by a report or copy generated by the sender's machine by which the transmission was made.

Third parties

12.1 Pursuant to s1(2)(a) of the 3rd Parties Act the parties intend that no term of this agreement may be enforced by a third party (as defined in that Act) except the Company.

12.2 The parties reserve the right pursuant to s 2(3)(a) of the 3rd Parties Act to rescind or vary the contract made by this agreement without the consent of the Company.

Interpretation

13.1 References to any party to this agreement shall where the context permits include his successors in title.

13.2 In this agreement:

(a) words expressed in any gender shall where the context so requires or permits include any other gender;

(b) words expressed in the singular shall where the context so requires or permits include the plural; and

(c) where any party is more than one person

- that party's obligations in this agreement shall take effect as joint and several obligations,

- anything in this agreement which applies to that party shall apply to all of those persons collectively and each of them separately, and

- the benefits contained in this agreement in favour of that party shall take effect as conferred in favour of all of those persons collectively and each of them separately.

12.5 Nothing contained in this agreement shall in any way affect the free exercise by any person of his powers as a director of the Company.

(*attestation as a deed*)

Table B-A private company limited by shares
MEMORANDUM OF ASSOCIATION

1. The company's name is 'The South Wales Motor Transport Company, Cyfyngedig'.
2. The company's registered office is to be situated in Wales.
3. The company's objects are the carriage of passengers and goods in motor vehicles between such places as the company may from time to time determine and the doing of all such other things as are incidental or conducive to the attainment of that object.
4. The liability of the members is limited.
5. The company's share capital is 50,000 pounds divided into 50,000 shares of one pound each.

We, the subscribers to the memorandum of association, wish to be formed into a company pursuant to this memorandum; and we agree to take the number of shares shown opposite our respective names.

Names and Addresses of Subscribers	Number of shares taken by each Subscriber
1. Thomas Jones, 138 Mountfield Street, Tredegar.	1
2. Mary Evans, 19 Merthyr Road, Aberystwyth.	1
Total shares taken	2

Dated

Witness to the above signatures.

Anne Brown, 'Woodlands', Fieldside Road, Bryn Mawr

Table A   Regulations for Management of a Company Limited by Shares

Table A as prescribed by the Companies (Tables A to F) Regulations 1985, SI 1985/805, amended by the Companies (Tables A to F) (Amendment) Regulations 1985, SI 1985/052) and the Companies Act 1985 (Electronic Communications) Order 2000, SI 2000/3373.

Interpretation

1. In these regulations:-

"the Act" means the Companies Act 1985 including any statutory modification or re-enactment thereof for the time being in force

"the articles" means the articles of the company

"clear days" in relation to the period of a notice means that period excluding the day when the notice is given or deemed to be given and the day for which it is given or on which it is to take effect

"executed" includes any mode of execution

"office" means the registered office of the company

"the holder" in relation to shares means the member whose name is entered in the register of members as the holder of the shares

"the seal" means the common seal of the company

"secretary" means the secretary of the company or any other person appointed to perform the duties of the secretary of the company including a joint, assistant or deputy secretary

"the United Kingdom" means Great Britain and Northern Ireland

Unless the context otherwise requires, words or expressions contained in these regulations bear the same meaning as in the Act but excluding any statutory modification thereof not in force when these regulations become binding on the company.

Share Capital

2. Subject to the provisions of the Act and without prejudice to any rights attached to any existing shares, any share may be issued with such rights or restrictions as the company may by ordinary resolution determine.

3. Subject to the provisions of the Act, shares may be issued which are to be redeemed or are to be liable to be redeemed at the option of the company or the holder on such terms and in such manner as may be provided by the articles.

4. The company may exercise the powers of paying commissions conferred by the Act. Subject to the provisions of the Act, any such commission may be satisfied by the payment of cash or by the allotment of fully or partly paid shares or partly in one way and partly in the other.

5. Except as required by law, no person shall be recognised by the company as holding any share upon any trust and (except as otherwise provided by the articles or by law) the company shall not be bound by or recognise any interest in any share except an absolute right to the entirety thereof in the holder.

Share Certificates

6. Every member, upon becoming the holder of any shares, shall be entitled without payment to one certificate for all the shares of each class held by him (and, upon transferring a part of his holding of shares of any class, to a certificate for the balance of such holding) or several certificates each for one or more of his shares upon payment for every certificate after the first of such reasonable sum as the directors may determine.

Every certificate shall be sealed with the seal and shall specify the number, class and distinguishing numbers (if any) of the shares to which it relates and the amount or respective amounts paid up thereon. The company shall not be bound to issue more than one certificate for shares held jointly by several persons and delivery of a certificate to one joint holder shall be a sufficient delivery to all of them.

7. If a share certificate is defaced, worn-out, lost or destroyed, it may be renewed on such terms (if any) as to evidence and indemnity and payment of the expenses reasonably incurred by the company in investigating evidence as the directors may determine but otherwise free of charge, and (in the case of defacement or wearing-out) on delivery up of the old certificate.

Lien

8. The company shall have a first and paramount lien on every share (not being a fully paid share) for all moneys (whether presently payable or not) payable at a fixed time or called in respect of that share. The directors may at any time declare any share to be wholly or in part exempt from the provisions of this regulation. The company's lien on a share shall extend to any amount payable in respect of it.

9. The company may sell in such manner as the directors determine any shares on which the company has a lien if a sum in respect of which the lien exists is presently payable and is not paid within fourteen clear days after notice has been given to the holder of the share or to the person entitled to it in consequence of the death or bankruptcy of the holder, demanding payment and stating that if the notice is not complied with the shares may be sold.

10. To give effect to a sale the directors may authorise some person to execute an instrument of transfer of the shares sold to, or in accordance with the directions of, the purchaser. The title of the transferee to the shares shall not be affected by any irregularity in or invalidity of the proceedings in reference to the sale.

11. The net proceeds of the sale, after payment of the costs, shall be applied in payment of so much of the sum for which the lien exists as is presently payable, and any residue shall (upon surrender to the company for cancellation of the certificate for the shares sold and subject to a like lien for any moneys not presently payable as existed upon the shares before the sale) be paid to the person entitled to the shares at the date of the sale.

Calls on Shares and Forfeiture

12. Subject to the terms of allotment, the directors may make calls upon the members in respect of any moneys unpaid on their shares (whether in respect of nominal value or premium) and each member shall (subject to receiving at least fourteen clear days' notice specifying when and where payment is to be made) pay to the company as required by the notice the amount called on his shares. A call may be required to be paid by instalments. A call may, before receipt by the company of any sum due thereunder, be revoked in whole or part and payment of a call may be postponed in whole or part. A person upon whom a call is made shall remain liable for calls made upon him notwithstanding the subsequent transfer of the shares in respect whereof the call was made.

13. A call shall be deemed to have been made at the time when the resolution of the directors authorising the call was passed.

14. The joint holders of a share shall be jointly and severally liable to pay all calls in respect thereof.

15. If a call remains unpaid after it has become due and payable the person from whom it is due and payable shall pay interest on the amount unpaid from the date it became due and payable until it is paid at the rate fixed by the terms of allotment of the share or in the notice of the call or, if no rate is fixed, at the appropriate rate (as defined by the Act) but the directors may waive payment of the interest wholly or in part.

16. An amount payable in respect of a share on allotment or at any fixed date, whether in respect of nominal value or premium or as an instalment of a call, shall be deemed to be a call and if it is not paid the provisions of the articles shall apply as if that amount had become due and payable by virtue of a call.

17. Subject to the terms of allotment, the directors may make arrangements on the issue of shares for a difference between the holders in the amounts and times of payment of calls on their shares.

18. If a call remains unpaid after it has become due and payable the directors may give to the person from whom it is due not less than fourteen clear days' notice requiring payment of the amount unpaid together with any interest which may have accrued. The notice shall name the place where payment is to be made and shall state that if the notice is not complied with the shares in respect of which the call was made will be liable to be forfeited.

19. If the notice is not complied with any share in respect of which it was given may, before the payment required by the notice has been made, be forfeited by a resolution of the directors and the forfeiture shall include all dividends or other moneys payable in respect of the forfeited shares and not paid before the forfeiture.

20. Subject to the provisions of the Act, a forfeited share may be sold, re-allotted or otherwise disposed of on such terms and in such manner as the directors determine either to the person who was before the forfeiture the holder or to any other person and at any time before sale, re-allotment or other disposition, the forfeiture may be cancelled on such terms as the directors think fit. Where for the purposes of its disposal a forfeited share is to be transferred to any person the directors may authorise some person to execute an instrument of transfer of the share to that person.

21. A person any of whose shares have been forfeited shall cease to be a member in respect of them and shall surrender to the company for cancellation the certificate for the shares forfeited but shall remain liable to the company for all moneys which at the date of forfeiture were presently payable by him to the company in respect of those shares with interest at the rate at which interest was payable on those moneys before the forfeiture or, if no interest was so payable, at the appropriate rate (as defined in the Act) from the date of forfeiture until payment but the directors may waive payment wholly or in part or enforce payment without any allowance for the value of the shares at the time of forfeiture or for any consideration received on their disposal.

22. A statutory declaration by a director or the secretary that a share has been forfeited on a specified date shall be conclusive evidence of the facts stated in it as against all persons claiming to be entitled to the share and the declaration shall (subject to the execution of an instrument of transfer if necessary) constitute a good title to the share and the person to whom the share is disposed of shall not be bound to see to the application of the consideration, if any, nor shall his title to the share be affected by any irregularity in or invalidity of the proceedings in reference to the forfeiture or disposal of the share.

Transfer of Shares

23. The instrument of transfer of a share may be in any usual form or in any other form which the directors may approve and shall be executed by or on behalf of the transferor and, unless the share is fully paid, by or on behalf of the transferee.

24. The directors may refuse to register the transfer of a share which is not fully paid to a person of whom they do not approve and they may refuse to register the transfer of a share on which the company has a lien. They may also refuse to register a transfer unless:-

- it is lodged at the office or at such other place as the directors may appoint and is accompanied by the certificate for the shares to which it relates and such other evidence as the directors may reasonably require to show the right of the transferor to make the transfer;

- it is in respect of only one class of shares; and

- it is in favour of not more than four transferees.

25. If the directors refuse to register a transfer of a share, they shall within two months after the date on which the transfer was lodged with the company send to the transferee notice of the refusal.

26. The registration of transfers of share or of transfers of any classes of shares may be suspended at such times and for such periods (not exceeding thirty days in any year) as the directors may determine.

27. No fee shall be charged for the registration of any instrument of transfer or other document relating to or affecting the title to any share.

28. The company shall be entitled to retain any instrument of transfer which is registered, but any instrument of transfer which the directors refuse to register shall be returned to the person lodging it when notice of the refusal is given.

Transmission of Shares

29. If a member dies the survivor or survivors where he was a joint holder, and his personal representatives where he was a sole holder or the only survivor of joint holders, shall be the only persons recognised by the company as having any title to his interest; but nothing herein contained shall release the estate of a deceased member from any liability in respect of any share which had been jointly held by him.

30. A person becoming entitled to a share in consequence of the death or bankruptcy of a member may, upon such evidence being produced as the directors may properly require, elect either to become the holder of the share or to have some person nominated by him registered as the transferee. If he elects to become the holder he shall give notice to the company to that effect. If he elects to have another person registered he shall execute an instrument of transfer of the share to that person. All the articles relating to the transfer of shares shall apply to the notice or instrument of transfer as if it were an instrument of transfer executed by the member and the death or bankruptcy of the member had not occurred.

31. A person becoming entitled to a share in consequence of the death or bankruptcy of a member shall have the rights to which he would be entitled if he were the holder of the share, except that he shall not, before being registered as the holder of the share, be entitled in respect of it to attend or vote at any meeting of the company or at any separate meeting of the holders of any class of shares in the company.

Alteration of Share Capital

32. The company may by ordinary resolution:-

- increase its share capital by new shares of such amount as the resolution prescribes;

- consolidate and divide all or any of its share capital into shares of larger amount than its existing shares;

- subject to the provisions of the Act, sub-divide its shares, or any of them, into shares of smaller amount and the resolution may determine that, as between the shares resulting from the sub-division, any of them may have any preference or advantage as compared with the others; and

- cancel shares which, at the date of the passing of the resolution, have not been taken or agreed to be taken by any person and diminish the amount of its share capital by the amount of the shares so cancelled.

33. Whenever as a result of a consolidation of shares any members would become entitled to fractions of a share, the directors may, on behalf of those members, sell the shares representing the fractions for the best price reasonably obtainable to any person (including, subject to the provisions of the Act, the company) and distribute the net proceeds of sale in due proportion among those members, and the directors may authorise some person to execute an instrument of transfer of the shares to, or in accordance with the directions of, the purchaser. The transferee shall not be bound to see to the application of the purchase money nor shall his title to the shares be affected by any irregularity in or invalidity of the proceedings in reference to the sale.

34. Subject to the provisions of the Act, the company may by special resolution reduce its share capital, any capital redemption reserve and any share premium account in any way.

Purchase of Own Shares

35. Subject to the provisions of the Act, the company may purchase its own shares (including any redeemable shares) and, if it is a private company, make a payment in respect of the redemption or purchase of its own shares otherwise than out of distributable profits of the company or the proceeds of a fresh issue of shares.

General Meetings

36. All general meetings other than annual general meetings shall be called extraordinary general meetings.

37. The directors may call general meetings and, on the requisition of members pursuant to the provisions of the Act, shall forthwith proceed to convene an extraordinary general meeting for a date not later than eight weeks after receipt of the requisition. If there are not within the United Kingdom sufficient directors to call a general meeting, any director or any member of the company may call a general meeting.

Notice of General Meetings

38. An annual general meeting and an extraordinary general meeting called for the passing of a special resolution or a resolution appointing a person as a director shall be called by at least twenty-one clear days' notice. All other extraordinary general meetings shall be called by at least fourteen clear days' notice but a general meeting may be called by shorter notice if it is so agreed:-

- in the case of an annual general meeting, by all the members entitled to attend and vote thereat; and

- in the case of any other meeting by a majority in number of the members having a right to attend and vote being a majority together holding not less than ninety-five per cent, in nominal value of the shares giving that right.

The notice shall specify the time and place of the meeting and the general nature of the business to be transacted and, in the case of an annual general meeting, shall specify the meeting as such.

Subject to the provisions of the articles and to any restrictions imposed on any shares, the notice shall be given to all the members, to all persons entitled to a share in consequence of the death or bankruptcy of a member and to the directors and auditors.

39. The accidental omission to give notice of a meeting to, or the non-receipt of notice of a meeting by, any person entitled to receive notice shall not invalidate the proceedings at that meeting.

Proceedings at General Meetings

40. No business shall be transacted at any meeting unless a quorum is present. Two persons entitled to vote upon the business to be transacted, each being a member or a proxy for a member or a duly authorised representative of a corporation, shall be a quorum.

41. If such a quorum is not present within half an hour from the time appointed for the meeting, or if during a meeting such a quorum ceases to be present, the meeting shall stand adjourned to the same day in the next week at the same time and place or [to] such time and place as the directors may determine.

42. The chairman, if any, of the board of directors or in his absence some other director nominated by the directors shall preside as chairman of the meeting, but if neither the chairman nor such other director (if any) be present within fifteen minutes after the time appointed for holding the meeting and willing to act, the directors present shall elect one of their number to be chairman and, if there is only one director present and willing to act, he shall be chairman.

43. If no director is willing to act as chairman, or if no director is present within fifteen minutes after the time appointed for holding the meeting, the members present and entitled to vote shall choose one of their number to be chairman.

44. A director shall, notwithstanding that he is not a member, be entitled to attend and speak at any general meeting and at any separate meeting of the holders of any class of shares in the company.

45. The chairman may, with the consent of a meeting at which a quorum is present (and shall if so directed by the meeting), adjourn the meeting from time to time and from place to place, but no business shall be transacted at an adjourned meeting other than business which might properly have been transacted at the meeting had the adjournment not taken place. When a meeting is adjourned for fourteen days or more, at least seven clear days' notice shall be given specifying the time and place of the adjourned meeting and the general nature of the business to be transacted. Otherwise it shall not be necessary to give any such notice.

46. A resolution put to the vote of a meeting shall be decided on a show of hands unless before, or on the declaration of the result of, the show of hands a poll is duly demanded. Subject to the provisions of the Act, a poll may be demanded:-

- by a chairman; or

- by at least two members having the right to vote at the meeting; or

- by a member or members representing not less than one-tenth of the total voting rights of all the members having the right to vote at the meeting; or

- by a member or members holding shares conferring a right to vote at the meeting being shares on which an aggregate sum has been paid up equal to not less than one-tenth of the total sum paid up on all the shares conferring that right; and

- a demand by a person as proxy for a member shall be the same as a demand by the member.

47. Unless a poll is duly demanded a declaration by the chairman that a resolution has been carried or carried unanimously, or by a particular majority, or lost, or not carried by a particular majority and an entry to that effect in the minutes of the meeting shall be conclusive evidence of the fact without proof of the number or proportion of the votes recorded in favour of or against the resolution.

48. The demand for a poll may, before the poll is taken, be withdrawn but only with the consent of the chairman and a demand so withdrawn shall not be taken to have invalidated the result of a show of hands declared before the demand was made.

49. A poll shall be taken as the chairman directs and he may appoint scrutineers (who need not be members) and fix a time and place for declaring the result of the poll. The result of the poll shall be deemed to be the resolution of the meeting at which the poll was demanded.

50. In the case of an equality of votes, whether on a show of hands or on a poll, the chairman shall be entitled to a casting vote in addition to any other vote he may have.

51. A poll demanded on the election of a chairman or on a question of adjournment shall be taken forthwith. A poll demanded on any other question shall be taken either forthwith or at such time and place as the chairman directs not being more than thirty days after the poll is demanded. The demand for a poll shall not prevent the continuance of a meeting for the transaction of any business other than the question on which the poll was demanded. If a poll is demanded before the declaration of the result of a show of hands and the demand is duly withdrawn, the meeting shall continue as if the demand had not been made.

52. No notice need be given of a poll not taken forthwith if the time and place at which it is to be taken are announced at the meeting at which it is demanded. In any other case at least seven clear days' notice shall be given specifying the time and place at which the poll is to be taken.

53. A resolution in writing executed by or on behalf of each member who would have been entitled to vote upon it if it had been proposed at a general meeting at which he was present shall be as effectual as if it had been passed at a general meeting duly convened and held and may consist of several instruments in the like form each executed by or on behalf of one or more members

Votes of Members

54. Subject to any rights or restrictions attached to any shares, on a show of hands every member who (being an individual) is present in person or (being a corporation) is present by a duly authorised representative, not being himself a member entitled to vote, shall have one vote and on a poll every member shall have one vote for every share of which he is the holder.

55. In the case of joint holders the vote of the senior who tenders a vote, whether in person or by proxy, shall be accepted to the exclusion of the votes of the other joint holders; and seniority shall be determined by the order in which the names of the holders stand in the register of members.

56. A member in respect of whom an order had been made by any court having jurisdiction (whether in the United Kingdom or elsewhere) in matters concerning mental disorder may vote, whether on a show of hands or on a poll, by his receiver, curator bonis or other person authorised in that behalf appointed by that court, and any such receiver, curator bonis or other person may, on a poll, vote by proxy. Evidence to the satisfaction of the directors of the authority of the person claiming to exercise the right to vote shall be deposited at the office, or at such other place as is specified in accordance with the articles for the deposit of instruments of proxy, not less than 48 hours before the time appointed for holding the meeting or adjourned meeting at which the right to vote is to be exercised and in default the right to vote shall not be exercisable.

57. No member shall vote at any general meeting or at any separate meeting of the holders of any class of shares in the company, either in person or by proxy, in respect of any share held by him unless all moneys presently payable by him in respect of that share have been paid.

58. No objection shall be raised to the qualification of any voter except at the meeting or adjourned meeting at which the vote objected to is tendered, and every vote not disallowed at the meeting shall be valid. Any objection made in due time shall be referred to the chairman whose decision shall be final and conclusive.

59. On a poll votes may be given either personally or by proxy. A member may appoint more than one proxy to attend on the same occasion.

60. The appointment of a proxy shall be executed by or on behalf of the appointor and shall be in the following form (or in a form as near thereto as circumstances allow or in any other form which is usual or which the directors may approve).

"   PLC/Limited

I/We,   , of   being a member/members of the above-named company, hereby appoint

of   , or failing him,

of   , as my/our proxy to vote in my/our name[s] and on my/our behalf at the annual/extraordinary general meeting of the company to be held on   20 , and at any adjournment thereof.

Signed on   20 ."

61. Where it is desired to afford members an opportunity of instructing the proxy how he shall act the appointment of a proxy shall be in the following form (or in a form as near thereto as circumstances allow or in any other form which is usual or which the directors may approve).

"   PLC/Limited

I/We   , of   , being a member/members of the above named company, hereby appoint

of   , or failing him,

of   , as my/our proxy to vote in my/our name[s] and on my/our behalf at the annual/extraordinary general meeting of the company, to be held on   20 , and at any adjournment thereof.

This form is to be used in respect of the resolutions mentioned below as follows:

Resolution No. 1 *for *against

Resolution No. 2 *for *against.

*Strike out whichever is not desired.

Unless otherwise instructed, the proxy may vote as he thinks fit or abstain from voting.

Signed this   day of   20 ."

62. The appointment of a proxy and any authority under which it is executed or a copy of such authority certified notarially or in some other way approved by the directors may:

(a) in the case of an instrument in writing be deposited at the office or at such other place within the United Kingdom as is specified in the notice convening the meeting or in any instrument of proxy sent out by the company in relation to the meeting not less than 48 hours before the time for holding the meeting or adjourned meeting at which the person named in the instrument proposes to vote; or

(aa) in the case of an appointment contained in an electronic communication, where an address has been specified for the purpose of receiving electronic communications:

(i) in the notice convening the meeting; or

(ii) in any instrument of proxy sent out by the company in relation to the meeting; or

(iii) in any invitation contained in an electronic communication to appoint a proxy issued by the company in relation to the meeting

be received at such address not less than 48 hours before the time for holding the meeting or adjourned meeting at which the person named in the appointment proposes to vote;

(b) in the case of a poll taken more than 48 hours after it is demanded, be deposited or received as aforesaid after the poll has been demanded and not less than 24 hours before the time appointed for the taking of the poll; or

(c) where the poll is not taken forthwith but is taken not more than 48 hours after it was demanded, be delivered at the meeting at which the poll was demanded to the chairman or to the secretary or to any director;

and an appointment of proxy which is not deposited delivered or received in a manner so permitted shall be invalid. In this regulation and the next "address" in relation to electronic communications, includes any number or address used for the purposes of such communications.

63. A vote given or poll demanded by proxy or by the duly authorised representative of a corporation shall be valid notwithstanding the previous determination of the authority of the person voting or demanding a poll unless notice of the determination was received by the company at the office or at such other place at which the instrument of proxy was duly deposited or, where the appointment of the proxy was contained in an electronic communication, at the address at which such appointment was duly received before the commencement of the meeting or adjourned meeting at which the vote is given or the poll demanded or (in the case of a poll taken otherwise than on the same day as the meeting or adjourned meeting) the time appointed for taking the poll.

Number of Directors

64. Unless otherwise determined by ordinary resolution, the number of directors (other than alternate directors) shall not be subject to any maximum but shall be not less than two.

Alternate Directors

65. Any director (other than an alternate director) may appoint any other director, or any other person approved by resolution of the directors and willing to act, to be an alternative director and may remove from office an alternate director so appointed by him.

66. An alternate director shall be entitled to receive notice of all meetings of directors and of all meetings of committees of directors of which his appointor is a member, to attend and vote at any such meeting at which the director appointing him is not personally present, and generally to perform all the functions of his appointor as a director in his absence but shall not be entitled to receive any remuneration from the company for his services as an alternate director. But it shall not be necessary to give notice of such a meeting to an alternate director who is absent from the United Kingdom.

67. An alternate director shall cease to be an alternate director if his appointor ceases to be a director; but, if a director retires by rotation or otherwise but is reappointed or deemed to have been reappointed at the meeting at which he retires, any appointment of an alternate director made by him which was in force immediately prior to his retirement shall continue after his reappointment.

68. Any appointment or removal of an alternate director shall be by notice to the company signed by the director making or revoking the appointment or in any other manner approved by the directors.

69. Save as otherwise provided in the articles, an alternate director shall be deemed for all purposes to be a director and shall alone be responsible for his own acts and defaults and he shall not be deemed to be the agent of the director appointing him.

Powers of Directors

70. Subject to the provisions of the Act, the memorandum and the articles and to any directions given by special resolution, the business of the company shall be managed by the directors who may exercise all the powers of the company. No alteration of the memorandum or articles and no such direction shall invalidate any prior act of the directors which would have been valid if that alteration had not been made or that direction had not been given. The powers given by this regulation shall not be limited by any special power given to the directors by the articles and a meeting of directors at which a quorum is present may exercise all powers exercisable by the

Directors.

71. The directors may, by power of attorney or otherwise, appoint any person to be the agent of the company for such purposes and on such conditions as they determine, including authority for the agent to delegate all or any of his powers.

Delegation of Directors' powers

72. The directors may delegate any of their powers to any committee consisting of one or more directors. They may also delegate to any managing director or any director holding any other executive office such of their powers as they consider desirable to be exercised by him. Any such delegation may be made subject to any conditions the directors may impose, and either collaterally with or to the exclusion of their own powers and may be revoked or altered.

Subject to any such conditions, the proceedings of a committee with two or more members shall be governed by the articles regulating the proceedings of directors so far as they are capable of applying.

Appointment and retirement of Directors

73. At the first annual general meeting all the directors shall retire from office, and at every subsequent annual general meeting one-third of the directors who are subject to retirement by rotation or, if their number is not three or a multiple of three, the number nearest to one-third shall retire from office; but, if there is only one director who is subject to retirement by rotation, he shall retire.

74. Subject to the provisions of the Act, the directors to retire by rotation shall be those who have been longest in office since their last appointment or reappointment, but as between person who became or were last reappointed directors on the same day those to retire shall (unless they otherwise agree among themselves) be determined by lot.

75. If the company, at the meeting at which a director retires by rotation, does not fill the vacancy the retiring director shall, if willing to act, be deemed to have been reappointed unless at the meeting it is resolved not to fill the vacancy or unless a resolution for the reappointment of the director is put to the meeting and lost.

76. No person other than a director retiring by rotation shall be appointed or reappointed a director at any general meeting unless:-

- he is recommended by the directors; or

- not less than fourteen nor more than thirty-five clear days before the date appointed for the meeting, notice executed by a member qualified to vote at the meeting has been given to the company of the intention to propose that person for appointment or reappointment stating the particulars which would, if he were so appointed or reappointed, be required to be included in the company's register of directors together with notice executed by that person of his willingness to be appointed or reappointed.

77. Not less than seven nor more than twenty-eight clear days before the date appointed for holding a general meeting notice shall be given to all who are entitled to receive notice of the meeting of any person (other than a director retiring by rotation at the meeting) who is recommended by the directors for appointment or reappointment as a director at the meeting or in respect of whom notice has been duly given to the company of the intention to propose him at the meeting for appointment or reappointment as a director. The notice shall give the particulars of that person which would, if he were so appointed or reappointed, be required to be included in the company's register of directors.

78. Subject as aforesaid, the company may by ordinary resolution appoint a person who is willing to act to be a director either to fill a vacancy or as an additional director and may also determine the rotation in which any additional directors are to retire.

79. The directors may appoint a person who is willing to act to be a director, either to fill a vacancy or as an additional director, provided that the appointment does not cause the number of directors to exceed any number fixed by or in

accordance with the articles as the maximum number of directors. A director so appointed shall hold office only until the next following annual general meeting and shall not be taken into account in determining the directors who are to retire by rotation at the meeting. If not reappointed at such annual general meeting, he shall vacate office at the conclusion thereof.

80. Subject as aforesaid, a director who retires at an annual general meeting may, if willing to act, be reappointed. If he is not reappointed, he shall retain office until the meeting appoints someone in his place, or if it does not do so, until the end of the meeting.

Disqualification and removal of Directors

81. The office of a director shall be vacated if:-

- he ceases to be a director by virtue of any provision of the Act or he becomes prohibited by law from being a director; or

- he becomes bankrupt or makes any arrangement or composition with his creditors generally; or

- he is, or may be, suffering from mental disorder and either:-

- he is admitted to hospital in pursuance of an application for admission for treatment under the Mental Health Act 1983 or, in Scotland, an application for admission under the Mental Health (Scotland) Act 1960, or

- an order is made by a court having jurisdiction (whether in the United Kingdom or elsewhere) in matters concerning mental disorder for his detention or for the appointment of a receiver, curator bonis or other person to exercise powers with respect to his property or affairs; or

- he resigns his office by notice to the company; or

- he shall for more than six consecutive months have been absent without permission of the directors from meetings of directors held during that period and the directors resolve that his office be vacated.

Remuneration of Directors

82. The directors shall be entitled to such remuneration as the company may by ordinary resolution determine and, unless the resolution provides otherwise, the remuneration shall be deemed to accrue from day to day.

Directors' Expenses

83. The directors may be paid all travelling, hotel, and other expenses properly incurred by them in connection with their attendance at meetings of directors or committees of directors or general meetings or separate meetings of the holders of any class of shares or of debentures of the company or otherwise in connection with the discharge of their duties.

Directors' Appointments and Interests

84. Subject to the provisions of the Act, the directors may appoint one or more of their number to the office of managing director or to any other executive office under the company and may enter into an agreement or arrangement with any director for his employment by the company or for the provision by him of any services outside the scope of the ordinary duties of a director. Any such appointment, agreement or arrangement may be made upon such terms as the directors determine and they may remunerate any such director for his services as they think fit. Any appointment of a director to an executive office shall terminate if he ceases to be a director but without prejudice to any claim to damages for breach of the contract of service between the director and the company. A managing director and a director holding any other executive office shall not be subject to retirement by rotation.

85. Subject to the provisions of the Act, and provided that he has disclosed to the directors the nature and extent of any material interest of his, a director notwithstanding his office:-

- may be a party to, or otherwise interested in, any transaction or arrangement with the company or in which the company is otherwise interested;

- may be a director or other officer of, or employed by, or a party to any transaction or arrangement with, or otherwise interested in, any body corporate promoted by the company or in which the company is otherwise interested; and

- shall not, by reason of his office, be accountable to the company for any benefit which he derives from any such office or employment or from any such transaction or arrangement or from any interest in any such body corporate and no such transaction or arrangement shall be liable to be avoided on the ground of any such interest or benefit.

86. For the purposes of regulation 85:-

- a general notice given to the directors that a director is to be regarded as having an interest of the nature and extent specified in the notice in any transaction or arrangement in which a specified person or class or persons is interested shall be deemed to be a disclosure that the director has an interest in any such transaction of the nature and extent so specified; and

- an interest of which a director has no knowledge and of which it is unreasonable to expect him to have knowledge shall not be treated as an interest of his.

Directors' Gratuities and Pensions

87. The directors may provide benefits, whether by the payment of gratuities or pensions or by insurance or otherwise, for any director who has held but no longer holds any executive office or employment with the company or with any body corporate which is or has been a subsidiary of the company or a predecessor in business of the company or of any such subsidiary, and for any member of his family (including a spouse and a former spouse) or any person who is or was dependent on him, and may (as well before as after he ceases to hold such office or employment) contribute to any fund and pay premiums for the purchase or provision of any such benefit.

Proceedings of Directors

88. Subject to the provisions of the articles, the directors may regulate their proceedings as they think fit. A director may, and the secretary at the request of a director shall, call a meeting of the directors. It shall not be necessary to give notice of a meeting to a director who is absent from the United Kingdom. Questions arising at a meeting shall be decided by a majority of votes. In the case of an equality of votes, the chairman shall have a second or casting vote. A director who is also an alternative director shall be entitled in the absence of his appointor to a separate vote on behalf of his appointor in addition to his own vote.

89. The quorum for the transaction of the business of the directors may be fixed by the directors and unless so fixed at any other number shall be two. A person who holds office only as an alternative director shall, if his appointor is not present, be counted in the quorum.

90. The continuing directors or a sole continuing director may act notwithstanding any vacancies in their number, but, if the number of directors is less than the number fixed as the quorum, the continuing directors or director may act only for the purpose of filling vacancies or of calling a

General Meeting.

91. The directors may appoint one of their number to be the chairman of the board of directors and may at any time remove him from that office. Unless he is unwilling to do so, the director so appointed shall preside at every meeting of

directors at which he is present. But if there is no director holding that office, or if the director holding it is unwilling to preside or is not present within five minutes after the time appointed for the meeting, the directors present may appoint one of their number to be chairman of the meeting.

92. All acts done by a meeting of directors, or of a committee of directors, or by a person acting as a director shall, notwithstanding that it be afterwards discovered that there was a defect in the appointment of any director or that any of them were disqualified from holding office, or had vacated office, or were not entitled to vote, be as valid as if every such person had been duly appointed and was qualified and had continued to be a director and had been entitled to vote.

93. A resolution in writing signed by all the directors entitled to receive notice of a meeting of directors or of a committee of directors shall be as valid and effectual as if it had been passed at a meeting of directors or (as the case may be) a committee of directors duly convened and held and may consist of several documents in the like form each signed by one or more directors; but a resolution signed by an alternate director need not also be signed by his appointor and, if it is signed by a director who has appointed an alternate director, it need not be signed by the alternative director in that capacity.

94. Save as otherwise provided by the articles, a director shall not vote at a meeting of directors or of a committee of directors on any resolution concerning a matter in which he has, directly or indirectly, an interest or duty which is material and which conflicts or may conflict with the interests of the company unless his interest or duty arises only because the case falls within one or more of the following paragraphs:-

- the resolution relates to the giving to him of a guarantee, security, or indemnity in respect of money lent to, or an obligation incurred by him for the benefit of, the company or any of its subsidiaries;

- the resolution relates to the giving to a third party of a guarantee, security, or indemnity in respect of an obligation of the company or any of its subsidiaries for which the director has assumed responsibility in whole or part and whether alone or jointly with others under a guarantee or indemnity or by the giving of security;

- his interest arises by virtue of his subscribing or agreeing to subscribe for any shares, debentures or other securities of the company or any of its subsidiaries, or by virtue of his being, or intending to become, a participant in the underwriting or sub-underwriting or an offer of any such shares, debentures, or other securities by the company or any of its subsidiaries for subscription, purchase or exchange.

- the resolution relates in any way to a retirement benefits scheme which has been approved, or is conditional upon approval, by the Board of Inland Revenue for taxation purposes.

For the purposes of this regulation, an interest of a person who is, for any purpose of the Act (excluding any statutory modification thereof not in force when this regulation becomes binding on the company), connected with a director shall be treated as an interest of the director and, in relation to an alternate director, an interest of his appointor shall be treated as an interest of the alternate director without prejudice to any interest which the alternate director has otherwise.

95. A director shall not be counted in the quorum present at a meeting in relation to a resolution on which he is not entitled to vote.

96. The company may by ordinary resolution suspend or relax to any extent, either generally or in respect of any particular matter, any provision of the articles prohibiting a director from voting at a meeting of directors or of a committee of directors.

97. Where proposals are under consideration concerning the appointment of two or more directors to offices or employments with the company or any body corporate in which the company is interested the proposals may be divided and considered in relation to each director separately and (provided he is not for another reason precluded from voting) each of the directors concerned shall be entitled to vote and be counted in the quorum in respect of each resolution except that concerning his own appointment.

98. If a question arises at a meeting of directors or of a committee of directors as to the right of a director to vote, the question may, before the conclusion of the meeting, be referred to the chairman of the meeting and his ruling in relation to any director other than himself shall be final and conclusive.

Secretary

99. Subject to the provisions of the Act, the secretary shall be appointed by the directors for such term, at such remuneration and upon such conditions as they may think fit; and any secretary so appointed may be removed by them.

Minutes

100. The directors shall cause minutes to be made in books kept for the purpose:-

- of all appointments of offices made by the directors; and

- of all proceedings at meetings of the company, of the holders of any class of shares in the company, and of the directors, and of committees of directors, including the names of the directors present at each such meeting.

The Seal

101. The seal shall only be used by the authority of the directors or of a committee of directors authorised by the directors. The directors may determine who shall sign any instrument to which the seal is affixed and unless otherwise so determined it shall be signed by a director and by the secretary or by a second director.

Dividends

102. Subject to the provisions of the Act, the company may by ordinary resolution declare dividends in accordance with the respective rights of the members, but no dividend shall exceed the amount recommended by the directors.

103. Subject to the provisions of the Act, the directors may pay interim dividends if it appears to them that they are justified by the profits of the company available for distribution. If the share capital is divided into different classes, the directors may pay interim dividends on shares which confer deferred or non-preferred rights with regard to dividend as well as on shares which confer preferential rights with regard to dividend, but no interim dividend shall be paid on shares carrying deferred or non-preferred rights if, at the time of payment, any preferential dividend is in arrear. The directors may also pay at intervals settled by them any dividend payable at a fixed rate if it appears to them that the profits available for distribution justify the payment. Provided the directors act in good faith they shall not incur any liability to the holders of shares conferring preferred rights for any loss they may suffer by the lawful payment of an interim dividend on any shares having deferred or non-preferred rights.

104. Except as otherwise provided by the rights attached to shares, all dividends shall be declared and paid according to the amounts paid up on the shares on which the dividend is paid. All dividends shall be apportioned and paid proportionately to the amounts paid up on the shares during any portion or portions of the period in respect of which the dividend is paid; but, if any share is issued on terms providing that it shall rank for dividend as from a particular date, that share shall rank for dividend accordingly.

105. A general meeting declaring a dividend may, upon the recommendation of the directors, direct that it shall be satisfied wholly or partly by the distribution of assets and, where any difficulty arises in regard to the distribution, the directors may settle the same and in particular may issue fractional certificates and fix the value for distribution of any assets and may determine that cash shall be paid to any member upon the footing of the value so fixed in order to adjust the rights of members and may vest any assets in trustees.

106. Any dividend or other moneys payable in respect of a share may be paid by cheque sent by post to the registered address of the person entitled or, if two or more persons are the holders of the share or are jointly entitled to it by reason of the death or bankruptcy of the holder, to the registered address of that one of those persons who is first named in the register of members or to such person and to such address as the person or persons entitled may in writing direct.

Every cheque shall be made payable to the order of the person or persons entitled or to such other person as the person or persons entitled may in writing direct and payment of the cheque shall be a good discharge to the company. Any joint holder or other person jointly entitled to a share as aforesaid may give receipts for any dividend or other moneys payable in respect of the share.

107. No dividend or other moneys payable in respect of a share shall bear interest against the company unless otherwise provided by the rights attached to the share.

108. Any dividend which has remained unclaimed for twelve years from the date when it became due for payment shall, if the directors so resolve, be forfeited and cease to remain owing by the company

Accounts

109. No member shall (as such) have any right of inspecting any accounting records or other book or document of the company except as conferred by statute or authorised by the directors or by ordinary resolution of the company.

Capitalisation of Profits

110. The directors may with the authority of an ordinary resolution of the company:-

- subject as hereinafter provided, resolve to capitalise any undivided profits of the company not required for paying any preferential dividend (whether or not they are available for distribution) or any sum standing to the credit of the company's share premium account or capital redemption reserve;

- appropriate the sum resolved to be capitalised to the members who would have been entitled to it if it were distributed by way of dividend and in the same proportions and apply such sum on their behalf either in or towards paying up the amounts, if any, for the time being unpaid on any shares held by them respectively, or in paying up in full unissued shares or debentures of the company of a nominal amount equal to that sum, and allot the shares or debentures credited as fully paid to those members, or as they may direct, in those proportions, or partly in one way and partly in the other; but the share premium account, the capital redemption reserve, and any profits which are not available for distribution may, for the purposes of this regulation, only be applied in paying up unissued shares to be allotted to members credited as fully paid;

- make such provision by the issue of fractional certificates or by payment in cash or otherwise as they determine in the case of shares or debentures becoming distributable under this regulation in fractions; and

- authorise any person to enter on behalf of all the members concerned into an agreement with the company providing for the allotment to them respectively, credited as fully paid, of any shares or debentures to which they are entitled upon such capitalisation, any agreement made under such authority being binding on all such members.

Notices

111. Any notice to be given to or by any person pursuant to the articles (other than a notice calling a meeting of the directors) shall be in writing or shall be given using electronic communications to an address for the time being notified for that purpose to the person giving the notice except that a notice calling a meeting of the directors need not be in writing.

In this regulation "address", in relation to electronic communications, includes any number or address used for the purposes of such communications.

112. The company may give any notice to a member either personally or by sending it by post in a prepaid envelope addressed to the member at his registered address or by leaving it at that address or by giving it using electronic communications to an address for the time being notified to the company by the member. In the case of joint holders of a share, all notices shall be given to the joint holder whose name stands first in the register of members in respect of the joint holding and notice so given shall be sufficient notice to all the joint holders. A member whose registered address is not within the United Kingdom and who gives to the company an address within the United Kingdom at which notices may be given to him or an address to which notices may be sent using electronic communications shall be entitled to have notices given to him at that address, but otherwise no such member shall be entitled to receive any notice from the company. In this regulation and the next, "address", in relation to electronic communications, includes any number or address used for the purposes of such communications.

113. A member present, either in person or by proxy, at any meeting of the company or of the holders of any class of shares in the company shall be deemed to have received notice of the meeting and, where requisite, of the purposes for which it was called.

114. Every person who becomes entitled to a share shall be bound by any notice in respect of that share which, before his name is entered in the register of members, has been duly given to a person from whom he derives his title.

115. Proof that an envelope containing a notice was properly addressed, prepaid and posted shall be conclusive evidence that the notice was given. A notice shall be deemed to be given at the expiration of 48 hours after the envelope containing it was posted.

116. A notice may be given by the company to the persons entitled to a share in consequence of the death or bankruptcy of a member by sending or delivering it, in any manner authorised by the articles for the giving of notice to a member, addressed to them by name, or by the title of representatives of the deceased, or trustee of the bankrupt or by any like description at the address, if any, within the United Kingdom supplied for that purpose by the persons claiming to be so entitled. Until such an address has been supplied, a notice may be given in any manner in which it might have been given if the death or bankruptcy had not occurred.

Winding up

117. If the company is wound up, the liquidator may, with the sanction of an extraordinary resolution of the company and any other sanction required by the Act, divide among the members in specie the whole or any part of the assets of the company and may, for that purpose, value any assets and determine how the division shall be carried out as between the members or different classes of members.

The liquidator may, with the like sanction, vest the whole or any part of the assets in trustees upon such trusts for the benefit of the members as he with the like sanction determines, but no member shall be compelled to accept any assets upon which there is a liability.

118. Subject to the provisions of the Act but without prejudice to any indemnity to which a director may otherwise be entitled, every director or other officer or auditor of the company shall be indemnified out of the assets of the company against any liability incurred by him in defending any proceedings, whether civil or criminal, in which judgement is given in his favour or in which he is acquitted or in connection with any application in which relief is granted to him by the court from liability for negligence, default, breach of duty or breach of trust in relation to the affairs of the company.

A NOVATION AGREEMENT

THIS NOVATION AGREEMENT made on   2005

between:

A (name) of (address) and (name) of (address) ("the Promoters");

B (name) Ltd a company registered in England & Wales under number (number) whose registered office is at (address) ("the Supplier"); and

C (name) Ltd a company registered in England & Wales under number (number) whose registered office is at (address) ("the Company").

Background

1.1 This agreement is supplemental to a contract ("the Contract") made on (date) between the Promoters and the Supplier for the provision by the Supplier of (describe) services to the Promoters.

1.2 The Promoters wishes to be released and discharged from the Contract and the Supplier has agreed to release and discharge the Promoters upon the terms of the Company's undertaking to perform the Contract and to be bound by the terms of the Contract in place of the Promoters.

Company's undertaking

2 The Company undertakes to perform the Contract and to be bound by the terms of the Contract in every way as if the Company were a party to the Contract in the place of the Promoters.

Release of Promoters

3 The Supplier releases and discharges the Promoters from all claims and demands of any kind in respect of the Contract.

Supplier's undertaking

4 The Supplier accepts the liability of the Company under the Contract in lieu of the liability of the Promoters and agrees to be bound by the terms of the Contract in every way as if the Company were named in the Contract as a party in place of the Promoters.

Third Party Rights

A person who is not a party to this deed has no rights under the Contracts (Rights of Third Parties) Act 1999 to enforce any terms of this deed

Company Law

Test yourself.

1. *"...a fundamental attribute of corporate personality...is that the corporation is a legal entity distinct from its members": Gower.* Which do you consider are the two outstanding advantages of incorporation? Give reasons for your choice and explain their dependence upon this fundamental attribute.

2. Three friends own and are also directors of a limited company carrying on the family business. They have it in mind to change the organisation to an ordinary partnership. What aspect of the business would be affected if this change were carried out?

The right to sue in the business name.

The right to mortgage the business assets.

The right of the partners to examine the firm's accounts.

The ability to create a floating charge over the business assets.

3. Alex and Angel are garage mechanics. They are considering changing their form of business association and trading as a private registered company limited by shares.

Explain to them the legal procedures that they must follow in order. to form such a company, and advise them on the advantages of trading as a private company as opposed to a partnership.

3. *Table A* will apply automatically except where it is excluded or modified by special articles of association in the case of:

private companies limited by shares only;

public companies limited by shares only;

all companies limited by shares; or

all limited companies.

4. A private company limited by shares must include in its memorandum a clause which states that:

the company is a private company limited by shares;

the liability of the members is limited;

the company is not a public company; or

the company is a private company.

5. The capital clause of a company limited by shares is contained in the memorandum. What does it state?

The amount of share capital which the directors can issue.

The amount of the share capital presently issued.

The amount of share capital which the company is entitled to issue.

The amount of share capital currently paid up.

3—Share Capital

Contents

What is capital?

A company's capital

Corporate organisation chart

Shares and ordinary shares

Preference shares

Glossary—capital and shares

Issue of shares—allotment

Issue of shares—allotment continued

Increases in capital

Other changes in capital—except reduction

Reduction in capital

Purchase of own shares—main

Purchase of own shares—other

Financial assistance

Financial assistance—continued

Class rights

Dividends—what is permitted

Dividends—how?

Transfers of shares

Test Yourself.

1   What is capital?

dictionary
> A capital stock or fund. The trading stock of a company corporation or individual on which profits or dividends are calculated. Accumulated wealth applied reproductively.

contrast
> capital and income

in business
> Money to run a business
> buy goods
> pay rent
> pay wages
> etc

sources
> own money
> borrowing
> (trade) credit

2   A company's capital

2 senses	1		economic
	2		ownership

source of money		shares (equity)
		borrowing
		credit

ownership		shareholders
	not	lenders

nature of shares		right to
		vote
		transfer
		dividends
		return of capital on winding up

3 Corporate organisation chart

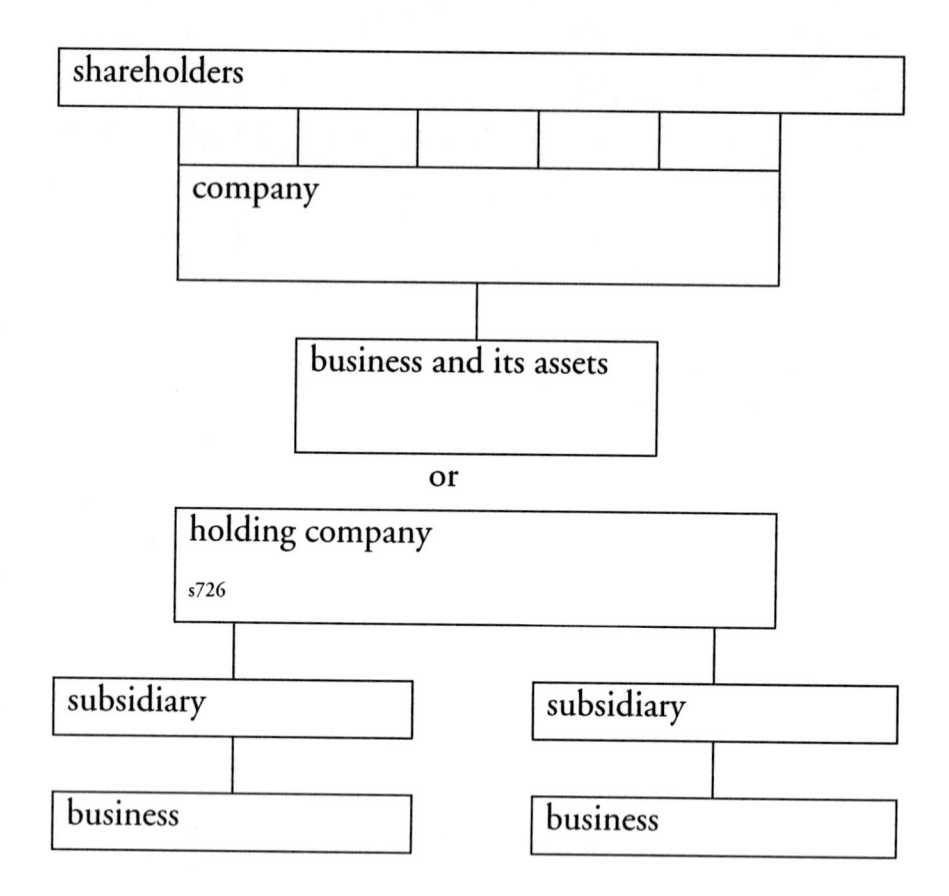

```
┌─────────────────────────────────────────────┐
│ shareholders                                │
├──┬──┬──┬──┬──┬──────────────────────────────┤
│  │  │  │  │  │
┌─┴──┴──┴──┴──┴──────────────────────────────┐
│ company                                     │
└──────────────────┬──────────────────────────┘
                   │
        ┌──────────┴──────────┐
        │ business and its    │
        │ assets              │
        └─────────────────────┘

                  or

┌─────────────────────────────────────────────┐
│ holding company                             │
│ s726                                        │
└────────┬────────────────────┬───────────────┘
         │                    │
┌────────┴────────┐   ┌───────┴─────────┐
│ subsidiary      │   │ subsidiary      │
└────────┬────────┘   └───────┬─────────┘
         │                    │
┌────────┴────────┐   ┌───────┴─────────┐
│ business        │   │ business        │
└─────────────────┘   └─────────────────┘
```

4 Shares and ordinary shares

s 744	'share' means share in the share capital of a company, and includes stock (except where a distinction between shares and stock is express or implied)
s 182	personal estate—transferable—numbered

basically	1	ordinary
	2	preference

ordinary		or, "ordinary"
	or	non-voting
	or	deferred
	or	'A', 'B', 'C'
	or	special right, etc
		as needed
		bonus

5 Preference shares

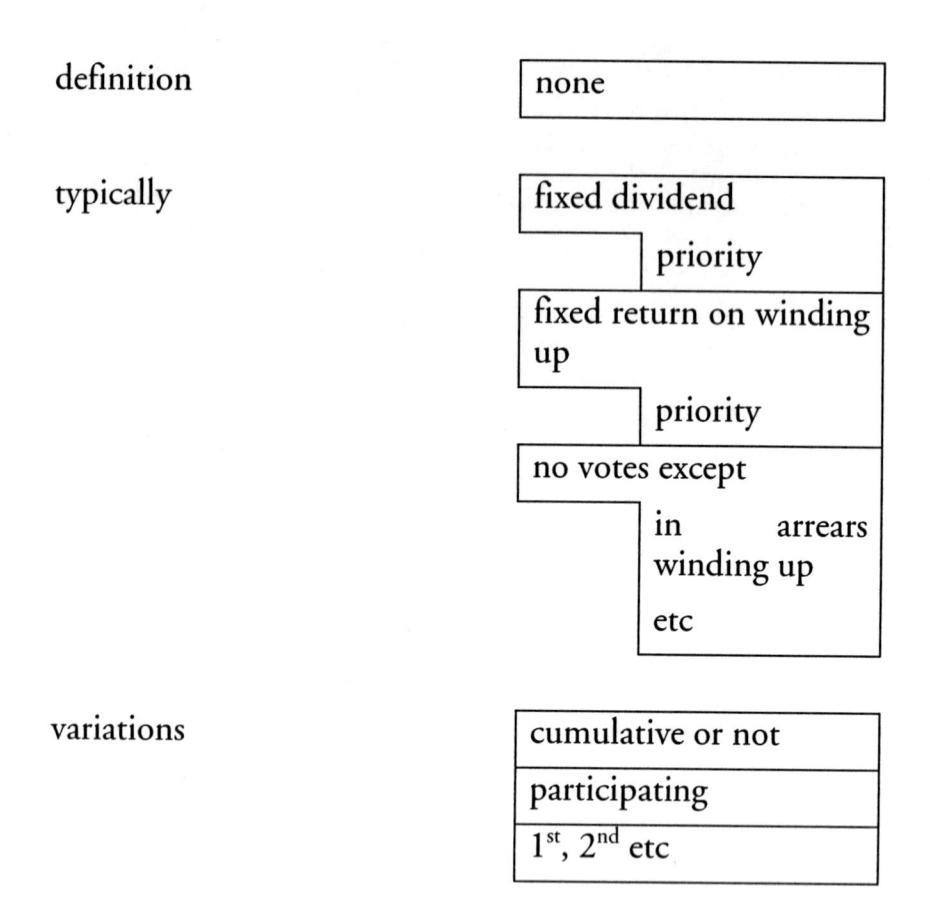

definition	none
typically	fixed dividend — priority
	fixed return on winding up — priority
	no votes except — in arrears / winding up / etc
variations	cumulative or not
	participating
	1st, 2nd etc

6 Glossary—capital and shares

Adam's Principle	The Court of Appeal in Adams v Cape Industries plc [1990] made a principled decision that corporate members of a group cannot be regarded as being anything but separate legal entities. This is known as the Adams Principle.
nominal or authorised	capital stated in the memorandum of association s 2(5)
allotted	capital which the company has issued
called-up	amount of allotted capital the company has called-up
paid up	actually paid by members
uncalled	amount on partly-paid shares not called up
equity	ordinary shares
reserve	Can be called only on winding up s 120
stock	amount of money rather than shares s 121(c)
warrants	"bearer" ss188, 355
	Value Added Tax. Registration under the Value Added Tax Act 1994 is by a 'person', a term defined to include a company or a group of companies. The registration also provided for division of a legal person or company.. Each division can be responsible for a VAT return. Also, a group can be

VAT

Limitation Periods

> The Companies Act sets out the period in which a shareholder may seek to enforce pre-emption rights. This is 2 years.

The Meridian Principles

> The Meridian Principles are variables which operate through the company's constitution or rules which are implied by Company Law and other statutes. These are the primary, general and special rules, three types of rules which determine whether a company is liable. Primary rules come from the company's constitution. General rules come from the law of agency, estoppel, ostensible liability and vicarious liability(tort). Special rules are those which come about from exceptional occasions when primary and general rules are not adequate. For example the House of Lords ruling in Tesco v Natrass is valid in dealing with the due diligence defence in the Trade Descriptions Act.

7 Issue of shares—allotment, start

2	to whom?
3	for how much?
4	Who does it and how?

answers		4	(Who?)—directors
s80	but		must be authorised
		1	Any
s2(5)	but		not more than authorised capital
		2	Anyone
(s81) Financial Services and Markets Act 2000	but		no offer to the public
s89	but		Only on pre-emption basis

8 Issue of shares—allotment, continued

answers continued

	3	any amount part or fully paid	
ss98, 100		no discount	but
s 97		except commission up to 10%	
		premium permitted	
		(ie at par or more)	
	4(a)	directors' resolution	
s 99(1)		pay in cash or kind	
s 99(2)		not services for PLC	but
s 103 et seq		valuation in PLC	
s 352	(b)	enter in register	
s 185	(c)	issue certificate	
s 88	(d)	return of allotments	

9 Increases in capital

s 121(2)(a)	how?		shareholders' resolution
Table A 32	unless provided	otherwise	ordinary resolution

s 80	NB - before issue	authority to allot
s 88		pre-emption

	effect	authorised capital increased
		note on memorandum
s 123		notice to registrar

	issuing them	back to sheets 7 and 8

summary	shareholders fix and alter capital (and pay for and take shares) but directors allot them issue certificates etc

10 Other changes of capital—except reduction

        what?

s 121(2)(b)	consolidate
s 121(2)(c)	convert into stock or reconvert to shares
s 121(2)(d)	subdivide
s 121(2)(e)	cancel

s 121(2)   how?   shareholders' resolution

Table A 32   unless   otherwise | ordinary resolution
                      provided

        effect

authorised capital unchanged or reduced
note on memorandum
notice to registrar

s 122

11 Reduction of capital

NB		MAINTENANCE OF CAPITAL
s 135(1)	how?	shareholders' special resolution
s 135(2), 136		confirmation by the court
s 135(2)(a)	what?	extinguish or reduce liability on shares
s 135(2)(b)		cancel paid-up shares lost or unrepresented by assets
s 135(2)(c)		pay off paid-up shares in excess of needs
	effect	issued capital reduced
s 135(2)		alter memorandum
s 138		notice to registrar

12 Purchase of own shares—main

NB MAINTENANCE OF CAPITAL

s 143(1)	in principle	prohibited
s 163	but may do	market or off market
s 164(1)	off only if	contract approved in advance
s 164(2)		contract terms authorised by special resolution
s 164(6)		contract displayed at R/O for 15 days before and at meeting
ss 168, 171		paid for out of distributable profits or (if private) "permissible capital payment"
s 169		reported to registrar of companies
s 170		"capital reserve redemption fund"

13 Purchase of own shares and redemption—other

           also

ss 159, 160 | redeemable shares |

s 143(3)(b) | acquisition as part of reduction of capital |

s 143(3)(d)
Table A 12 – 22 | forfeiture of shares |

ss 163, 166 | market purchase |

s 165 | contingent purchase |

ss 176, 177 | dissenting shareholders |

14 Financial assistance

NB MAINTENANCE OF CAPITAL

s 151 in principle | prohibited |

meaning …where a person is acquiring…shares in a company, it is not lawful for the company…to give financial assistance for the purpose of the acquisition …

eg
| gift |
| loan |
| guarantee or security for loan |
| release of liability |
| etc |

consequences
| transaction unlawful |
| company fined |
| officers fined imprisoned or both |

15   Financial assistance—continued

exceptions

s 153(1)	the company's principal purpose in giving the assistance is not to give it for the purpose of the acquisition or was an incidental part of a larger purpose and the assistance was given in good faith

also

s 153(4)(a)	lending in the ordinary course of business where lending is part of the company's ordinary business
s 153(4)(b), (bb), (c)	lending for the purposes of an employees' share scheme or enabling employees and families to acquire shares in the company

relaxation of prohibition for private companies

s 155(1), (2)	if	net assets not reduced
	or	if reduced assistance given out of distributable profits

1 156, 157	NB	statutory declaration and special resolution

16 Class rights

see sheet 4 for examples

	what?	direct change
		not change of other classes
	how?	depends on articles of association or terms of issue
s 125(2)		not if in memorandum
s 125	in default	shareholders' special resolution
s 125(2)	and either	consent of ¾ of the class by value
	or	sanction of class meeting and extraordinarily resolution
s 128	plus	registration of rights and new rights

17   Dividends—what permitted?

NB   MAINTENANCE OF CAPITAL

	basic rule	distributions prohibited

sheet 4	except	bonus shares
sheet 11		reductions of capital
sheets 12, 13		purchase of shares
		dividends

s 263(1)	prohibited	distribution except out of available profits
s 263(2)		distributions in cash or kind
s 263(3)	available profits	accumulated profits (not previously distributed) less accumulated realised losses (not written off)

18 Dividends—how?

	how?	depends on articles of association
Table A 102	default	declared by shareholders' ordinary resolution
Table A 102		in accordance with rights of members
Table A 102		only if recommended by directors
		paid (if declared) by directors
Table A 103		directors may pay interim dividends

19 Transfers of shares

	how?	depends on articles of association
s 183(1)		must be on proper transfer NB stamp duty
1 183(5)		must be registered within 2 months
		quoted company cannot restrict transfers
Table A, 23		private companies usually restrict
	eg	transfer notice and pre-emption clauses
Table A, 23		transmission eg on death or bankruptcy

20 Illustrations of changes in capital

	bonus		increase		loss of assets		return of assets		purchase of own shares		dividend	
	sheet 4		sheet 9		sheet 11		sheet 11		sheet 12		sheet 17	
	Bfr	after	bfr	after	bfr	after	bfr	after	bfr	after	bfr	after
fixed assets	500	500	500	500	500	500	500	500	500	500	500	500
current assets	300	300	300	350	250	250	400	350	300	250	400	350
assets	800	800	800	850	750	750	900	850	800	750	900	850
liabilities	600	600	600	600	700	700	600	600	600	600	600	600
net	200	200	200	250	50	50	300	250	200	150	300	250
share capital	100	150	100	150	100	50	100	50	100	50	100	100
P & L account	100	50	100	100	(50)	0[2]	200	200	100	50	200	150
reserve[1]	0	0	0	0	0	0	0	0	0	50	0	0
shareholders' funds	200	200	200	250	50	50	300	250	200	150	300	250

1   This is the "capital reserve redemption fund" in s170 Companies Act 1985, see sheet 12

2   The reduction of capital clears the P&L account so dividends may be paid if there are profits in the next year

Company Law

Test Yourself

1. Distinguish the meaning of capital in a business sense from capital in the sense of a company's equity capital.

2. Explain and distinguish between:

preference shares;

participating preference shared;

ordinary shares;

part-paid shares; and

premium.

3. Can a shareholder find out the rights of his or her shares from:

the share certificate?

the share certificate and the memorandum of association?

the share certificate and the articles of association? or

the articles of association and the terms of issue?

4. Explain what it meant by "capital maintenance"

5. Discuss how the provision of the UK Companies Act 1985 attempt to ensure capital maintenance by regulating:

the payment of dividends

the issue of shares at a premium

6. Salome and Sam formed a company called TESTAMENT Ltd. They became the sole directors and took up 50% of the shares, the other shares being allotted to 15 other people. They sold their business to TESTAMENT Ltd for £130,000 although it was valued at £120,000. How should the profit be dealt with?

They may keep it.

They may keep it if they disclose it to the board of directors and obtain the consent of the board.

They may keep it if they disclose it to all the other shareholders and obtain their consent.

They cannot keep it in any circumstances.

7. ALEX Ltd has an authorized share capital of £150,000. It is divided into 50,000 £1 preference shares and 100,000 £1 ordinary shares. All shares have been issued. The rights attached to the preference shares include the right to have capital repaid before the ordinary shareholders in the event of the company being wound up. The articles contain no such provision. The articles are also silent on how to vary class rights. Advise ALEX Ltd on whether and how it may convert its preference shares into ordinary shares.

8. ANGELS Ltd has an issued share capital of £2 million. In 1999 it made a trading profit of £100,000 but the value of its assets fell to £1 million. In 1998, it made a trading loss of £50,000. Advise the directors whether, and how much, of the 1999 profit is available for distribution as dividend

9. FREDERICK, a director and member, proposes to transfer his shares in BOXMOOR Ltd in breach of a pre-emption clause in the articles of BOXMOOR

which provides that members will offer their shares to other members first and that the other members may purchase them. What action can the other shareholders take?

a) Restrain the transfer through an action by the company.

b) Bring an action against Frederick through the company for breach of his fiduciary duties as a director.

c) Bring a personal action to prevent the transfer as being in breach of contract.

d) They can take no action.

4—Meetings

Contents

Introduction

Shareholders' meetings

Annual general meeting

Extraordinary general meetings & resolutions

Elective resolutions

Special notice

Special notice & written resolutions

Procedure—1

Procedure—2

Directors' meetings—standard

Directors' meetings—alternatives

Specimen Notice of annual general meeting

Specimen Notice of extraordinary general meeting

Specimen members' written resolutions

Meetings of shareholders, notices and resolutions

Company law: how many votes do you need?

1   Introduction

how a company operates

Nb   formal | Companies Act |
      informal | The real day to day exercise of power depends more on informal meetings and lines of communication. |

formal | through meetings |

mainly | members |

                 | directors |

also 1 | classes of shareholders |

                 | creditors |

also 2 | written resolutions |

2   Shareholders' meetings

s 366

annual general meeting
annual
1ˢᵗ within 18 months
max 15 months between
21 days' notice

Table A, reg 36

extraordinary general meetings
if and when needed
14 or 21 days' notice

NB | short notice |
NB | elective resolution |

3   Annual general meeting

purpose	Companies Act	not specified
		directors' accountability to the members

	Table A 1985	nothing

Table A (1948) reg 52	1948	ordinary business
		dividends
		accounts
		reports
		directors
		auditors

Table A (1948) reg 52	1948	special business
		anything else

4 extraordinary general meetings & resolutions

purpose	anything to be done by the company	

s 369(1)(b)	ordinary	14 days prior notice 7 if unlimited
Table A, regs 46, 50		simple majority ie 50% + 1
		anything except where special or extraordinary is required

s 378(2)	special	21 days prior notice
s 378(2)		75%
		see notes

s 378(1)	extra ordinary	14 days prior notice
s 378(1)		75%
		see notes

5 Elective resolutions

Companies Act 1989 — **simplification** / reduction of formalities

only private companies

s 379A(2) — 21 days prior notice or consent to short notice; 100%

	purposes	
s 80A		duration of authority to allot shares
s 252		dispense with accounts and reports at agm
s 366A		dispense with agm
s 369(4) s 378(3)		majority for short notice
s 386		dispense with annual appointment of auditors

s 379A(3) — revocation — ordinary resolution

6 special notice

s 379	special notice	to the company
		by a member
		of his intention
		to move
		at next general meeting
		28 days before the meting

s 303(2)	purpose	remove a director from office
s 293(4)		appoint a director over age 70
s 391A(1)(b)		appoint new auditor
s 388(3)		re-appoint auditor appointed to fill casual vacancy
s 391A(1)(a)		removing auditors before expiry of term of office

7 short notice & written resolutions

Reference	Condition	Threshold
s 368(3)(a)	if agreed by	AGM—100%
s 369(3)(b), s 387(3)		EGM—95%
s 379A(2A)		elective—100%
	but	
s 369(4), s 378(3)	if elective resolution	95% reduced to not below 90%

written resolution

two regimes

Table A reg 53		articles of association
	and	
s 381A		statutory

s 381A (6)	statutory	expressly includes special, extraordinary and elective
Sch 15A para 1	but	excludes removing director or auditor before expiry of term

8 Procedure—1

calling meetings

s 370(1)	normally directors acting by company secretary
s 368 also	requisition by members (10%)
s 370(3)	two members (10%)
s 376	members' resolution and statements (5%)
s 392A	requisition by auditor
s 367	DTI on member's application
s 371	Court on member's or director's application

at meetings

s 370 (4), s 370A, Table A 40, 41	quorum
s 372, Table A reg 60 – 62	proxies
s 375, Table A reg 58, 63	representatives
s 370(6), Table A reg 54	show of hands
ss 373, 374, Table A reg 47 – 52, 59	poll
Table A reg 50	casting vote

9 Procedure—2

s 370(5) Table A 42,43	control of meeting	chairman
Table A reg 40	adjournment	no quorum at start
		ceases during meeting
		to next week
s 381		date of resolution
s 380	after meeting	registration
ss 382, 383 Table A reg 100	minutes	all proceeding sign by chairman inspection sole member (!)
s 380	registration	14 days after
		special, extraordinary elective equivalents by all members s 80, s 166 and others

10 Directors' meetings—standard

	sources	
		Companies Act - nothing
		articles of associations everything

	procedures	
		Table A
reg 98		as they think fit
reg 98		called by director or secretary as director's requisition
(reg 98)		reasonable notice
reg 98		not if overseas
		one vote per person
reg 98		simple majority
reg 98		casting vote
reg 99		quorum two
reg 103		committee
reg 106		written resolutions

11 Directors' meetings—alternatives

special articles instead of Table A

fixed meeting dates
fixed notice of meetings
corporate directors and representatives
teleconference meetings
no casting vote
delegation and committee to include non-directors
majority shareholder to have votes = membership votes
all votes proportionate to membership votes

> NB   This precedent is © Butterworths and is from chapter 13 of Kelly's Draftsman 18th Edition (2003), general editor Roderick Ramage, with modifications taken from the Encyclopaedia of Forms and Precedents.
>
> This precedent is supplied by kind permission of Roderick Ramage only to illustrate what is commonly contained in a notice and is not to be used in any particular case.

Notice of annual general meeting[1]

(*name*) Ltd

company (*number*)

The Companies Acts 1985 to 1989

company limited by shares

NOTICE IS GIVEN that the Company's [third] annual general meeting will be held at (*address*) on [Monday] the (*date*) at (*time*) am/pm when there will be transacted the following ordinary business:[2]

1 to receive and consider the report of the directors and the statement of accounts and balance sheet of the Company for the year ended (*date*) with the auditors' report on it;[3]

---

1   Minutes must be kept of all proceedings of all general meetings, and all meetings of the directors and, where there are any, the managers: CA 1985, s382(1). Any minute purporting to be signed by the chairman of the meeting at which the proceedings were held or the following meeting shall be evidence of the proceedings: CA 1985, s382(2). There is no general principle of law that resolutions need a seconder as well as proposer: Re Horbury Bridge Coal, Iron and Wagon Co (1879) 11 Ch D 109, CA. The auditors are entitled to receive all notices and other communications to which the members are entitled and to attend general meetings (CA 1985, s390).
Every company must hold an annual general meeting in every year, with not more than fifteen months between each meeting, but if the first meeting is held not more than eighteen months after incorporation, a meeting need not be held in the first or the following year: CA 1985, s366(2). Twenty-one days' notice in writing must be given (CA 1985, s369(1)(a)) unless all the members entitled to attend and vote agree to accept shorter notice (CA 1985, s369(3)(a)). A copy of the balance sheet, profit and loss account, where appropriate group accounts, directors' report and auditors' report must be sent within the same period (CA 1985, s240) unless supplied electronically (see note 4 below). By ss369(4A) to (4G) inserted by the Companies Act 1985 (Electronic Communications) Order 2000, notification may be made by an electronic communication.

2   The notice must state that the meeting is the annual general meeting: CA 1985, s66(1). The articles of association may specify what is the normal business of the AGM (eg items 1, 2, 3, 5 and 6 of this precedent under reg 52 of the 1948 Table A), in which case there is no need to set out the general business in the notice, although it has been common practice to do so. The 1985 Table A does not specify what is the normal business of an AGM, in which case it will be necessary to specify the nature of the business in the notice. If The articles determine what is the ordinary business of an AGM, strictly speaking no notice need be given of the business, and everything else is special business of which notice is required.

3   By ss12(4A) to (4D) and 239(2A) and (2B) of the CA 1985 inserted by the Companies Act 1985 (Electronic Communications) Order 2000, accounts and reports may with the member's agreement be supplied electronically instead of being sent in legible form. Under the CA 1985, s241(1) the directors must lay the accounts and reports before the company in general meeting. This business merely requires consideration, and it is unnecessary (unless the articles provide otherwise) to adopt, approve or pass any resolution about this matter.

2   to declare a dividend;[4]

3   to re-elect as directors the following who retire by rotation namely:

>   (*name*)

>   (*name*)

>   (*and/or*)

> to elect the following as directors in the place of those retiring;[5]

>   (*name*)

>   (*name*)

>   (*and/or*)

> to elect (*name*) as an additional director;

>   (*and/or*)

to consider, and if thought fit pass, a resolution that (*name*), the director who retires by reason of his having attained the age of [70], shall notwithstanding that fact be reappointed as a director of the company for the further period of (*specify*) years[6].

4   to reappoint (*name*) as auditors for the ensuing year[7] and authorise the directors to fix their remuneration;

>   (*or*)

to elect (*name*) as auditors for the ensuing year and authorise the directors to fix their remuneration[8];

>   (*or*)

---

[4] The Companies Acts do not state who has power to declare dividends, and the question is usually governed by the articles of association. Table A, reg 102 (1948 Table A, reg 114) states that the dividends may be declared by the general meeting but not of any amount exceeding that recommended by the directors, and reg 103 (1948 Table A, reg 115) gives the directors power to pay such interim dividends as appear to be justified by the profits. As to what dividends may be distributed, see the CA 1985, Part VIII, ss 263 to 281. An auditors' statement (required under s271(4) if the accounts have been qualified) must be available before the distribution is made: Precision Dippings Ltd v Precision Dippings Marketing Ltd [1986] Ch 447.

[5] This note assumes that Table A, regs 73 to 80 (1948 Table A, regs 89 to 97) apply unaltered. All the directors retire at the first AGM of the company and thereafter they retire by thirds in rotation. Retiring directors are eligible for re-election. The company in general meeting may also fill a casual vacancy (arising out of such retirement, the removal of a director or otherwise) and appoint additional directors. However, except for persons eligible for re-election, no person who is not recommended by the directors may be elected unless not less than three nor more than 21 days before the meeting there is left at the company's registered office written notice of the intention to propose his election and notice signed by him of his willingness to be elected.

[6] Special notice of this resolution is required: see the Companies Act 1985 s293(5).

[7] An auditor must be appointed at every meeting before which the accounts of the company are laid (in normal, but not Companies Act, parlance, the AGM), who will hold office until the end of the next such meeting: CA 1985, s384. He is not automatically re-elected, and if no auditor is appointed or reappointed, the company must within one week notify the Secretary of State of the fact, and he may fill the vacancy: CA 1985, s384(5).

[8] Special notice is required of a resolution appointing as auditor a person other than a retiring auditor: see the Companies Act 1985 s391A(1) as inserted by the Companies Act 1989 s122(1).

to pass a resolution that (auditors) not be reappointed[9];

And the following special business.

5   To consider and, if thought fit, pass the following as an ordinary resolution:

      (*set out resolutions*)

Dated (*date*)

By order of the Board

(*signature*)

Secretary

Notes:

1. The registers of members will be closed from the (*date*) to (*date*) inclusive, and no transfers will be registered during that time.

2. A member entitled to attend and vote at the meeting is entitled to appoint a proxy [or more than one proxy] to attend and vote in his or her place. A proxy may demand, or join in demanding, a poll. A proxy need not be a member of the Company.[10]

3. We the undersigned being members or representatives of members[1] of the Company holding not less than [all (*or*) [95]%] of the nominal value of the shares giving a right to attend and vote at the meeting consent to the convening of the extraordinary meeting for the date and place above mentioned and the passing at it of the resolution(s) above set out.[11]

      [*signatures*]

4. Copies of all directors' service contracts of more than one year's duration are available for inspection at (address) during usual business hours on each business day and at (place of meeting) for at least 15 minutes prior to and during the meeting convened by this notice.

There are no directors' service contracts of more than one year duration[12].

---

[9] See note 8 above.

[10] This statement must appear if the company has a share capital. A member of a private company may not appoint more than one proxy unless the articles otherwise provide: CA 1985, s372(2)(b), and Table A, reg 59 (but no 1948 equivalent). If the company's securities are listed THE Listing Rules require it to send two-way proxy forms with this notice in respect of all resolutions except those which are merely procedural. By ss372(2A) and (2G) inserted by the Companies Act 1985 (Electronic Communications) Order 2000, the appointment of a proxy may be made by an electronic communication..

[11] CA 1985, s 369(3)(a). The consent of all the members entitled to attend and vote is necessary.

[12] One of these statements, whichever is applicable, is usually included if the company has listed securities as evidence of compliance with the Listing Rules. The are not applicable to unquoted companies.

Notice of extraordinary general meeting[13]

(*name*) Ltd

company (*number*)

The Companies Acts 1985 to 1989

company limited by shares

NOTICE IS GIVEN that a general meeting of the Company will be held at (*address*) on [Monday] (*date*) at (*time*) am/pm [for the purpose of considering and if thought fit passing the following resolution[s] which will be proposed as to resolutions 1 and 2 as ordinary resolutions, as to resolution 3 as an extraordinary resolution and as to resolution 4 as a special resolution.

as ordinary resolutions

1   (*resolution*)

2   (*resolution*)

as a special resolution

3   (*resolution*)]

(*or*)

for the purpose of considering (*matters to be considered*) and passing such resolutions in relation to them as is thought fit.

[*add where special notice of a resolution has been given to the Company*[14]]

AND NOTICE IS ALSO GIVEN that notice has been received by the Company of the intention to move at the [meeting (*or*) meeting convened by the accompanying notice to be held on (*date*)[15]] the following resolution [and that there have been received representations, of which a copy is enclosed[16]]:

5   (*resolution*)

Dated (*date*)

By order of the Board

---

[13] For the length of prior notice and the electronic communication of notices, see note "Meetings of shareholders, notices and resolutions". The notice of a special resolution must either set out the resolution in full or the entire substance of it: Re Moorgate Mercantile Holdings Ltd [*1980*] *1 All ER 40*, [*1980*] *1 WLR 227*. It is prudent to set out the resolution in full in all cases. The requisitionists of an EGM may, if the directors do not do so within 21 days from the requisition, themselves convene the meeting. In this case the notice should be signed by the requisitionists instead of the company secretary and the following should be added in the place of the words 'By order of the Board': 'This meeting is being convened by us who have signed below pursuant to the powers conferred by s368 of the 1985 Act'. Alternatively, if the articles do not otherwise provide (Table A (both 1948 and 1985) is silent on the point), two or more members holding not less than one tenth of the issued share capital may call a meeting without any prior requisition in which case in these alternative words, 's370(3)' should be substituted for 's368'.

[14] See CA 1985, s379.

[15] This notice need not be set out in the notice convening the meeting, but should be given at the same time and in the same manner as the latter.

[16] The words in brackets are not required in the case of the election of a director over the age of 70.

(*signature*)

(Company Secretary)

Notes:

1. A member entitled to attend and vote at the meeting is entitled to appoint a proxy [or more than one proxy] to attend and vote in his or her place. A proxy may demand, or join in demanding, a poll. A proxy need not be a member of the Company[17].

2. We the undersigned being members or representatives of members[1] of the Company holding not less than [all (*or*) [95]%] of the nominal value of the shares giving a right to attend and vote at the meeting consent to the convening of the extraordinary meeting for the date and place above mentioned and the passing at it of the resolution(s) above set out[18].

---

17. This statement must appear if the company has a share capital. A member of a private company may not appoint more than one proxy unless the articles otherwise provide: CA 1985, s372(2)(b), and Table A, reg 59 (but no 1948 equivalent). If the company's securities are listed THE Listing Rules require it to send two-way proxy forms with this notice in respect of all resolutions except those which are merely procedural. By ss372(2A) and (2G) inserted by the Companies Act 1985 (Electronic Communications) Order 2000, the appointment of a proxy may be made by an electronic communication.

18. CA 1985, s369(3)(b). The requisite majority is 95% of the nominal value of shares with a right to attend and vote at the meetings or, if there is no share capital, 95% of the voting rights at that meeting: s369(4). If the appropriate elective resolution has been passed the requisite majority may be not less than 90%

Basic form of members' written resolution[19]

(*name*) Ltd

company (*number*)

The Companies Acts 1985 to 1989

company limited by shares

RESOLUTION of the members passed on (*date*) under regulation [(*number*) in the Company's articles of association (*or*) 53 in the Companies (Tables A to F) Regulations 1985] (*or*) [73A (*or*) 5 in Part II] of Table A in the first Schedule to the Companies Act 1948 incorporated in the Company's articles of association].

Resolved as [an] [ordinary (*or*) extraordinary (*or*) special] resolution[s]

---

[19] The Companies Act 1989 introduced a new regime for written resolutions of private companies, contained in the CA 1985, ss381A, 381B, 381C and Schedule 15A. This regime:
  (i) enables private companies to pass resolutions in writing in the absence of any power to do so in their articles or even despite any prohibition in the memorandum or articles (but in view of the statutory restrictions it may be quicker and easier to alter the articles); and
  (ii) remove any lingering doubts about the existing system, eg matters expressly required to be done by the company in meeting including special and elective resolutions. Written resolutions under s381A may not be used to remove a director or auditor before the expiration of their term of office: CA 1985, Sch 15A. The Schedule also contains other detailed provisions about written resolutions passed under s381A. Probably a director cannot be removed from office under s303 by a written resolution pursuant to the articles (eg Table A, reg 53), because by s304 he is entitled to be heard on the resolution at the meeting at which his removal is considered.

The Deregulation (Resolutions of Private Companies) Order 1996, SI 1996/1471 introduced a new s381B into the CA 1985, to replace the s 381B introduced by the 1989 Act and to remove some of the problems created by that section. It is now sufficient that the auditors are given a copy of the resolution or 'otherwise notified of its contents' at or before the time that the resolution is supplied to any member for signature, and the auditors no longer have seven days in which to respond. There is now however a criminal offence (with a maximum fine of £1,000) for failure to comply with the section, but the failure does not invalidate the resolution. The section expressly states that the obligation to send a copy to the auditors does not apply so companies exempt from the requirement to appoint auditors. The previous doubts, whether the statutory procedure supplemented or supplanted existing procedures for written resolutions in companies' articles of association, eg reg 53 in Table A have been resolved: s381C has been altered to provide that the statutory regime applies notwithstanding anything in the company's memorandum or articles of association and does not prejudice any power given in them.

Regulation 53 of Table A, which states that a resolution signed by all the members (including the authorised representatives of corporations) entitled to receive notice of and attend and vote at general meetings shall be as valid and effective as if it had been passed at a general meeting of the company duly convened and held.

All the shareholders acting together can do anything intra vires the company, notwithstanding the lack of any notice, meeting or written and signed document: Cane v Jones *[1981] 1 All ER 533, [1980] 1 WLR 1451*. In the light of this decision and of s380(4)(c) of the CA 1985, there should be little doubt that this means of passing a resolution may apply to extraordinary, special and elective resolutions and not only to ordinary resolutions; notwithstanding that extraordinary and special resolutions must by the CA 1985, s378(1) and (2) and that elective resolutions by s379A(1) be passed at a general meeting and that reg 53 applies subject to the provisions of the CA 1985. However, see Re Barry Artists Ltd *[1985] 1 WLR 1305, [1985] BCLC 283*, in which Nourse J confirmed with great reluctance a resolution to reduce capital passed in writing by all the shareholders and not by a special resolution at a duly convened meeting. He did not doubt the effectiveness of the resolution, but was troubled on account of the court's discretion to confirm or refuse to confirm it.

(*resolution*)

(*resolution*)

(*resolution*)

Signed

(*all the members*)

Basic form of members' written resolution passed under s 381A[1]

(*name*) Ltd

company (*number*)

The Companies Acts 1985 to 1989

company limited by shares

RESOLUTION of the members passed on (*date*) under the Companies Act 1985, s 381A. Resolved as a (*or*) an ordinary (*or*) extraordinary (*or*) special (*or*) elective resolution[s]

(*resolution*)

(*resolution*)

(*resolution*)

Signed

(*all the members*)

Meetings, Notice and Resolutions

1   Meetings (of members)

(a)   Annual general meeting

    CA 1985, s 366.

(b)   Other general meetings

There is no statutory definition of other meetings, although the CA 1985, s 368(1) provides for extraordinary general meetings to be convened on a requisition by members. Thus the matter is one to be determined by the articles of association. Regulation 36 of Table A (1948 Table A, reg 48) states that all meetings other than annual general meetings shall be called extraordinary general meetings.

2   Notices [20]

(a)   Annual general meetings—21 days: CA 1985, s369(1)(a);

(b)   Other general meetings of limited companies—14 days; and of unlimited companies—7 days: CA 1985, s369(1)(b);

(c)   General meetings to consider a special resolution—21 days: CA 1985, s378(2);

(d)   General meetings to consider an elective resolution—21 days: CA 1985, s379A.

(e)   Special notice to the company—28 days: CA 1985, s 379.

(f)   Short notice

for an annual general meeting with consent of all persons entitled to attend and vote: CA 1985, s 369(3)(a);

for other meeting with consent of a majority of 95% of the nominal value of the shares giving a right to attend and vote: CA 1985, ss369(3)(b) and (4) and 378(3) or a majority not below 90% in the appropriate elective resolution.

3   Resolutions

(a)   *Extraordinary*

CA 1985, s378(1). Majority of not less than three-quarters. Fourteen days' notice.

Required under the following sections of the 1985 Act:

s125(2), (6): to sanction a variation of rights at a separate general meeting of the class;

Required under the following sections of the 1986 Act:

s84(1)(c): to resolve that the company cannot by reason of its liabilities continue its business and that it is advisable to wind up;

s165(1)(a): to permit the liquidator to exercise certain powers under Part I of Sch 4 to the Insolvency Act 1986 in the case of a members' voluntary winding up.

---

[20] By Table A regulation 116 (1948 Table A regulation 131) service of notices, when sent by post, are deemed to be effected 48 hours (1948 version, 24 hours) after posting.

(b) *Special*

CA 1985, s378(2). Majority of not less than three-quarters. Twenty-one days' notice. Required by a company for the following purposes:

s4: to alter its objects in its memorandum;

s9: to alter its articles;

s17: to alter conditions in its memorandum which could have been in its articles;

s28: to change its name;

s35(3): to ratify action by directors beyond capacity of company;

s35(3): to relieve directors from liability from action beyond capacity of company;

s43(1)(a): to enable a private company to re-register as public

s51(1): to re-register an unlimited company as limited;

s53(1)(a): to re-register a public company as private;

s95(1), (2): to empower the directors to disregard the statutory pre-emption rights on the allotment of equity securities;

s120: to reserve uncalled capital for winding-up;

s135: to reduce its capital;

s155(4): to authorise a private company to give financial assistance for the purchase of its own shares;

s164(2): to authorise a company to make an off-market purchase of its own shares;

s164(3): to vary, revoke or review an authority under s164(2);

s164(7): to agree to a variation of a contract by a company to purchase its own shares;

s165(2): to approve a contingent purchase contract by a company to purchase its own shares;

s167(2): to approve an agreement by a company to release its rights under a contract approved under ss164 or 165;

s173(2): to approve a payment out of capital by a company for the redemption or purchase of its own shares;

s250(1): to enable a dormant company to make itself exempt from the obligation to appoint auditors.

s307: to make the liability of its directors unlimited;

s308: to approve an agreement enabling a director or manager to assign his office;

s690(1): to enable such a company to alter its form of constitution by substituting a memorandum and articles for a deed of settlement; and

s21, para 6(2): to enable a company, not formed under the Act but registered under Part VIII of it, to adopt Table A.

Required under the Insolvency Act 1986 for the following purposes:

s84(1)(a) and (b): to be wound up voluntarily;

s110(3): in a members' voluntary winding up to authorise the liquidator to receive, for distribution amongst members, shares, policies or other like interests in another company acquiring the whole or part of the business of the company being wound up;

s122(1)(a): to be wound up by the court.

(c) *Elective*[21]

CA 1985, s379A(1): Only a private company. Unanimous. Twenty one days' notice. Required under the following sections of the CA 1985:

s80A: as to duration of authority to allot shares;

s252: to dispense with laying of accounts and reports before general meeting;

s366A: to dispense with holding of annual general meeting;

s369(4) or 378(3): as to majority required to authorise short notice of meeting; and

s386: to dispense with appointment of auditors annually.

(d) *Under CA 1985, s425*

Majority of not less than three-quarters. Notice etc as the court directs. Purpose of agreeing a compromise between creditors and members.

(e) *Others*

Normally called ordinary resolutions.

---

21 By Companies Act 1989, s117 the Secretary of State may make regulations for other elections by private companies.

Company law: how many votes do you need?

Sally Ramage presented a Paper at the Annual Soico-Legal Conference at Liverpool University in March 2005, partl of a table comprising similar data for UK, France and Germany, used to discuss whether the new European Company Statute would oust shareholder power.

one member or more

change of status from limited to unlimited: s49, s78(2)

quorum: s370, Table A reg 42, 43

meetings called by the court: s371.

meetings called by the DTI: s367.

elective resolution: s379A

winding up because it is just and equitable: s122(1) IA 1986

unfair prejudice: ss459 to 461

rights of contributors in insolvency: IA 1986 s27(1), s92(2), s111(2), s112(1), s116, s124(1), s126(1), s139(4), s147(1), s167(3), s170(2), s195(1), s201(3), s212(3), s218(1),(6)

declaration that dissolution is void: s651

application for restoration to register: s653

short notice at annual general meetings: s369, s378, s369(3)(a), s379A(2A)

5% or 100 members average sum of not less than £100 paid up

members' requisition for resolution and statement: s376 circulation of about it

10%

meetings requisitioned by members: s368

meetings called by members: s370(3)

meetings called by liquidator on request of members: s168(2) IA 1986

demand a poll: s 373 (or five members)

maximum non-cash transfer to plc: s104

15%

change of memorandum of association: s4, s17

variation of shareholders' rights: s127

20% (one fifth)

director's association with body corporate: s346(4)

"associated" for the purpose of group accounts; sched 4A para 20

25% + 1 vote

"negative control" to block extraordinary or a special resolution: s378(1), s378(2)

arrangements and reconstruction: s425(2)

registration of companies not formerly under Act: s681(1) [25%], s681(4) [any]

Part XXII of the CA 1985 contains provisions for the under the CA 1985 companies not formed under it: s681(1) [25%], s681(4) [any]

powers of creditors in a liquidation: IA 1986 s136(5)(c), s168(2), s171(2)(b)

resolutions in insolvency requiring majority of three fourths: s192(2)(b), s192(4), s425(2), s681(2), sch15B 1 s425(2).

one-third or one-half

alteration of a floating charge in debentures: s70(2)(b)(ii) IA 1986, s466(3)(c) (Scotland only)

one-half

director's control of a body corporate (enforcement of fair dealing by directors): s346(5)

50%

"normal" control by ordinary resolutions

requesting a meeting in winding up: s171(3)(a) IA 1986.

one-half, three-quarters

public examination of officers of company in liquidation: s133(2) IA 1986.

three-quarters

requisite majorities at creditors' meetings: Part I (Company Voluntary Arrangements): Insolvency Rules, r1.19(1).

Conclusion to "shareholders' powers"

These examples of minority rights show that minorities have in general no say in the day to day running and control of a company. Although they may cause meetings to be called and resolutions to be put forward their rights are largely negative and relate to basic questions such as the constitution of the company. It is when a company is in liquidation that minorities however small have the largest opportunity to take the initiative.

In certain cases the prescribed majorities are based on the numbers actually present and voting, whereas in other cases they are based on the numbers entitled to attend and vote whether or not they actually do so.

Company Law

Test Yourself.

1. Which, if any, of these answers is correct?

   The Companies Act 1985 requires that when equity shares are allotted for cash they must be offered first to existing shareholders in proportion to their holding in the company. Such an issue of shares is known as:

   a rights issue?

   a preference issue?

   an issue of founders' shares?

2. The articles of private companies often provide that members wishing to sell their shares must offer them first to existing members. What is such a clause called?

   An expropriation clause.

   A compulsory purchase clause.

   A pre-emption clause.

3. The Registrar may accept a copy of a resolution in a form other than a printed copy, but the document must be durable and legible.

   True?

   (b) False?

4. Explain how and in what circumstances a general meeting of a company will be called.

   Explain what minimum period of notice must be given to call an extraordinary general meeting and whether and how such period may be shortened/lengthened.

5. What members' meetings are held by registered companies?

6. What is an extraordinary resolution and when is such a resolution required under the Companies Act 1985?

   What is special business? Identify two matters which would be included under such business.

   What is a requisitioned circular? Who may demand it and who bears the cost?

7. Certain ordinary resolutions require special notice. Which of the following resolutions require special notice?

The removal of a director before the expiration of his period of office?

The appointment of a director who is over seventy years old?

The appointment of an auditor to replace the present auditor?

The removal of an auditor before the expiry of the term of office?

8. Is a special resolution required for the alteration of the objects clause?

9. In what circumstance may the members of a company who have requisitioned an EGM call the meeting themselves?

a) If the directors do not call a meeting to be held within 21 days of the deposit of the requisition.

b) If the directors do not within 21 days from the date of the deposit of the requisition call a meeting for a date not more than 28 days after the notice calling the meeting.

10. If a company is a member of another company, it may appoint a representative to act on its behalf at a meeting. Is this true?

11. Which section of the UK Companies Act applies to the following statement ?

12. If a company's directors send invitations to members at the company's expense, to appoint specified persons as proxies, invitations must be sent to all the members who are entitled to the notice of the meeting.

Why do you think this was a necessary section of the legislation?

13. What is the minimum period of notice which must be given to the members of a limited company who are entitled to be present and vote in person or by proxy at an EGM to pass an ordinary resolution?

a) 28 days.

b) 1 days.

c) 14 days.

d) 7 days.

5—Directors, Secretary and Powers of Companies and Officers

Contents

Who does what in a registered company?

Directors and secretary—what and why?

Appointment of directors

Retirement and removal by rotation

Removal by members—registration

Small print detail

Division and exercise of power

What can the company do? Ultra vires

Authority of directors

Directors' duties

Director's interest in shares

Dealings between director and company

Disqualification and personal liability

Company secretary and duties

Draft minutes of first meeting of directors

1 Who does what in a registered company?

members

provide the capital
owners (of the company, not the business)
entitled to profits
normally no liability
appoint the directors
no powers of management

directors

manage the company
answerable to the company
may work for it but not necessarily
risk of personal liability, but normally none

employees

work
but (in theory) not manage

2 Directors and secretary—what and why?

s 741	directors	what?	as statutorily defined
			"director" includes any person occupying the position of director, by whatever name called
		also	shadow directors
s 282		why?	public—at least two
			private—at least one
Table A, reg 64		NB	articles may alter
s 283	secretary		no definition
			typical—see note
s 283		why?	must have one
			but not sole director
Table A, reg 99		NB	articles may alter

3   Appointment of directors

s 282 Table A, reg 64	how many	but	1 or 2 (sheet 2) articles - - - - - - - - might be more
s 10 (2)(b)	original		subscribers articles (perhaps)
	subsequently	but	theoretically members actually directors
Table A regs 76, 77	by general meeting only if		recommended by directors prior notice to company and members notice of willingness
Table A reg 79	by directors		any time, anyhow

4 Retirement by rotation and removal

Table A reg 81	retire	resignation by notice
	by rotation	articles not statute
Table A reg 73		1st AGM all
Table A reg 73	then	1/3rd each year
Table A reg 74		by seniority
Table A reg 79	if appointed by directors	next AGM
Table A reg 84		except executive
Table A reg 75	deemed reappointment if	vacancy not filled and willing to act
	unless	resolution to reappoint put and lost
Table A reg 81	also removed if	prohibited by law bankrupt mental disorder 6 months' absence
s 303		ordinary resolution

5   Removal by members—registration

s 303(1)	removal by	ordinary resolution
s 303(1)		notwithstanding articles
s 303(2)		special notice
s 304(2)	director's right	written representations
s 304(1)		to be heard at meeting

	rigmarole therefore	alter articles, eg removal by extraordinary resolution

s 10	Registrar of Companies	original appointment
s 288		subsequent changes

s 288	the company	register of directors and secretaries

s 299	details	name, former name, usual residential address, nationality, business occupation other directorships, date of change

6 Small print detail

s 292	voted on individually	if PLC ie not "en bloc"
s 293	age limit	age 70 if PLC or subsidiary of PLC
s 305	age limit	company notepaper names not necessary if one appears all must
Table A reg 84	employment	may be (in addition to office)
Table A reg 82, 83, 87	payments	remuneration expense pensions
s 312		compensation for loss of office
Company Accounts (Disclosure of Directors' Emoluments) Regulations 1997		disclosure
s 318	contacts	open for inspection
s 319	approval	GM if term > 5 years

7 Division and exercise of power

	company and directors	can do anything permissible
	allocation	articles
reg 70	Table A	business managed by directors
	subject to	directions by special resolution
	delegation by directors	to committee to managing director to other executive directors
	otherwise	collective decisions
s 285	defective appointment	directors' acts are valid

8 What can the company do? Ultra vires

capacity of company—NOT authority of directors etc

	reminder		artificial legal body
		so	do only what is permitted by its rules
s 3	objects clause		memorandum of association
	old view		protection of shareholders
	actually		trap for unwary creditors
s 3A	therefore		general commercial company
s 35A	protection of 3rd parties		directors' powers deemed to be unrestricted
s 35B			no 3rd party bound to enquire
s 711A			no one deemed to have notice of registered documents

9 Authority of directors

authority of directors etc—NOT capacity of company

    see sheet 7—Table A and delegation

s 35, 35A	3rd parties	may assume directors have authority
s 35A(2)(b)		even if actual knowledge of lack of authority

s 35(2)	company	obtain injunction to prevent ultra vires act by directors
s 35(3)		sue for damages if directors act ultra vires
		sue for damages if directors act outside authority
s 35(3)		liability removed by special resolution

s 322A	between company and directors	voidable if outside directors' authority

10   Directors' duties

	to company	fiduciary
		skill and care
	to shareholders	basically none
		exception if quoted
s 309	to employees	none—but must have regard to interests of employees
s 719		provide for employees on cessation or transfer of business
IA s187		liquidator may make payments decided under s 719
	to creditors	none while solvent
		but different in insolvency

11 Director's interest in shares

s 324, Sch 13	directors must notify company	interest in shares or debentures on becoming director
		becoming or ceasing to have interest in shares or debentures
		within five days of event
s 327		including spouse and children
s 325, Sch 13	company must keep	register of interests
		open to inspection by members
	enforcement	fine or imprisonment
		applies to shadow directors

12 Dealings between director and company

s 317	transactions	must disclose interest in contracts with company
		to whole board
Table A, regs 94-98		articles may (eg) exclude vote
s 320	substantial property transactions	approval by ordinary resolution

s 330	loan to directors	prohibited
s 331		includes guarantees and quasi loans
s 334		OK if < £5 ie "small"
s 337		OK if to fund expenses
		also to director of holding company
		also to connected persons

13 Disqualification and personal liability

Companies Directors Disqualification Act 1986

s 2	indictable offence
ss 3, 5	breach of company law
s 4	fraudulent trading
ss 6, 7, 9	unfitness
s 8	DTI inspection

personal liability   main examples

	pre-incorporation
s 35(3)	ultra vires
s 349(1)	orders cheques etc
CDDA s 15	contravention of a disqualification order
IA s 213	fraudulent trading
IA s 214	wrongful trading
IA s 217	"phoenix companies"

Duties of Company Secretary

Every company must have a company secretary (Companies Act 1985, s283). If the company is a PLC, the secretary must be qualified (ibid, s286).

The secretary is the company's principal administrative officer whose duties normally include:

issuing notices of directors' and shareholders' meetings;

keeping minutes of the meetings;

keeping the company's statutory registers (members, directors' interest in shares, charges and mortgages etc);

filing returns to the Registrar of Companies (increases of capital, allotments of shares, appointment and removal of directors and secretary, annual returns etc);

registering transfers of shares;

issue of communications to shareholders and directors;

maintaining up to date copies of the memorandum and articles of association;

payment of dividends; and

receipt of communications to the company (formal communications often being addressed to "the Secretary").

The functions of a company secretary are often combined with other office (eg director, but not sole director) and administrative accounting or commercial duties, which typically could include responsibilities for:

accounts;

administrative staff or staff generally;

insurances;

management of directors' and employees' company cars;

office management;

pension scheme;

printing and stationery; and

purchase and maintenance of administration and office equipment.

> NB   This precedent is © Butterworths and is from chapter 13 of Kelly's Draftsman 18th Edition (2003), general editor Roderick Ramage.
>
> This precedent is supplied by kind permission of Roderick Ramage only to illustrate what is commonly contained at a first meeting of the directors and is not to be used in any particular case.

Minutes of first meeting of directors after incorporation

(*name*) Ltd

company (*number*)

MINUTES of the first meeting of the directors

Present   (*name-A*)

(*name-B*)

(*name-C*)

in attendance

Place

Date

Time

DOCUMENTS PRODUCED

The following documents were produced to the meeting:

the Company's certificate of incorporation on (*date*) as company number (*number*);

a copy of the Company's memorandum and articles of association;

"Appointment Resolution" a written resolution passed on (*date*) by the subscribers appointing (*name*) and (*name*) as directors;

"Resignations" signed but undated resignations by (*name*) and (*name*) as directors and secretary;

"Transfers" signed and stamped but undated transfers by (*name*) and (*name*) of [the right to subscribe for] the subscriber shares;

"Contracts Account" an account setting out particulars of assets acquired, contracts entered into, moneys expended, liabilities incurred by (*name*) and (*name*) to the intent that they should be adopted and acquired by the Company after its incorporation;

(*name*) Bank plc's printed mandate and specimen signature form;

applications by (*name-A*) for (*number*) shares and (*name-B*) for (*number*) shares;

"Sale Agreement" an agreement intended to be made between (*name-A*) and the Company for the acquisition by the Company of (*name-A*)'s business of (*description*);

"Debenture-A" a debenture intended to be given by the Company to (*name-A*);

"Debenture-B" a debenture intended to be given by the Company to (*name-B*);

"Service Agreement-A" a service agreement intended to be made between (*name-A*); and

"Service Agreement-B" a service agreement intended to be made between (*name-B*).

REPORTED

The Company had been incorporated by its subscribers (*name*) and (*name*) on (*date*) with number (*number*) and with the memorandum and articles of association a copy of which with the certificate of incorporation were produced to the meeting.

The subscribers had appointed themselves to be the Company's first directors and (*name*) to be its secretary [and that they had lodged the Appointment Resolution and the Resignations with the Company].

The Company's registered office as filed with the Registrar of Companies by the promoters is (*address*).

The two subscribers had each undertaken to subscribe for one share in the Company's capital [and had lodged the Transfers with the Company duly stamped].

DECLARATIONS OF INTERESTS

(*name*) and (*name*) declared their interests in the subject matter of resolutions (*number*), (*number*) and (*number*).

RESOLUTIONS

APPOINTMENTS OF DIRECTORS, et cetera.

[*where the first directors are (eg) the promoters' solicitors or accountants and attend the meetings*]

(*name*) and (*name*) be appointed additional directors of the Company until the next annual general meeting. the Company's certificate of incorporation on (*date*) as company number (*number*);

[*Where the promoters are the original directors, they simply take office without further resolution*]

The [written] resignations [produced [to the meeting (*or*) with these resolutions]] of (*name*) and (*name*) as directors and of (*name*) as the Company's secretary be accepted with [immediate effect (*or*) effect from (*date*)].

(*name*) be appointed chairman of the board of directors.

name) be appointed the Company's secretary.

(*name*) & Co be appointed the Company's auditors.

(*name*) Bank Ltd at its branch at (*address*) be appointed the Company's bank. (Attached to these minutes is the copy of the resolution and mandate form required by the bank.)

(*name*) & Co be appointed the Company's solicitors.

REGISTRATION ETC FORMALITIES

The Company's registered office be moved to (*address*).

The Company's statutory registers be kept at the registered office.

The Company's accounting reference date be (*date*).

SEAL [*if any*]

The seal impressed on these minutes be adopted as the Company's seal.

TRANSFER OF SUBSCRIBER SHARES ALLOTMENT

[*if the memorandum and articles of association are subscribed by nominees or law agents, add the following*]

The transfer[s] from (*name*) to (*name*) [and from (*name*) to (*name*)], each of [the right to subscribe for] one share in the Company's capital, be accepted [the share[s] having been subscribed for in the memorandum of association but not having been issued and [the (*or*) each] transferee assuming the liability to pay the subscription price of £[1] to the Company.

ALLOTMENT OF SHARES

The following shares [including the subscriber shares] be allotted for cash at par and that the allottees be entered in the register of members and that share certificates be executed by the Company and issued to them as follows:

	Shares		
Allottee	number	from	to
(*name*)	500	1	500
(*name*)	300	501	800
(*name*)	200	801	1,000
Total	1,000	1	1,000

BUSINESS

(*name*) and (*name*) declared their interests in the matter as Sellers. The Company adopts and acquires from them the whole of the assets acquired and the contracts entered into by them all of which are listed in the account produced to the meeting and annexed to these minutes and in consideration for them [pays to them in cash (*or*) acknowledges that it is indebted to them by way of [unsecured and interest-free] loans for such amounts as have been expended by them respectively in respect of those assets and are shown in the account] and undertakes to adopt and accept all liability for all of such contracts as have not been performed and to compensate (*name*) and (*name*) in full on demand for all liabilities in respect of them. (*name*)

(*Name-A*) and (*name-B*) declared their interests as seller and lender respectively in the matters dealt with in this resolution. The Company (having received from (*name-B*) an application for (*number*) shares to be issued at the price of £(.....) ((.....) pounds) per share and a cheque for the total price of £(.....) ((.....) pounds)):

- acquires from (*name-A*) the business of a (*description*) carried on by [him] and for that purpose enter into the [Sale Agreement (or) agreement produced to the meeting marked '(*name*)-1' ("Sale Agreement")];
- that the Sale Agreement be signed by (*name*) on behalf of the Company;
- the following shares [including the subscriber shares] be allotted as follows:

(a) to (*name-A*) (*number*) £[1] shares credited as fully paid pursuant to the Sale Agreement and in [part] consideration for the transfer of the business to the Company under it; and

(b) to (*name-B*) (*number*) £[1] shares credited as fully paid for cash at [the issue price of £[2] per share (*or*) par];

- the Company's seal be affixed to the share certificates and the certificates be delivered to the respective allottees;
- the Company acknowledges its indebtedness to (*name-A*) and (*name-B*) in respect of the [unsecured interest free] loans made as follows:

(a) by (*name-A*) for £(.....) ((.....) pounds) representing the balance of the consideration payable to [him] under the sale agreement, and

(b) by (*name-B*) for £(.....) ((.....) pounds) paid to the Company in cash; and

- the Company issues to (*name-A*) and (*name-B*) as security for the loans debentures in the form of the documents produced to the meeting and marked respectively "(*name*)-2" and "(*name*)-3" and accordingly that the Company's seal be affixed to the debentures.

SERVICE AGREEMENTS

(*name*) and (*name*) declared their interests in the matter. Service agreements be offered to (*name*) and (*name*) in the form of the documents produced to the meeting and marked respectively "(*initials*)" and "(*initials*)" and (*name*) be authorised to sign them on behalf of the Company.

CONCLUSION

There being no other business, the meeting was declared closed.

SIGNED

(*name*)

chairman

TEST YOURSELF

PRACTICAL QUESTION

You work for a firm of solicitors and have attended the first meeting with some business people who need advice about the establishment of a company. The following is a file note taken at that meeting. Whilst it is reasonably clear what the parties wish to achieve, it is clear that they have not worked out all the detail and are not aware of all the legal issues. Read the following note carefully and prepare the advice requested in paragraphs 5 and 6.

SALLY RAMAGE and CHARLOTTE TONKINSON are partners under the name RAMAGE & TONKINSON in the business of manufacturing corkscrews, which is carried on in an industrial unit held on a lease which will expire on Lady day 2005. They have ten employees, plant and machinery on hire purchase from COPEHALE Finance plc, various contracts with suppliers for commonly available components and materials and a long term supply agreement with French Steel Ltd, terminable on six months' prior notice, for the supply of a key component which cannot readily be obtained elsewhere. Apart from the hire purchase agreement, the partners have an overdraft with their bank secured by mortgages on their houses. Part of their sales come directly through the internet and other advertising and the rest from an exclusive agent, ANGELA WHEELER, whose contract can be terminated on three months' notice.

SALLY RAMAGE and CHARLOTTE TONKINSON are negotiating to supply corkscrews to WINES-ARE-US Ltd, a major supplier of accoutrements to UK wine merchants. If they win the contract, it will double their production and they will need a bigger factory and additional capital to finance their increased level of business. An adviser at the local Chamber of Commerce recommended that they form a company to carry on the business and invited them to a meeting at which they made presentations to a number of so-called "business angels". Three of the business angels, Samantha, Michael and Edward, are interested in participating in a new company to carry on the increased Ramage & Tonkinson business, if they win the WINES-ARE-US Ltd contract.

Samantha owns a suitable factory for the business but is not prepared to invest any money in the company. Michael and Edward are both prepared to put money in the company if the other does, but want a guaranteed income plus a share of profits and security for their money, so that they can be paid out in five years time or, if the company goes into liquidation, ahead of Sally Ramage and Charlotte Tonkinson and, if possible ahead of the ordinary trade creditors. Samantha would like similar preferred treatment for her investment of the factory she owns. Each of Samantha, Michael and Edward will give part time help to the business and be directors of the company. Sally Ramage and Charlotte Tonkinson insist that they must have day to day control of the business and an agreed share or amount of profit before any is paid to the business angels. They also want the bank to release their houses from the mortgages.

They decide to form a new company, Ramage & Tonkinson (2005) Ltd, to take over the business Ramage & Tonkinson on 1 October 2005. Sally Ramage and Charlotte Tonkinson will receive shares in exchange for the business. They will each have 35% of the ordinary shares in the company and each of the business angels will have 10%. It has not been decided whether any other classes of shares or other security should be made available to the latter. It is assumed that the bank will want a first fixed and floating charge to secure the overdraft, which the company will need in spite of the introduction of additional capital by the business angels.

You have been consulted by all five of them and asked to advise about the company structure and what contracts and other documents will be needed to establish the above arrangements. You are not advising any of them individually and each of them understands that he must taken independent advice about his personal interest in the arrangements.

In particular you will consider the followings issues:

how (if at all) to deal with the existing Ramage & Tonkinson contracts, ie

the lease,

the employees,

the hire purchase agreement with Copehale Finance plc,

the bank,

the ordinary trade suppliers and creditors,

the supply contract with French Steel Ltd

the ordinary customers,

the agent Angela Wheeler[22], and

the new customer, WINES-ARE-US Ltd;

the documents needed to

establish the company,

transfer the Ramage & Tonkinson business to it; and

secure the interest of the bank and, if required, the various interests of Samantha, Michael and Edward and

how the share capital of Ramage & Tonkinson(2005) Ltd should be structured, what resolutions need to be passed and by whom and what provisions should be contained in the articles of association[23] or any other documents to deal with the different interests of the parties.

You are not required to draft any legal documents, but should identify what documents will be required and the matters which will be dealt with them. You must identify and describe the legal issues and the problems (legal rather than commercial) that the parties might face. You are expected to suggest alternative solutions for the parties to consider. There is no single answer and credit will be given for the number of material legal points which are identified.

---

[22] Pretend that the Commercial Agents (Council Directive) Regulations 1993, SI 1993/3053 and SI 1993/3173 do not exist and that this relationship is governed by contract without any statutory interference.

[23] These should be based on Table A with appropriate modifications.

Company Law

Test Yourself some more…

1. An additional director is to be appointed to the board of a company. What steps must taken:

a) if the appointments is by the members; and

b) if by the directors?

2. Unless the articles of a company carry a contrary provision directors must retire from office:

a) every five years but may be re-elected any number of times;

b) every three years with re-election any number of times;

c) every three years with re-election only three more times; or

d) every five years with re-election only three more times.

3. 'A modern company secretary is not a mere clerk but an officer of the company with extensive duties and responsibilities and he has ostensible authority to sign contracts in connection with the administration side of a company's affairs.' Discuss this statement.

4. A director can be removed at a general meeting of his company. What kind of resolution is required?.

5. What principle is illustrated in the case Hogg v Cramphorn Ltd (1967)?

6. Directors can be disqualified under the Company Directors Disqualification Act 1986. The power is NOT LIMITED to offe3nces involving the internal management of a company. What can you research about R v Corbin (1984) 6 Cr App Rep (s) 17, R v Austen(1985) 7 Cr App Rep 214, CA, R v Young (1990) 12 Cr App Rep (S) 262, CA, and R v Holmes (1992) 13 Cr App Rep (S) 29, CA ?

7. Part 1V of the Companies Act 1985, Investigation of Companies and their affairs, Requisition of Documents, section 434 states:

"Production of documents and evidence to inspectors.

When inspectors are appointed under section 431 or 432, it is the duty of all officers and agents of the company, and of all officers and agents of any other body corporate whose affairs are investigated under section 433

to produce to the inspectors all [documents] of or relating to the company or, as the case may be, the other body corporate which are in their custody or power....

....

Which document did Earnest Saunders of the GUINNESS serious Fraud Case infamously destroy?

a) an email?

b) a letter?

c) a set of management accounts?

d) his diary?

8. Which section of the 1985 Companies Act contains the equivalent or near equivalent of section 188 of the 1945 Companies Act "where a person is convicted on indictment of any offence in connection with the promotion, formation or management of a company....the court may make an order that that person shall not , without the leave of the court, be a director of or in any way, whether directly or indirectly,, be concerned or take part in the management of a company for such period not exceeding 5 years....?

9. 'The matters to which the directors of a company are to have regard in the performance of their functions include the interests of the company's employees in general as well as the interests of its members'

What is the effect of this provision and how may it be enforced?

10. A managing director is usually appointed by the other directors and his powers and duties will depend on his contract of service with the company.

Explain the degree of skill and care which the law requires of a company director.

6—Borrowings, Securities and Debentures

Contents

Sources of capital

What do the parties want?

Loans—characteristics

Security—characteristics

Typical debenture

Multiple lenders

Power to borrow and mortgage

Companies Act requirements

preference under Insolvency Act 1986

avoidance under Insolvency Act 1986

enforcement of charges

1 Sources of capital
(reminder from classes 2 & 1)

source of money

| shares (equity) |
| borrowing |
| credit |

distinguish   from

| loan |
| security |

NB <u>not</u>   "I have a mortgage"
(meaningless twaddle)

loan contract

| offer and acceptance |
| consideration |
| intention to create legal relations |

eg   I

| lend money |

you

| repay money and until repaid pay interest |

2 What do the parties want?

borrower		
	1	money
	2	as long as possible
	3	as cheaply as possible
	4	freedom of action
	5	keep all profits

lender		
	1	interest
	2	repayment (but not premature)
	3	security
perhaps 4		transferability
	5	convertibility
	6	profit

3 Loans—characteristics

NB—these are examples and not exhaustive

interest

| interest free |
| fixed rate |
| variable |
| "penalty" |

repayment

| on demand |
| end of term |
| instalments |
| early |

instalments

| include interest |
| capital only |

security

| secured |
| unsecured |

4   Security—characteristics

words	"debenture" "mortgage" "charge"
essence	power to manage
and	power of sale
plus	loan contract
"charge"	fixed or floating
	legal or equitable
personalty	transfer of title & reconvey
"real" property	"charge by way of legal mortgage"
trade credit	retention of title
chattel mortgages	bill of sale (if not company)

5 Typical debenture

lender	(usually in facility letter)	
		lends fixed amount
(if bank)		provides variable "facility"

borrower

financial		fixed instalments
		overdraft on demand
		interest
security	for	all money owing present or future including interest and costs
fixed		land & buildings present and future
		plant machinery etc
floating		everything else

6 Multiple lenders

A   priorities

1st lender ranks first
must be repaid before others
2nd 3rd etc lenders

ie / then

negotiated priorities

1	existing debenture 1st charge
2	borrow to buy new property
3	fixed mortgage
4	negotiate priorities

B   series

to number of lenders
eg 100 5% 1st debentures

B   "unitised" security

debenture stock trust deed
trustee is mortgagee
trustee is intermediary between company and lenders

ie

7 Power to borrow and mortgage

s 3A   company

trading company has implied power
express power in memorandum
non-trading must have express power

may have

ss 35, 35A   but

public protected

Table A reg 70   directors

power to manage
no express borrowing power
1948 Table reg 79 limited to issued capital

NB

in practice

banks may want members' resolution

8 Companies Act requirements

	borrowing	none

s 395(2)	charges		defined
s 398			registration in 21 days
s 397			register of charges
s 399		if not	charge void
s 407			debt payable on demand
s 403			memorandum of ceasing to have effect
s 410			notice of crystallisation
s 416			chargee's deemed notice

s 190	company	register of debentures
s 185		debenture certificates
s 184		transfers of debentures
s 411		register of charges
s 412		open for inspection
s 192		trustee of debentures

9 Preference under Insolvency Act 1986

IA s 239	meaning	if	company does or fails to do anything
		so	a creditor or guarantor of its debts
			is in a better position on insolvent liquidations
	consequence		apply to court
			transaction void
IA s 240	timing		in 2 years before insolvency if person connected with company
			otherwise 6 months
	and		unable to pay its debts
	So?		secured creditor ahead of unsecured
	but		debenture voidable

10 Avoidance under Insolvency Act 1986

IA s 245	floating charge	void
	except	value of cash, good or services (market value)
		discharge or reduction of debts
		interest on above
	timing	in 2 years before insolvency if person connected with company
		otherwise 12 months
	and	unable to pay its debts (only if person <u>not</u> connected)

11   Enforcement of charges

If the borrower defaults

practical alternatives—to rescue the business

reorganise debt
new lender(s)
extend repayment period
capitalise interest
convert to equity

legal remedies

sue for debt
take possession
sell
foreclose
appoint receiver

Company Law

Test Yourself

Leyland Daf/Barleycorn precedents

A company is able to grant an effective form of security in the form of a **floating charge** in order to raise money for its activities. In other words, a lender may obtain an effective security on a company's present and future undertakings and assets.

In 2004 there was the House of Lords decision in the <u>Leyland Daf</u> case which caused heated discussion because this House of Lords judgement overturned the lower court's decision and at the3 same time over-ruled the decision in <u>Re: Barleycorn Enterprises</u> that has stood as authority for over thirty years.

The Barleycorn judgement, given by Lord Denning was overturned because it was said that Denning misconstrued the relevant statutory provisions. Denning had held that ALL assets of a company, including those subject to a floating-charge, were available to meet the proper expenses incurred in the winding up of a company,

<u>in priority</u> to the debt owed to the floating-charge holder.

The new precedent is now this—

free assets, together with <u>any surplus</u> from the floating charge fund, constitute the second fund which is held in trust for the general creditors. Therefore the costs of realising or preserving a particular asset are recoverable from floating charge realizations.

<u>This gives a new meaning to the word floating—charge.</u>

There is already a newer consideration that affects floating charges.

Is the newer development—

(a) Securitization? or

(b) New legislation?

7—Administration, Winding Up and Striking Off

Contents

Overview

Receivership

Administration & floating charges—Enterprise Act 2002

Appointment of administrator

Purpose, duration and effect of administration

Administrative receivers qualification and duties

Company voluntary arrangements

Members' voluntary winding up

Creditors' voluntary liquidation

Liquidation by the court

Liquidation procedures

Dissolution and striking off

Test Yourself

1   Overview

the rescue of a company

    or | receivership |

    or | administration |

The End of a Company

    either | winding up |

    or | striking off |

winding up   1 | compulsory |

    or

    2 | voluntary |

voluntary   1 | members |

    or

    2 | creditors |

2 Receivership

application		all mortgages not just companies
if		borrower defaults
lender may		sell
		etc (week 6)
		appoint receiver
receiver	is	appointed by lender
		agent of borrower
	may	take possession
		receive rents etc
		sell
on sale	must	pay own expenses
		repay loan
		pay balance to borrower
	or	discharge mortgage

3 Administration & floating charges
Enterprise Act 2002

    old law   before 15 Sept 2003

debenture holder	of	(substantially whole of company's property
	may appoint	receiver and manager
		ie administrative receiver
	ie	may manage
	eg	sell as going concern

transitional

floating charges
created before 15.9.03
retain power

s 72A   new law

holder of floating charges
created on and after 15.9.03
may not appoint administrative receiver

s 72B to s 72G   except for   capital market arrangements, public private partnerships, utility projects, project finance, financial market contracts and registered social landlords

                 ie

in practice unimportant

4 Appointment of administrator

2	3 methods	(a)		by court
		(b)		by QFC
IA sched B1 inserted by EA 2002 the above and following are para numbers in that schedule		(c)		by company or directors

10	by court			administration order
11		if	(a)	unable to pay debts
			(b)	achieve purpose
12		on		application by company, directors, creditors, magistrates court

14	by QFC			holder of a qualifying floating charge in respect of a company's property
		but		see sheet 3 (s72B etc)

22	by company			company or directors
25		not if		winding up petition, adminstrations application or administrative receiver in office

5 Purpose, duration and effect of administration

3	purpose	(a)	rescuing the company as a going concern
		(b)	better result for creditors as a whole than w/u
		(c)	realising assets for secured or preferred creditor

40	effect	w/u petition dismissed
41		other receiver dismissed
42		moratorium on insolvency proceedings
43		moratorium on other legal process

76,	duration		1 year unless
		extension	by court
		or	creditors (6 months)
79 to 84		ends on	court order, objective achieved, CV liquidation, dissolution

6 Administrative receivers qualification and duties

insolvency practitioner ie a person acting

IA s 388	as	liquidator provisional liquidator administrator administrative receiver supervisor of voluntary arrangements
IA s 390	must be	individual
IA s 389 IA s 392	and	qualified or authorised by DTI
IA ss 390, 391 SI 2001/1090	qualifying body	various accountancy bodies, Insolvency Practitioners Association, Law Society etc

old law—administration before 15 Sept 2003

	duties owed to	debenture holder
	not	other creditors

new law

		share for unsecured creditors
	floating charge assets	50% of 1st £10,000 then 20% up to £600,000 ie £123,000

7 Voluntary arrangements

	either	compromise with creditors (and members)
		company voluntary arrangements

s 425	compromise		
	between	company and creditors
		company and members
		or an class of either
	majority	3/4^{ths} majority
		sanction by court

IA s 1	voluntary arrangements	
IA s 1	proposed by	directors, administrator or liquidator
IA s 1	nominee	as trustee (insolvency practitioner —sheet 6)
IA s 2	procedure	trustee's report to court
IA ss 3, 4, 4A		meeting to approve (creditors 75%, members simple)
IA ss 4, 4A		approval by court

8 Members' voluntary winding up

when?

expiry of term
any other time

IA s 84(1)(a)   expiry of term

if in articles
not automatic
ordinary resolutions

IA s 84(1)(b)   any other time

special resolution

effect and practicalities

IA s 89	declaration of solvency
IA s 86	starts on resolution
IA s 91(a)	liquidator appointed
IA s 91(b)	directors' powers cease
IA s 84(3)	file copy registration
IA s 85	advertise resolution
IA s 86	business ceases
IA s 85	no share transfers

9 Creditors' voluntary liquidation

	how?		exit from administration (sheet 5)
IA s 84(1)(c)			extraordinary resolution
IA s 95			liquidator's decision during MVL
	by resolution		similar to MVL
IA s 90		Except	no declaration of solvency
IA s 84(1)(c)			extraordinary resolution
IA s 98(1)(a)			creditors' meeting
IA s 98(1)(a)			not <14 days after members' EGM
IA s 98(1)(b)			not <7 days notice to creditors
IA s 98(1)(c)			advertise in LG & local papers
IA s 99			directors' statement of affairs and affidavit
IA s 100			nominate liquidator
IA s 101			appoint liquidation committee

10 Liquidation by the court

IA s 122	grounds		special resolution
			PLC s117 not issued within 1 year
			not commence business within 1 year
			suspends business for 1 year
IA s 123			unable to pay its debts £750 or assets < liabilities
			end of moratorium
			just and equitable
IA s 124	how?		petition
		by	company, directors, creditors(s), etc
IA s 125	court may		dismiss petition
			make such order as it thinks fit

11 Liquidation procedures

IA s 129	commencement	presentation of petition
IA s 126	after petition	proceedings stayed
IA ss 135, 136		appointment of liquidator
IA s 130(1)		notify Registrar of Companies
IA s 130(2)		no proceedings
IA s 132		investigation by OR
IA s 141		liquidation committee

	1	secured (fixed)
	2	preferential
IA s 40	3	secured (floating)
	4	unsecured

SI 1986/1925	preferential	pension schemes (1 year previous)
		wages (4 months previous, max £800 + holiday pay)
EA 2002 s 252	but (from 15.9.03)	not Crown debts

12 Dissolution and striking off

    dissolution
    when?

after liquidation
after administration
other

    after liquidation

IA s 201   Voluntary

3 months after liquidator's final return

IA s 202   compulsory

3 months after   liquidator's notice of final meeting OR's notice w/u complete OR's application for early dissolution

    after administration

IA shed B1 para 84

if no property

    striking off

s 652

s 652A

reasonable cause to believe defunct
directors' application

Company Law

Test Yourself

1. The prime intention of the Insolvency Act 1986 with regard to companies is to provide various alternatives to the winding-up of an insolvent company.

Explain.

2. When the court makes an administration order, when should an administrative receiver in post vacate office?

a) If required to do so by a majority of the creditors only.

b) Automatically.

c) If required to do so by the administrator only.

d) If required to do so by a majority in number of the creditors and the administrator.

3. A person who is not qualified to act as an insolvency practitioner may nevertheless act as:

a) administrator.

b) Official Receiver.

c) provisional liquidator.

4. What kind of resolution is required to commence a voluntary winding-up when no declaration of solvency can be given?

a) Special.

b) Extraordinary.

c) Ordinary.

d) Ordinary with special notice.

5. Who can fill the office of administrator if there is a vacancy?

a) The court.

b) The creditors.

c) Anyone entitled to appoint an administrative receiver.

d) Anyone entitled to appoint an administrative receiver provided the court approves of the appointee.

8—Reconstruction, Merger, Acquisitions, Disposals

Contents

What and why?

How?

Subsidiaries and divisions

Part owned subsidiaries

Shareholder leaving—Table A unaltered

Shareholder leaving—special articles

Sale of or by private company

Sale of shares in private company

Sale of shares in private company and other

Offer for shares—"takeovers"

Test Yourself

1 What and why?

changes to | business |
| ownership |

business | what |
| more of the same |
| new |
| give up |

| capital |
| increase |
| decrease |
| change classes |

| where |
| move |
| branches |
| abroad |

ownership | new owners |
| new participants |
| ("exit") |

2　How?

capital	see week 3 notes

grow business:

organically
acquisition   vertical   horizontal
methods   companies   joint venture   agency etc   outsourcing

reduce business:

organically
close down
disposal   companies   joint venture   agency etc   outsourcing

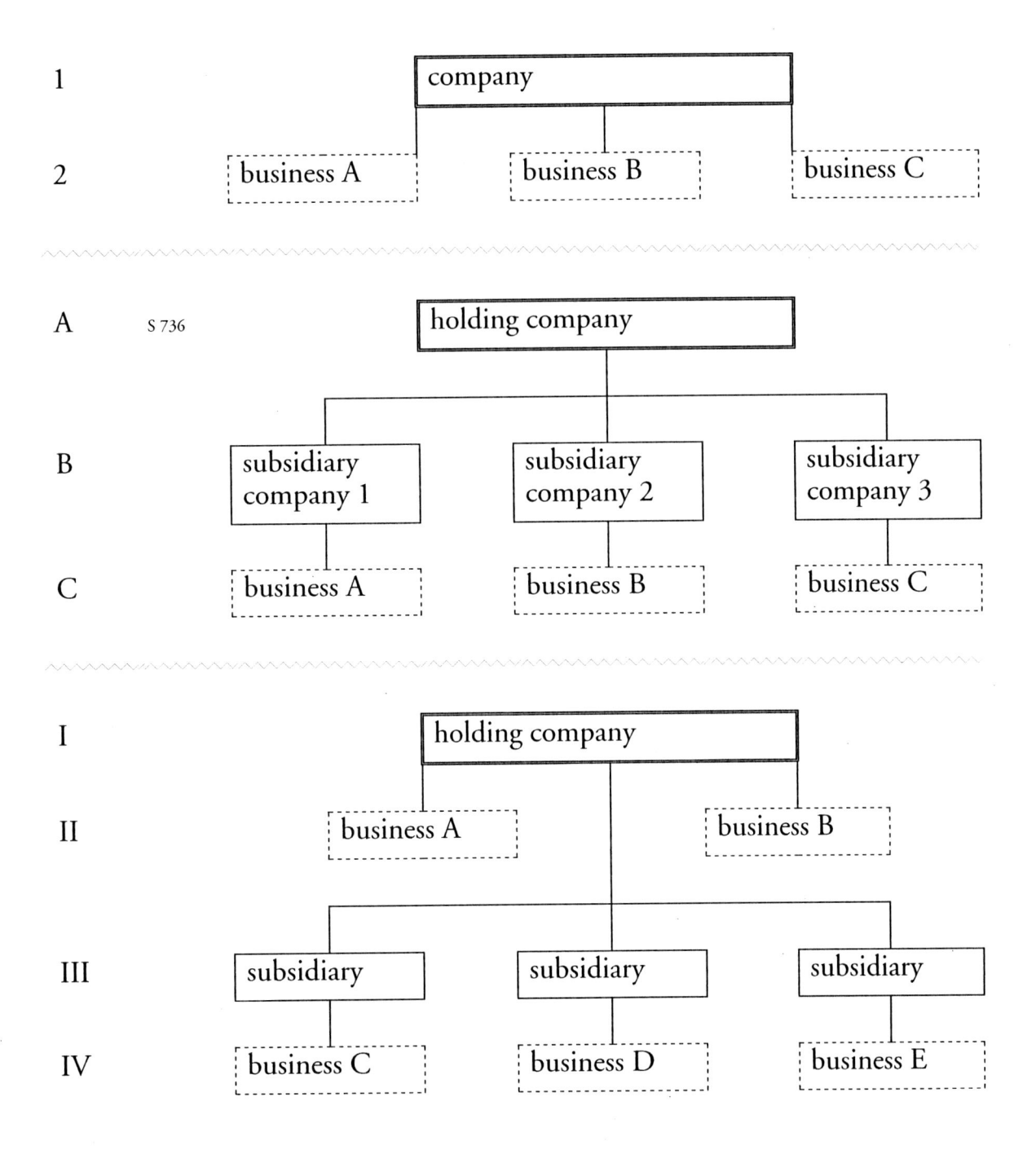

3 Subsidiaries and divisions

1   company

2   business A   business B   business C

A   S 736   holding company

B   subsidiary company 1   subsidiary company 2   subsidiary company 3

C   business A   business B   business C

I   holding company

II   business A   business B

III   subsidiary   subsidiary   subsidiary

IV   business C   business D   business E

4 Part owned subsidiaries (mainly ss 258 (sched 10A) and 736)

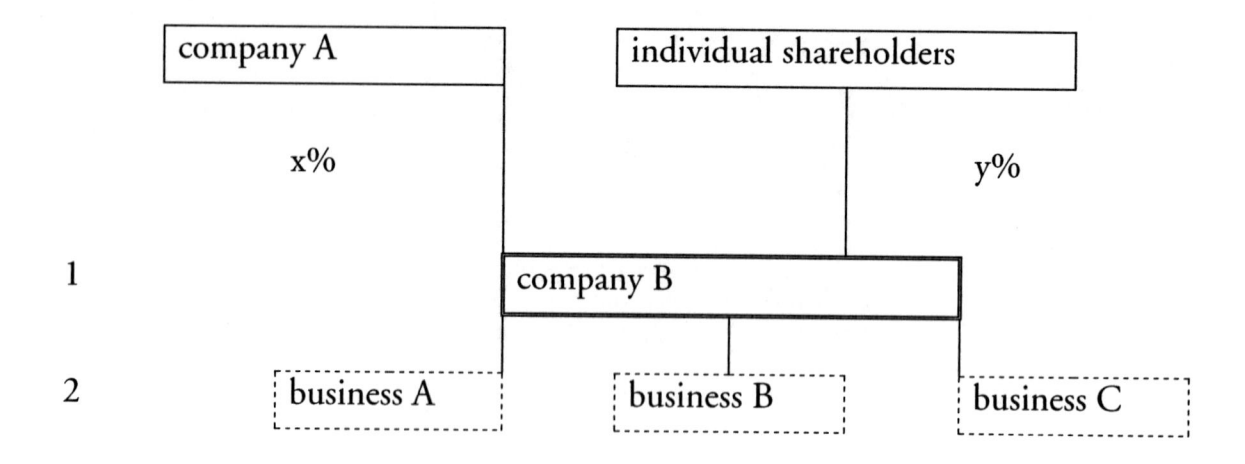

```
┌──────────────┐         ┌────────────────────────┐
│  company A   │         │ individual shareholders│
└──────┬───────┘         └───────────┬────────────┘
       │ x%                          │ y%
       │         ┌───────────────┐   │
1      └─────────┤   company B   ├───┘
                 └───┬───────┬───────┬───┘
2          ┌─────────┴─┐ ┌───┴─────┐ ┌──┴────────┐
           │business A │ │business B│ │business C│
           └───────────┘ └─────────┘ └───────────┘
```

x = > 50%	B is subsidiary
x = < 50%	B is (probably) not subsidiary
x = < 50%	B is subsidiary if A can appoint and remove majority of directors
x = < 50%	B is subsidiary and others control > 50%
x = 0%	B is not subsidiary
x = 20%	group accounts

s 260

5 Shareholder leaving—Table A unaltered

scenario

shareholders	
A	33 $\frac{1}{3}^{rd}$
B	33 $\frac{1}{3}^{rd}$
C	33 $\frac{1}{3}^{rd}$
C wishes to retire	
1 Table A	
2 Special articles	

SI 1985/805   what happens?

Table A unaltered

3rd party

if C offers his shares to D
transfer form signed and D delivers it to company

if friendly

directors approve transfer and enter D as member

if hostile

directors (2:1) refuse transfer
C remains a member

but

probably excluded (week 9)

6 Shareholder leaving—special articles

Table A plus pre-emption typical

	"transfer notice" given or enforced
	price negotiate or valuation
or	company to buy?
	offered to remaining members
	all or none
	transfer form signed and D delivers it to company
	price paid
	if company buys A & B 50/50 see class 3 sheets 12 & 13
or	directors approve transfers and enter A & B as transferees of C's shares still 50/50 but paid out of net income

7 Sale of or by private company

scenario

shareholders
A   33 $^1/_3{}^{rd}$
B   33 $^1/_3{}^{rd}$
C   33 $^1/_3{}^{rd}$
All wishes to sell to D

NB

private company
no stock exchange etc
Table A etc not relevant
simply contract

but what is sold?

1	shares
2	assets

shares

sellers get cash
buyer gets everything including skeletons

assets

buyer cherry-picks assets
sellers left with company

NB

tax, tax and tax

8 Sale of shares in private company (sort of) typical

stages

approach & negotiation
confidentiality
price and payment
seller's work after sale
buyer's finances
disclosure and warranties
completion

sale agreement

parties
definitions
sell and buy
price and payment
warranties
indemnities
completion

9 Sale of business in private company

similar to sale of shares except

| no shares transferred |
| assets transferred individually |
| liabilities retained |
| employees transferred under TUPE |
| cash in company |
| seller keeps the company |

SI 1981/1794   Nb

OTHER

NB all variations on the theme

| merger |
| MBO |
| MBI |
| hive down |
| hive out |
| hive up |
| compromise |
| share distribution |

s 425

IA s 110

10 Offer for shares—"takeovers"

quoted PLCs

regulated

City Code on Take-Overs and Mergers
Takeover Panel
Stock Exchange Listing Rules
Financial Services and Markets Act 2002

either

agreed or contested

offer document

to members
prospectus
acceptance form

s 429   finally

compulsory purchase

Specimen clause in share sale agreement setting out what is to be done on completion

> This precedent is © Butterworths from chapter 30 of Kelly's Draftsman 18th Edition (2003), general editor Roderick Ramage.
>
> This precedent is supplied by kind permission of Roderick Ramage only to illustrate what might typically take place on the completion of a share sale agreement and is not to be used in any particular case.

x   On completion the following shall take place.

x.1   The Seller shall deliver to the Buyer:

the certificates for the Sale Shares and signed transfers of them in favour of the Buyer or its nominees;

a waiver in the agreed terms by all the members of the Company of any pre-emption or other rights which they have in respect of shares in the Company;

the written resignation in agreed terms of (specify names) as directors and the secretary of the Company;

compromise agreements in the agreed terms for the purposes of the Employment Rights Act 1996 confirming the termination of the employments of (names) without claim against the Company;

the written resignation in the agreed terms of (name) as auditors of the Company in accordance with section 394 of the Companies Act;

the certificate[s] of incorporation [and on change of name], seal and statutory registers of the Company;

the title deeds to the Properties and all ancillary documents;

a certificate from the Seller' solicitors in agreed form as to the title of the Company to the Properties;

a tax deed in the form set out in schedule [A] duly executed by each of the Seller and the Company;

certificates from the Company's bankers certifying the current and deposit account balances of the Company at the close of business on the last business day preceding Completion;

appropriate forms to amend the mandates given by the Company to its bankers;

written confirmation from the Seller that there are no subsisting guarantees given by the Company in its favour and that after compliance with clause [y] none of the Seller or their Associates will be indebted to the Company or vice versa;

original certificates of all registered trademarks patents and designs and the originals of all licences or Environmental Authorisations obtained by or issued to the Company or any other person in connection with the business carried on by it;

evidence (in a form reasonably satisfactory to the Buyer) of the release from all charges debentures and other security interests created by the Company or to which any of its assets is subject or (as appropriate) certificates of non-crystallisation;

the Disclosure Letter;

such other papers and documents as the Buyer (by notice from the Buyer's Solicitors to the Seller' Solicitors given not less than five business days prior to Completion) reasonably requires.

x.2   The Seller will procure that a meeting of the directors of the Company will be held at which:

such persons as the Buyer nominates will be appointed as directors and the secretary of the Company;

there shall be submitted and accepted the resignations of the directors referred to in clause [x].1(c);

(*name*) shall be appointed auditors of the Company;

the transfers of the Shares (subject to stamping) shall be approved for registration;

the existing bank mandates given by the Company shall be cancelled;

the registered offices of the Company shall be changed as the Buyer directs;

the Company and (*name*) shall enter into service agreements in agreed form; and

the Seller shall repay all money then owing by it to the Company (whether then due for payment or not).

x.3   The Buyer shall:

pay to the Seller's solicitors (whose receipt shall be a good discharge to the Buyer) £(…) ((…) pounds) [on account of] the Price;

[allot and issue to the Seller in due proportion the Consideration Shares and issue to them definitive share certificates;]

procure that the Company repays to the Seller the Seller's Loans; and

deposit in the joint names of the respective solicitors of the Seller and the Buyer £(…) ((…) pounds) being the balance of the Price which or the balance of which (if any) shall be released to the Seller's solicitors after the application of it or any part of it in or towards any adjustment of the price in favour of the Buyer made under clause [z]. Any interest which accrues on these monies shall be credited to the joint account and any payment out of the account (to whichever party) shall carry the interest earned on that sum.

Business Sale Agreement—short form (eg) between connected companies: no warranties

THIS AGREEMENT is made on (*date*)

between:

(*name*) **Ltd** a company registered in England and Wales under number (*number*) whose registered office is at (*address*) ('the Seller'); and

(*name*) **Ltd** a company registered in England and Wales under number (*number*) whose registered office is at (*address*) ('the Buyer').

DEFINITIONS

1.1 In this agreement the following terms shall have the following meanings.

'Business'	means the business of the manufacture and supply of (*description*) products carried on by the Seller under the name (*name*).
'Cash'	means all cash both at bank and in hand at the Effective Date [amounting to £(...) ((...) pounds)].
'Completion Date'	means (*date*).
'Debts'	means all book and other debts due to the Seller at the Effective Date [listed in schedule (*number*)] [except the debt of £(...) (...) pounds in respect of the consideration payable under this agreement].
'Effective Date'	means (*date*).
'Employees'	means the employees of the Business employed in the Business at the Effective Date whose particulars are in schedule (*number*) [and all other persons who are or are deemed to be employed in the Business immediately before the transfer effected by this agreement].[4]
'Excluded Assets'	means [all the Seller's assets except the Sale Assets (*or*) the Cash, the Debts, the Group Securities, and the Properties (*etc*)].
'Goodwill'	means the goodwill of the Business including the exclusive right for the Buyer to use all the trade names now or previously used by the Seller and to represent itself as carrying on the Business in succession to the Seller.
'Group Securities'	means all shares and other securities in and all loans and other indebtedness owing by the Seller's subsidiary companies.

'Holding Company'	means (*name*) Ltd company (*number*).
'Insurance Policies'	means the benefit of all insurance policies listed in schedule (*number*).
'IP Rights'	means the full benefit of all patents trade marks rights (registered or unregistered) in designs discoveries inventions and secret processes and any applications for any of the foregoing as listed in schedule (*number*).
'Liabilities'	means the Seller's debts, liabilities and other obligations of or in respect of the Business outstanding at the Effective Date.
'Other Assets'	means all other assets (if any) which are:
	used by the Seller in the Business [(except the Excluded Assets)]
	not expressly mentioned in this (*document*) above, and
	not assets used in connection with the Retained Business.[6]
'Plant'	means all fixed and loose plant and machinery, fixtures, fittings, equipment and motor vehicles [listed in schedule (*number*)].
'Prepayments'	means all prepayments and deposits received by the Seller in respect of any orders or contracts [whether or not] assumed by the Buyer.
'Properties'	means the leasehold and freehold properties described in schedule (*number*).
'Purchase Contracts'	means the full benefit (subject to the burden) of all purchase leasing hire-purchase maintenance and other contracts [listed in schedule (*number*)].
'Retained Business'	means the business carried on by the Seller of [consultancy and the provision of services in the field of (*description*) under the (*name*)].
'Sale Assets'	means the Properties, the Goodwill, the Plant, the Stocks, the Debts, the Sale Contracts, the Purchase Contracts, the IP Rights, the Insurance Policies, the Cash and the Other Assets.

(*or*)

'Sale Assets'	means all the Seller's assets used by it in connection with the Business at the Effective Date [except the Excluded Assets].
'Sale Contracts'	means the full benefit (subject to the burden) of all contracts for the sale of (*description*) products [listed in schedule (*number*)].
'Stocks'	means all stocks and materials listed in schedule (*number*) and all other stock and work-in-progress of the Business at the Effective Date.
'Sale Contracts'	means the full benefit of all current and pending contracts, licences, agencies and orders listed in schedule (*number*).
'Transfer Regulations'	means the Transfer of Undertakings (Protection of Employment) Regulations 1981 (SI 1981/1794) as amended.

1.2 [*add standard interpretation clauses*]

BACKGROUND

2.1 All the issued shares in the Seller's capital are owned beneficially by the Holding Company.

2.2 [All] the issued shares in the Buyer's capital are owned beneficially by the [the Seller (*or*) Holding Company].

SALE

3.1 The Seller agrees to sell with full title guarantee and the Buyer agrees to buy the Business and the Sale Assets [free from all encumbrances].

3.2 The sale and purchase shall be effective as at the commencement of business on the Effective Date when title to and risk in the Sale Assets shall pass to the Purchaser.

ENCUMBRANCES

4 The Sale Assets and each of them shall be sold subject to all charges, covenants, restrictions, liens, and other encumbrances which affect all or any of them.

EXCLUDED ASSETS

5 The sale and purchase effected by this agreement does not include the Excluded Assets.

PURCHASE PRICE

6 The purchase price for the sale and purchase shall be the obligations undertaken by the Buyer under clause [12.1] [and £(…)] ((…) pounds) in cash] to be apportioned between the Sale Assets as the parties agree or in default of such agreement as designated by the [Seller (*or*) the Buyer].

COMPLETION

7 The sale and purchase shall be completed on the Effective (*or*) Completion Date at the Seller's solicitors' offices at (*address*) immediately following the execution of this agreement.

PAYMENT OF THE PURCHASE PRICE

8.1　On completion the Buyer shall pay [£(…) ((…) pounds)] of the purchase price to the Seller or as the latter directs.

8.2　The balance of the purchase price payable in cash shall be left owing by the Buyer to the Seller on an interest free inter-company loan account payable on demand.

TRANSFER OF SALE ASSETS

9　On completion the Seller shall:

put the Buyer into possession of all the Sale Assets capable of being transferred by delivery;

execute all documents necessary to transfer those Sale Assets which cannot be transferred by delivery; and

do all other things reasonably required by the Buyer to vest the Sale Assets in the Buyer and give the Buyer the full benefit of this agreement.

UNTIL COMPLETION

10　The Seller shall retain possession of the Sale Assets until completion and:

continue to carry on the Business as previously;

but from Effective Date as agent for and on behalf of the Buyer and all necessary accounting entries shall be made in the books of account of the Seller and the Buyer to reflect this agency.

NOVATION OF CONTRACTS

11　The Buyer shall, subject to all necessary consents of other contracting parties, discharge adopt and perform all Purchase Contracts and Sale Contracts outstanding as at the Effective Date binding on the Seller and shall at all times following Effective Date compensate the Seller in full on demand for all liability in respect of them.

LIABILITIES

12.1　The Buyer shall discharge all the Liabilities and shall at all times following Effective Date compensate the Seller in full on demand for all liability in respect of the Liabilities.

12.2　Nothing in this agreement shall impose on the Buyer any responsibility for any of the Seller's debts, liabilities and other obligations in respect of the Retained Business.

DEBTS

13.　The Debts shall remain the property of the Seller, [but the Buyer shall use all reasonable endeavours to collect the Debts on behalf of the Seller and remit any Debts so collected to the Seller on a weekly basis].

TITLE

14.1　The Buyer shall accept without investigation or objection such title as the Seller has to all the (*subject matter*).

(*or if warranted free from encumbrances etc*)

14.1　The Seller warrants that it is the beneficial owner of the Sale Assets of free from any encumbrance, charge, lien or claims in favour of or by any other person and the Buyer shall accept without investigation or objection such title as the Seller has to them.

14.2　The Seller shall use its best endeavours to obtain the concurrence of any person having any interest in any of the Sale Assets to the transfer to the Buyer of the Sale Assets including the benefit and burden of any [business] contract or of any agreement affecting the Sale Assets.

EMPLOYEES

15 The Seller and the Buyer acknowledge that the Transfer Regulations apply to the transfer of the Business as regards the Employees and that on completion they will be transferred to the employment of the Buyer by operation of law and the Buyer shall compensate the Seller in full on demand against all liabilities in respect of the Employees which arise on or after the transfer of the Business.

PENSIONS

16 Schedule (*number*) will apply in relation to pensions.

ACCOUNTS AND RECORDS

17.1 The Seller shall deliver to the Buyer on completion all its accounts and records relating to the Business.

17.2 The Buyer shall retain all the accounts and records for a period of [10] years from the Effective Date and permit the Seller to inspect and make copies of them in person or by agents at all reasonable times during that period.

CONTINUING OBLIGATIONS

18 The provisions of this (*document*) which require or are capable of imposing any liability after completion shall continue in force notwithstanding completion of [the sale and purchase] and any corresponding right conferred on either party shall be enforceable after completion.

VAT

19.1 The purchase price for the transfer of the Sale Assets is exclusive of value added tax but the parties shall use their best endeavours to obtain the relief available under article 5 of the Value Added Tax (Special Provisions) Order 1995.

19.2 If the relief is not available then the Buyer shall pay to the Seller a sum equal to the value added tax at the appropriate rate in respect of such of the Sale Assets as are chargeable to value added tax immediately on the Seller issuing a tax invoice for them.

STAMP DUTY

20 The parties acknowledge that this agreement is not made in pursuance of or in connection with an arrangement as specified in s27(3) Finance Act 1967 such as would cause the stamp duty relief provisions in s42 Finance Act 1930 not to apply to this agreement.

GOVERNING LAW

21 This (*document*) shall be governed by English law and the Buyer consents to the exclusive jurisdiction of the English courts in all matters regarding it except to the extent that the Seller invokes the jurisdiction of the courts of any other country.

SCHEDULE 1

The freehold land and buildings known as (*description*) is registered at HM Land Registry with absolute title under title number (*number*).

(*or*)

The leasehold land and buildings known as (*description*) which are comprised in a lease dated (*date*) and made between (*name*) and (*name*).

SCHEDULE [1], [2], [3] etc

(*plant and machinery*)

(stock and materials)
(debts due to the Seller)
(sale contracts, orders, etc)
(purchase, hire-purchase, maintenance contracts, etc)
(patents, trade marks, etc)
(insurance policies)
(debts due by the Seller)
(employees)
(pensions)

[attestation clauses]

Warranties by sellers of shares or assets

What topics need to be considered?

The accounts of the company

Taxation

Companies Act

Capital

Employees and directors

Pension scheme and pensions2

Land and buildings

Other assets

Compliance with legislation and contractual and other obligations

Finances and borrowings

Miscellaneous

Company Law

Test Yourself

1. Tansy plc is in financial difficulties and wants its debenture holders to exchange their debentures for shares in order to get rid of the requirement to pay interest on the debentures. How should Thames proceed?

Under s110 of the Insolvency Act 1986.

Under s425 of the Companies Act 1985.

By a reduction of capital.

By unilaterally altering the terms of issue of the debentures.

2. What is the legal position of a person who buys shares on the faith of a share certificate issued by a company to a transferee on the basis of a forged transfer?

The person gets an equitable interest in the shares.

The transfer is valid and the person gets a good title if he has acted in good faith.

The transfer is void and the person cannot claim against the company.

The transfer is void but the person has a claim for compensation against the company.

3. Roger, a financier, has made a personal bid for the equity shares of HOUSING plc. He has acquired 92 per cent of the shares in Brick and intends to compulsorily acquire the rest. What is the legal position?

a) He will be able compulsorily to acquire the shares under the Companies Act 1985.

b) He cannot compulsorily acquire the shares under the Companies Act 1985 because he did not get 95 per cent.

c) There are no legal provisions which allow compulsory acquisition.

d) The compulsory acquisition provisions of the Companies Act 1985 do not apply in this situation.

9—Crime

Contents

A	Oppression of minorities
1	Reminder—How many votes?
2	The Rule in Foss v Harbottle (1843)
3	Fraud on minority (company)
4	Fraud on minority (individual)
5	"Oppression of minority"
6	Quasi partnership
7	More examples—prejudicial conduct
8	More examples—valuation
B	Crime and tort
9	Some statutory offences
10	Crimes—whose mind?
11	Crime—more controlling minds
12	Theft from own company
13	Corporate manslaughter

1 Reminder—How many votes?

day to day control		ordinary resolution > 50%
major decisions		special or extraordinary resolution 75%
also (class 4)	1 or more	Ltd to unlimited quorum unfair prejudice just and equitable
	5%	members' requisition for resolution
	10%	requisition or call meeting
	15%	object to change to memorandum class rights
	25%	negative control
what else?	NB	what else can the aggrieved shareholder do?
		directors manage

2 The Rule in <u>Foss v Harbottle</u> ([Fo1843] 2 Hare 461)
"The majority rules"

Reminder	who does what?
Chapter 5	directors manage shareholders own
Facts	2 shareholders sued directors and others
	alleged fraud
Held	shareholders had no standing to sue
Exceptions	fraud on minority
	derivative actions
Cook v Deeks [1916] 1 AC 554	directors negotiated contract for company but took it themselves
	must account for profit
NB	shareholders' collective not private interests

3 Fraud on minority (company)

Daniels v Daniels [1978] ChD 406, [1978] 2 All ER 89

facts	majority caused company to sell land to one of themselves
	buyer made profit on resale
claim	by minority's claim
held	minority entitled to claim
reason	if no other remedy, may sue when directors benefits themselves at expense of company

Wallersteiner v Moir (No 2) [1975] 1 All ER 849, CA

facts	W 80%, M 20%
claim	M claimed that W obtained his 80% majority by a cheat
	sought order for costs
held	costs to be paid by company
reason	action for benefit of company not individual shareholder

4 Fraud on minority (individual)

Brown v British Abrasive Wheel Co [1919] 1 Ch 290

facts	98% majority to provide capital if 2% bought out
	articles changed for compulsory purchase by 9/10^{ths}
claim	(by 2%) sought injunction to block the resolution
held	injunction granted
reason	not for benefit of company

Clemens v Clemens Bros [1976] 2 All ER 268

facts	shareholders 45%/55%
	increased capital to go partly to directors and mainly to EBT reducing 45% to < 25%
claim	(by 45%) to set aside resolution
held	declaration granted
reason	voting rights restrained by equitable principle that particular exercise was unjust

5 "Oppression of minority"

S 459	either	unfair prejudice
IA s 122	or	just and equitable
	or	both

ss 459, 461

> a member
>
> May petition the court
>
> affairs conducted…unfairly prejudicial to interests of members
>
> such order as the court thinks fit
>
> eg regulate conduct in future
> company to refrain from act
> civil proceedings to be brought
> purchase of member's shares

IA s 122(1)(g)

> a company may be wound up by the court if—
>
> the court is of the opinion that it is just and equitable that the company should be wound up

6 Quasi partnership

Ebrahimi v Westbourne Galleries [1973] 3 AC 360, [1972] 2 All ER 492, House of Lords

Facts:
- Ebrahimi & Nazar partners sharing equally
- transferred into company
- Nazar junior joined
- E removed as director

S 459

IA s 122

E petitioned for:
- N & N Jnr to buy E's shares

or
- company to be w/u

Court ordered:
- s 459 refused
- but w/u ordered

Why w/u?
- personal relationships essentially a partnership
- loss of mutual confidence so remove stake & leave

7 More examples—prejudicial conduct

re Sam Weller Ltd [1990] Ch 682, [1990] BCLR 133

Facts	increasingly profitable company failed to increase dividends
claim	(by 43%) that unfairly prejudicial conduct
defence	affected all shareholders
held	claim could proceed
reason	prejudicial to <u>interests</u> of some members

O'Neill v Phillips [1999] 2 All ER 961, HL

facts	75% resumed control and 25% no longer to have half profits
claim	(by 25%) unfair prejudice
held	not unfair
reason	no legal obligation broken, nothing to prevent majority from withdrawing from negotiations

8 More examples—valuation

re Bird Precision Bellows [1986] Ch 658, [1985] 3 All ER 523

facts	petitioners removed from office and court order made for purchase of shares
issue	valuation of shares
held	pro rata
reason	quasi partnership terminated by majority's conduct
but	discounted in minority's fault

Virdi v Abbey Leisure Ltd [1990] BCLR 342, CA

facts	company formed to buy, refurbish and sell nightclub
	assets: just cash
claim	(by 40%) to be wound up
defence	Offer to buy shares
held	wound up
reason	risk of under valuation

9 Some statutory offences

tables of offences

> Companies Act 1985 Schedule 24
>
> Insolvency Act 1986 Schedule 10

s 733

> directors etc (also members)
> if consent, connivance, neglect
> liable for specified offences

s 210 — notice of interest in shares

s 216(3) — investigation of takeovers

s 394A(1) — statement on ceasing to be auditor

ss 447 - 451 — investigation of companies

similarly under

> Companies Act 1989
>
> Company Directors Disqualifications Act 1986
>
> Business Names Act 1985
>
> Insolvency Act 1986
>
> Theft Act 1968

10 Crimes—whose mind?

Tesco Supermarkets Ltd v Nattrass [1972] AC 153, [1971] 2 All ER 127, HL

facts	inaccurate price information
offence	Trade Descriptions Act
defence	management system
decision	not guilty
reason	manager is not the "directing mind and will"

DG of Fair Trading v Pioneer Concrete (UK) Ltd and Anor [1995] 1 AC 456, [1995] 1 All ER 135

facts	price fixing cartel
offence	restrictive trade practices
defence	against express company policy
decision	guilty
reason	"an employee who acts for the company within the scope of his employment is the company"

11 Crime—controlling minds

Lennard's Carrying Co Ltd v Asiatic Petroleum [1915] AC 705

facts	fire on unseaworthy ship
claim	damage to goods
defence	no liability without actual fault
held	company liable
reason	the managing director was in full control of the ship and company responsible for his act

DPP v Kent and Sussex Contractors Ltd [1944] KB 146[24]

facts	false documentation
claim	breach of fuel rationing regulations
defence	de facto done by transport manager
held	company guilty
reason	acts thought people acting for it and can for intention to deceive

---

[24] The PROSECUTION of a CORPORATION has not taken place in the United Kingdom since this case in 1944. Only certain culpable directors are now prosecuted.

12 Theft from company

TA s 1   **Theft Act 1968**

A person is guilty of theft if he dishonestly appropriates property belonging to another with the intention of permanently depriving the other of it

AG's Reference (No 2 of 1982) [1984] QB 624, [1994] 2 All ER 216

facts	sole directors and shareholders stole from their company
offence	theft
defence	were the "directing minds" an could not steal from themselves
decision	guilty
reason	Tesco inapplicable as company was victim

R v Appleyard (1985) CA

similar	arson - defence (company must have assented) failed

13 Corporate manslaughter

R v British Steel plc [1995] IRLR 310, CA

facts	unsecured metal platform collapsed killing an employee
offence	breach of Health & Safety at Work etc Act 1974
defence	employees in charge not part of senior management team
decision	guilty
reason	absolute offence not limited to acts of directing mind of company
Manslaughter	problems identifying the "controlling mind" in a corporation or an individual who is directly responsible for the fatality.
Eg	P&O European Ferries 1991 (Herald of Free Enterprise) R v F Howe 1999 (Great Western Trains—Southall crash)
Corporate Killing Bill —2004	The Law Commission proposed a new offence of 'corporate killing' which makes it unnecessary to identify a guilty 'mind'.

Company Law

Test Yourself.

1 Explain the Rule in *Foss* v *Harbottle* and describe the limits to this Rule.

2 'For a minority shareholder who has suffered a wrong at the hands of the majority to establish a case under the alternative remedy he must show both that he suffered "unfairly prejudicial conduct" and that this was suffered in his capacity as a member of the company.'

Discuss.

3 John, who is the majority shareholder in Thames Ltd, is refusing to recommend the payment of dividends in spite of healthy profits. Instead he has recently increased his salary as a director by £40,000. What action can the minority shareholders take?

a) Bring a derivative action under an exception to *Foss* v *Harbottle*.

b) Petition under CA 1985, s 459.

c) Bring an action under the CA 1985 which requires that the directors recommend a dividend if there are distributable profits.

d) No action is possible in this situation.

4 Which, if any, of the following can petition the court for relief under CA 1985, s 459?

a) The company.

b) Members holding not less than 10 per cent in number of the company's issued shares.

c) A member of the company.

10—Partnerships

Contents

1. Legal structure—sole trader, partnership, company (reminder from class 1)
2. Legal structure—natural persons reminder from class 1)
3. Agency—meaning
4. Agency—authority, enforcement &c
5. Partnership—characteristics
6. Partners and 3rd parties
7. Partners—terms with each other
8. Partnership names
9. Small print
10. Termination—grounds
11. Termination—consequences
12. Limited Partnerships
13. Limited Liability Partnerships—introduction
14. LLPs—formation and regulation

1   **Legal structure—sole trader, partnership, company (reminder from class 1)**

two basic categories	natural persons
	legal persons

natural persons	sole traders
	partnerships

legal persons	corporations sole
	corporation aggregate

normally	Companies Act 1985

possibilities	public	private
	limited liability	unlimited liability
	quoted	unquoted
	shares	guarantee

in commercial reality	company limited by shares "ltd" or "plc"

2 Legal structure—natural persons reminder from class 1)

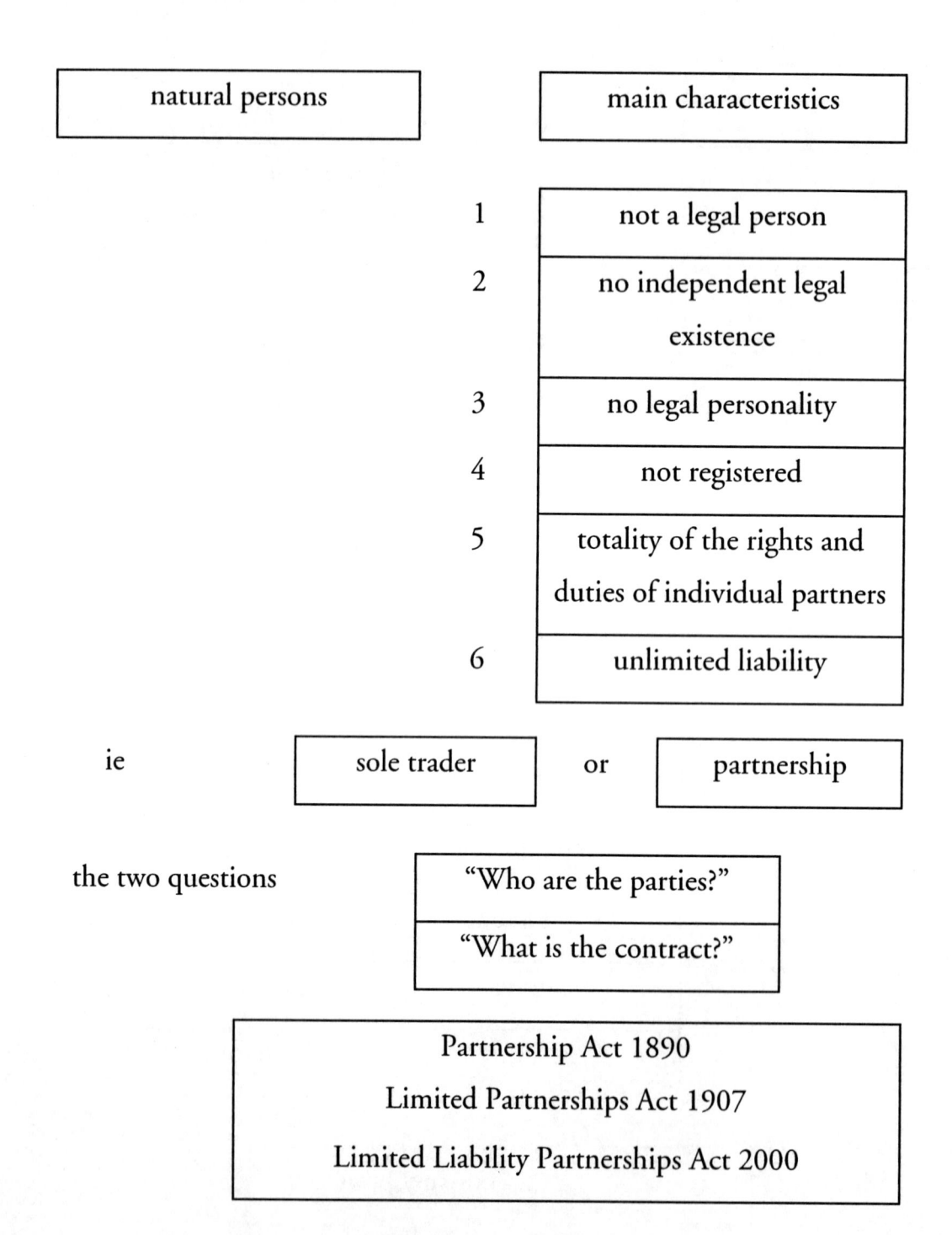

natural persons		main characteristics
	1	not a legal person
	2	no independent legal existence
	3	no legal personality
	4	not registered
	5	totality of the rights and duties of individual partners
	6	unlimited liability

ie   sole trader   or   partnership

the two questions   "Who are the parties?"

"What is the contract?"

Partnership Act 1890

Limited Partnerships Act 1907

Limited Liability Partnerships Act 2000

3   Agency—meaning

NB — legal meaning

relationship between:
- the "principal"
- with whose authority
- the "agent"
- deal with 3rd parties
- on the principal's behalf

NOT dictionary meaning

eg:
- Rover, Ford etc agent
- sales agent (if actually distributor)
- Contributions Agency
- agent for change

characteristics eg:
- intermediary
- not employee
- not on own behalf

4 Agency—authority, enforcement &c

in principle		principal liable for all acts in agent's ostensible authority

contract enforceable			by and against principal
	if		authorised
		and	name or existence of principal disclosed to 3rd party when contract made
but	if		contract authorised
			but in agent's name
		and	principal not disclosed
			agent personally liable
	Unless		3rd party elects for principal alone
	if		contract unauthorised
			only agent liable
	Unless		unless ratified by principal

5 Partnership—characteristics

PA s 1(1)		'Partnership is the relation which subsists between persons carrying on a business in common with a view of profit'	
PA s 45		' "business" includes every trade, occupation, or profession'	
PA s 1(2)		but not	members of a company
PA s 2(1)			joint ownership
PA s 2(2)			sharing gross returns
PA s 2 (3)			profit share if remuneration, interest
(obvious)			employment
(obvious)			agency
	NB	no	separate legal personality
PA s 4(1)		but	"a firm"

6 Partners and 3rd parties

NB **no separate legal entity**

therefore | no legal body |
to	hold property
	make contracts
	be sued

the firm — a ghostly fiction

PA s 5
> 'Every partner is an **agent** of the firm and his other partners for the purpose of the business of the partnership…and the acts of every partner who does any act for carrying on in the usual way business of the kind carried on by the firm of which he is a member bind the firm and his partners…'

PS s 6
> 'Any act or instrument relating to the business of the firm done or executed in the firm-name…by any person thereto authorised, whether a partner or not, is binding on the firm and all the partners.

agency — inward (partners) outward (3rd parties)

7 Partners—terms with each other

subject to special agreement

PA s 24

share equally capital profits and losses
each partner indemnified by firm for liability
interest at 5% pa for excess capital
no interest on capital
participate in management
no remuneration
new partner only if agreed unanimously
decisions by majorities
no change of business except unanimously
partnership books at place of business

8 Partnership names

Business Names Act 1985

- no register
- no restrictions on similarity etc
  - except
    - passing off
    - prohibited

BNA s 4 — disclosure
- on all business letters written orders, invoices, demands for payment etc
  - name of each partner
  - address in GB for service of documents
- at each place of business
  - prominent display of names and addresses
- exception: if >20 partners
- and: document states address of principal place of business where names open for inspection

9 Small print

PA s 9, 12	liability	all partners jointly and severally
PA s 14	holding out	non-partner can be liable
PA s 16	notices	to any partner
PA s 17(1)	new partner	not liable for existing debts
PA s 17(2),(3)	outgoing partner	not relieved from debts by retirement unless agreed with partners and creditors
PA s 19	variation	by consent of all partners
PA s 20,21	partnership property	if brought into partnership stock or acquired belongs to the firm (ie held on trust for partners)
PA s 25	expulsion	not possible

10 Termination—grounds

PA s 32(a)	how	expiry of fixed term	
PA s 32(b)		completion of venture	
PA s 32(c)		notice by any partner	
PA s 33(1)		death or bankruptcy	
PA s 33(2)		charge of share	
PA s 34		subsequent illegality	
PA s 35		court order	if any partner permanently incapable
			prejudicial conduct by any partner
			wilful etc breach by any partner
			loss
			just and equitable
	or	in accordance with partnership agreement	

11 Termination—consequences

    winding up

PA s 38

partners' authority continues as far as necessary	
to	wind up partnership
	complete unfinished transactions

PA s 44

distribution of assets	
	losses paid from
	1 profits
	2 capital
	3 partners
then	debts to non-partners
	debts to partners
	repay capital
	residue per profit shares

12 Limited Partnerships

Limited Partnerships Act 1907

based on 1890 act and general partnership law

	formation	
LPA 1907 s 4		1 or more general and 1 or more general partners
LPA 1907 s 5		limited on registration
LPA 1907 s 8		particulars for registration
LPA 1907 s 9		particulars of change
LPA 1907 s 13		certificate of registration and changes

	limited partner	
		investor
LPA 1907 s 4(3)		not withdraw capital
LPA 1907 s 6(1)		not manage
LPA 1907 s 6(1)		not bind firm
LPA 1907 s 6(5)		may assign share
LPA 1907 s 6(5)		not terminate by notice
	general partner	manages
		personally liable

13 Limited Liability Partnerships—introduction

Limited Liability Partnerships Act 2000

Limited Liability Partnerships Regulations 2001, SI 2001/1090

applies and modifies company legislation

LLPA s1(5)	NOT based on existing partnership law – 1890 Act does not apply	
LLPA s 1(1)	nature	new form of legal entity
LLPA s 1(2)		body corporate with a legal personality separate from that of its members
LLPA s 1(3)		unlimited legal capacity
LLPA s4(2)		any 'person' can be a member
LLPA s1(4), s6(4)	Regs Sch 3 & IA 1986	liability limited
	NB	members not liable for other members' negligence
LLPA 2 6		members agents of LLP

14 LLPs—formation and regulation

LLPA s 3	incorporation		by registration
LLPA s 2(1)(a)			2 or more persons
			associated for carrying on business with a view to profit
LLPA s 2(1)(b)			registered incorporation document and statement of compliance
		but	no M & A of A
LLPA sched	names		similar to companies
		end in	limited liability partnership or LLP
		or	partneriaeth atabolrwydd cyfyngedig or PAC
LLPA sched	registered office		similar to companies
egs Sched 1	disclosure		accounts, annual returns as for companies
		but	no AGMs
LLPA s8	designated members		not less than 2

Company Law

Test Yourself

1   a)   What kinds of liquidation or windings-up are there and what distinguishes them from each other?

      b)   Distinguish between fraudulent trading and wrongful trading and say what consequences may follow if a person is found guilty of either of them.

2   a)   What are the statutory requirements in respect of calling an annual general meeting?
      b)   What is the usual business at an annual general meeting of a company?
      c)   What is an extraordinary general meeting?
      d)   When must the directors call such a meeting?
      e)   What consequences may follow the directors' failure to call such a meeting?

3   An additional director is to be appointed to the board of a company. What steps must taken:
      a)   if the appointments is by the members; and
      b)   if by the directors?

4   A is to be recruited as a company's works director and so will be both an employee and a director. His service agreement says that either party may terminate it on giving not less than six months notice to the other.
      a)   He dismissed summarily for gross misconduct. Does this terminate his directorship?
      b)   If the company is aware of the problems of s303, what alternative arrangements can it make in anticipation of the need to remove a director at short notice?

5   Explain and distinguish between:
      a)   preference shares;
      b)   participating preference shared;
      c)   ordinary shares;
      d)   part-paid shares; and
      e)   premium.

11—Revision—Law Cases

Separate Legal Personality

> **Salomon v A Salomon & Co Ltd [1897] AC 33, HL**
>
> Boot manufacturer as sole trader for over 30 years.
>
> Company was formed to purchase the business
>
> Mr Salomon 94 of the shares and six members of his family owned one share each as nominees him
>
> The purchase price £39,000 paid by:
>
> £10,000 worth of fully paid shares;
>
> debenture worth £10,000 secured over the company; and
>
> the balance by the company discharging of Mr S's trade debts and liabilities
>
> In less than one year the company had trading difficulties and went into liquidation. Mr S brought proceedings to enforce the debenture. If successful he would be paid first. There were not enough assets to discharge the debenture so the other creditors would get nothing. The liquidator objected saying that the debenture was invalid as a 'fraud', ie forming a one man company amounted to a fraud. Both the court of first instance and the CA found that the company as nothing more than Mr S's nominee, refused to recognise its existence as a separate legal person and decided in favour of the liquidator.
>
> *Held* The company exists at law as a separate being from its shareholders and it made no difference that one member owned the beneficially all or substantially all of the shares. Mr S's debenture was valid.

Separate Legal Personality

Macaura v Northern Assurance Co [1925] AC 619, HL

Mr Macaura owned timber estates in Ireland and sold the timber to a company for £42,000 paid by the issue of 42,000 fully paid shares. He had also financed the company for about £19,000 as an unsecured creditor. He took out insurance on the timber in his name, but when most of the timber was destroyed by fire, the insurance company refused to pay.

Held The claim failed. The timber was owned by the company and not by him so he had no insurable interest in it. It made no difference that Mr M the only shareholder and a major creditor, because the company was an independent entity.

Separate Legal Personality

Lee v Lee's Air Farming ltd [1961] AC 12, PC

The appellant was the widow of

Mr Lee owned 2,999 of the 3,000 shares in the company, which carried on an aerial crop spraying business. He was its sole director, had been employed by it and was killed in an air crash while working. His widow claimed compensation under the New Zealand Workers Compensation Act 1922 and the question arose as to whether he was a 'worker' within the meaning of that legislation. The New Zealand CA had found that for all intents and purposes he was the company and as such was the employer so could not be a worker.

Held The appeal was allowed applying Salomon v Salomon. The company had a separate legal personality so contractual relations could exist between him and it.

Lifting The Veil of Incorporation

> **DHN Food Distributors Ltd v Tower Hamlets London Borough Council [1976] 1 WLR 852, CA**
>
> DHN Food Distributors Ltd carried on a food distribution business and had two wholly-owned subsidiaries, all with the same directors. The subsidiaries were Bronze Investments Ltd, which owned the land used in the business, and DHN Food Transport Ltd, which owned the lorries. The local authority issued a compulsory purchase order over the land and paid compensation for the land value to Bronze Investments Ltd, but it refused to pay compensation disturbance to the business. The business was carried on by the parent company and not Bronze and the parent was a separate legal entity and not subject to the CPO
>
> *Held* Lord Denning lifted the corporate veil on the basis that, on the facts of the case the doctrine of corporate personality was applied artificially and unfairly. He treated the group as one entity for the purposes of that particular statute. DHN Food Distributors Ltd should receive compensation for business disruption to its business.

Promoters—definition

> **Whaley Bridge Calico Printing Co v Green [1880] 5 QBD 109**
>
> Bowen J said:
>
> 'The term promoter is a term not of law, but of business, usefully summing up in a single word a number of business operations familiar to the commercial world by which a company is generally brought into existence.'
>
> What the promoter does as analogous to a trustee for the company's benefit. So a company may enforce the personal claims of a promoter against a party who has undertaken to pay the promoter a profit or other benefit in connection with its promotion.

Promoters—personal profit

> **Gluckstein v Barnes [1900] AC 240, HL**
>
> The National Agricultural Hall Co Ltd went into liquidation and Mr Gluckstein and three other purchased its premises for £140,000 and re-sold them for £180,000 to a Olympia Company Ltd, a company they had promoted. In the prospectus they disclosed the £40,000 profit, but they did not disclose the £20,000 profit they made out of dome discounted debentures of the old company. The new company, Olympia, went into liquidation and the liquidator claimed Mr G's share of the £20,000.
>
> *Held* (Upholding the findings of the lower courts)' Mr G was liable to account to the company for the amount sought. The directors of the company were Mr G and his associates and were not independent. It was therefore not sufficient that knew the details, but full disclosure should have been made to the company.

Promoters' contracts

> **Phonogram Ltd v Lane [1982] QB 938, CA**
>
> It was planned to form a new company to manage, 'Cheap Mean & Nasty' was the name of a rock band, which was to be managed by a new company to be called Fragile Management Ltd. Before Fragile was formed Mr Lane, who was promoting it, entered negotiations with Phonogram Ltd and for a loan 'for and on behalf of the proposed company. The load was made but the company was never formed and an action was brought against Mr Lane for repayment of the money.
>
> *Held* Mr L was personally liable to repay the loan.

Articles of association—contract between members

> ### Rayfield v Hands [1958] 2 All ER 194
>
> The articles of association of a private company provided:
>
> 'Every member who intends to transfer his shares shall inform the directors who will take the said shares equally between them at a fair value.'
>
> The plaintiff wished to sell his shares and asked the three directors of the company to buy them in accordance with the articles, but they refused. He sued them without joining the company in the action.
>
> *Held* The court found that the directors were bound to buy the shares. The articles were to create a contractual relationship between the plaintiff as shareholder and vendor and the defendants as directors and purchasers. Vaisey J dealt with the problems raised by the reasoning of the courts examined below, 4.1.3 by saying:
>
> Now the question arises at the outset whether the terms of [the] article…relate to the rights of the members *inter se*…or whether the relationship is between a member as such and directors as such, I may dispose of this point very briefly by saying that, in my judgment, the relationship here is between the plaintiff as a member and the defendants not as directors but as members.
>
> The said that this might not apply to all companies but this was a quasi-partnership in which the directors owned all of the shares between them.

Memorandum of association—objects—*ultra vires* or outside the terms of business

<u>Ashbury Railway Carriage & Iron Co Ltd v Riche [1875] LR 7 HL 653</u>

The company bought a concession to build a railway in Belgium and entered into an agreement with Mr Riche to finance its construction. The company got into difficulties the contract with Mr R was repudiated and Mr R sued for damages. The company in its defence argued that the financing agreement was void and ineffective as it was *ultra vires* its powers. The objects clause in its memorandum of association empowered the company to make railway carriages and rolling stock, to carry on business as mechanical engineers, and to trade in timber, coal, metals etc. *Held* The agreement was *ultra vires* and therefore void. Lord Cairns LC emphasised that the memorandum states the outer limits of what constitutes a company's 'vitality and power'. It cannot exceed those limits. Even if all the shareholders unanimously consent, it makes no difference; if a contract is beyond the competence and power of a company, then it is void *ab initio* and nothing the members subsequently do can save it.

Memorandum of association—Multiple Separate Objects

<u>Cotman v Brougham [1918] AC 514, HL</u>

The objects clause of a company included power to carry on almost every type of commercial activity and had a final sub-clause stating that each sub-clause should be construed as a separate and independent object. A dispute arose as to whether or not the company was authorised to underwrite a share issue in another company.

Held The objects clause of the memorandum was so widely drafted that the transaction was in fact *intra vires*. The HL regarded this type of blanket objects clause as an abuse but because of the express wording of the memorandum there was no basis upon which they could cut down the company's powers.

Memorandum of Association—Ancillary to Business

> **Bell Houses Ltd v City Wall Properties Ltd [1966] 2 All ER 674, CA**
>
> The plaintiff company's business was as a property developer in accordance with its objects clause. It put the defendant company in touch with a financier but the introducer's fee was not paid on the grounds that mortgage broking was *ultra vires* its plaintiff's business, so it was not entitled to the fee. The plaintiff's objects clause contained a phrase permitting it 'to carry on any other trade or business whatsoever which can, in the opinion of the board of directors, be advantageously carried on by the company in connection with or as ancillary to any of the above businesses or the general business of the company'.
>
> *Held* The plain and natural meaning of the sub-clause was such as to render this ancillary business *intra vires*.

Memorandum of Association—Borrowing not an Object

> **Re Introductions Ltd (1970) CA**
>
> This company started business offering hospitality services, then changed to deck chair rental and finally pig breeding, after which it went into liquidation. When the bank tried to enforce its security but the liquidator that it was unenforceable as the company's borrowing had been *ultra vires* and so the security granted was void. The company's memorandum contained a wide objects clause in similar terms to that used in *Cotman v Brougham*. It did not include pig farming but one sub-clauses gave power to borrow. The bank knew of the purpose of the loan.
>
> *Held* The breeding of pigs was clearly *ultra vires* and the bank had notice of it. Borrowing is not capable of being an independent substantive object and is no more than an incidental power. It cannot be elevated to an object by the wording of the memorandum. Borrowing for the purposes of an *ultra vires* object (pig breeding) was not an *intra vires* object.

Articles of association—Effect on earlier contract

> **Southern Foundries (1926) Ltd v Shirlaw [1940] AC, HL**
>
> Mr Shirlaw had been appointed managing director of Southern Foundries Ltd in 1933 pursuant to a written agreement. Southern Foundries Ltd was taken over by Federated Industries Ltd in 1936 and altered its articles of association to insert a new article which empowered Federated Industries Ltd, by written instrument, to remove any of its directors. In 1937, Federated Industries Ltd used that power to remove Mr S from office and the latter sued for breach of contract.
>
> *Held* Mr S was awarded damages. Lord Porter stated as a matter of general principle:
>
> A company cannot be precluded from altering its articles thereby giving itself power to act upon the provisions of its altered articles—but so to act may nevertheless be a breach of contract if it is contrary to a stipulation validly made before the alteration. Nor can an injunction be granted to prevent the adoption of the new articles and in that sense they are binding on all and sundry, but for the company to act upon them will none the less render it liable in damages if such action is contrary to the previous engagements of the company.

Company's name—passing off

> **Exxon Corp v Exxon Insurance Consultants International Ltd [1982] 1 Ch 119**
>
> Exxon Corp an global oil company sought an injunction preventing Exxon Insurance was a motor insurance brokers from using of the word 'Exxon' in its company name.
>
> *Held* The common law tort of passing off extended to prevent the Exxon Insurance from using the name 'Exxon' even though it was not in the same business as the plaintiff. Because the name 'Exxon' is so widely known, it was possible that the sue of that name might lead the public to do business with the defendant company under the impression that a connection exists the companies.

Class Rights—whether varied

White v Bristol Aeroplane Ltd (1953) CA

The company had preference shares and ordinary shares. A bonus issue was proposed of both preference and ordinary shares which would have the effect of proportionately increasing the number of ordinary shares in issue in relation to the preference shares in issue. The literal voting rights of both classes were unaffected by the bonus issue but the ordinary shareholders' relative voting strength was increased afterwards simply because there were more of them. The preference shareholders challenged the bonus issue arguing that it constituted a variation of their class rights and they should have the protection of the s 125 procedure.

Held The Court of Appeal rejected the preference shareholders' argument. Their voting power as a class may have been affected but their literal rights remained the same after the bonus issue as before. It was the enjoyment of the right that had been affected, not the legal nature of the right itself.

Class Rights—rights to individual

Cumbrian Newspapers Group Ltd v Cumberland and Westmorland Herald Newspaper and Printing Co Ltd (1986)

The plaintiff company had, as part of a scheme of amalgamation, acquired 10.67% of the ordinary shares of the defendant company. In order to make it difficult for anyone outside the Cumbrian Newspapers Group Ltd to ever gain control of newspapers owned by the defendant company, the articles of association of the defendant company were altered so that the plaintiff company had three types of special right attaching to any ordinary shares it held in the defendant at any time. These three categories of rights were: (1) rights of pre-emption on the transfer of any other issued ordinary shares in the defendant company; (2) pre-emption rights over any unissued shares in the defendant company; (3) the right to appoint a director of the defendant so long as the plaintiff owned at least 10% of its shares. The question before the court was—if the company wanted to alter those particular articles, did this constitute a variation of class rights even though the 'class' was defined by reference to any ordinary shares held by one person?

Held These rights, although they did not attach to particular shares but inured to an individual, were still capable of being 'class rights'.

Class Rights—shareholders' agreement

Harman v BML Group Ltd [1994] 2 BCLC 674, CA

A shareholders' agreement was in existence and it provided that a meeting of the company was only quorate if B or his proxy were present at it. A resolution to remove B as a director was passed at a meeting in his absence and he brought a s459 action in protest at his removal.

Held The Court of Appeal upheld the effect of the shareholders' agreement saying that B's rights were in effect class rights which could not be overridden. They had the same effect as if they were class rights contained in the company's articles of association.

Directors—remuneration, unlawful distribution

Re Halt Garage (1964) Ltd (1982)

Mr and Mrs C were the sole directors of the company and owned all its shares. They both worked in the business, drawing directors' remuneration as authorised to do under the company's constitution. However, Mrs C became ill in 1967 and withdrew from involvement in the company's business. She continued to be a director and received payment as such at a reduced rate. By 1968, the company was no longer profitable and it went into insolvent liquidation in 1971. The liquidator applied for repayment of sums allegedly overpaid to Mr and Mrs C as directors' remuneration. He argued that Mrs C should not have been entitled to any remuneration from the time she became ill onwards and that the level of Mr C's remuneration was unreasonable and disproportionate to the benefit gained by the company in the light of the company's unprofitability.

Held The liquidator's claim against Mr C failed as the court thought that it was not for the courts to pronounce on the level of directors' remuneration but rather this was a question for the shareholders and in the absence of fraud or of the company making a distribution of its capital then although the law required shareholders to be honest it did not require them to be wise in setting the level of directors' remuneration.

However, the court agreed with the liquidator with regard to those sums paid to Mrs C, ostensibly as remuneration, after she had become ill and withdrawn from active participation in the company. This, said the court, was not genuine remuneration but was a disguised gift of capital and thus repayable to the company.

Role of Chairman

> **John v Rees (1969)**
>
> The plaintiff was the president and chairman of the Pembrokeshire Divisional Labour Party. At a properly constituted meeting, a conflict of views arose and there was evidence of noise, disorder and some minor violence. The plaintiff, as chairman, warned that it would be impossible to continue the meeting if the disorder persisted. Upon the continuance of the disorder, the chairman announced the adjournment of the meeting and left, accompanied by a number of others. The meeting continued without the chairman and new officers were elected. The plaintiff sought an order invalidating these actions.
>
> *Held* The chairman possessed an inherent power to adjourn a meeting in the event of disorder if he acted *bona fide* and if the adjournment were for no longer than necessary for the restoration of order. However, in the present case, the disorder was not sufficient to warrant an adjournment. The meeting remained in being and the elections of the new officers were thus valid.

Members' Resolutions—deemed to be passed

> **Re Duomatic Ltd (1969)**
>
> For a period of 15 months, the two directors of the company were its only ordinary shareholders. Under the articles of the company, remuneration of directors had to be determined from time to time by resolution of the company in general meeting. No such resolutions were passed but the two directors drew sums according to their needs and entered them into the accounts as 'directors' salaries'. The liquidator of the company sought to recover these sums from the two directors.
>
> *Held* Although none of the payments were authorised by resolution, the clear assent of all the ordinary shareholders was as binding as a resolution and the payments could not be disturbed. Buckley J said: 'Where it can be shown that all the shareholders who have a right to attend and vote at a general meeting of the company assent to some matter which a general meeting of the company could carry into effect, that assent is as binding as a resolution in general meeting would be.'

Members' Resolutions without meeting

Cane v Jones (1980)

Two brothers, H and P, formed a company and were the sole directors of that company. The shareholding of the company was divided equally between members of H's family and members of P's family. The company's articles provided for the election of a chairman by the directors, who should have a casting vote at board meetings and should preside over and have a casting vote at general meetings of the company. An agreement was made between all the shareholders that the chairman should cease to be entitled to use his casting vote. The management of the company became deadlocked. The plaintiff claimed the informal agreement was effective to alter the company's articles, and thus the defendants could not exercise a casting vote.

Held Despite the lack of a meeting or a resolution in writing to comply with the statutory requirements regarding the alteration of a company's articles, the agreement was effective. The agreement represented the unanimous will of the shareholders acting together and had the same effect as would a special resolution altering the company's articles so as to deprive the chairman of his casting vote.

Directors—Balance of power with General Meeting

Quin & Axtens Ltd v Salmon (1909) HL

The articles of association of the appellant company vested in the directors the general management of the company. With regard to certain matters, however, the articles provided that no resolution of the directors should be valid if either of the two managing directors dissented. The respondent, one of the two managing directors, so dissented from such a resolution. At an extraordinary general meeting, the company purported to ratify the original resolution by a simple majority. The respondent, as original plaintiff, was granted an injunction restraining the company from acting on the resolutions of the board and the general meeting. The company appealed.

Held The House of Lords dismissed the appeal. The resolutions were inconsistent with the provisions of the articles and the company was properly restrained from acting thereon. The right of management veto, as contained in the articles, was therefore upheld.

Directors—Removal—Weighted Voting

> **Bushell v Faith [1970] AC, HL**
>
> The Company had 300 shares issued. The plaintiff, defendant and their sister held 100 each. The plaintiff and the defendant were the only directors. The company's articles of association weighted the voting rights attached to the shares from the normal one vote per share to three votes per share where, and only where, the issue before a general meeting of the company was the removal of the director holding those shares. The plaintiff and her sister tried to remove the defendant from office as a director. The issue thus arose as to whether a court should give effect to the weighted voting rights attached by the articles to the defendant's shares which would, if recognised, have the effect of blocking the resolution to remove him by 300 votes to 200.
>
> *Held* The House of Lords decided to recognise the weighted voting rights accorded by the articles. In so doing they drew a distinction between the voting rights attached to shares and the mandatory scope of s303 of the Companies Act 1985. They thought that Parliament, in enacting s303, did not mean to fetter the scope for a company to issue a share with such rights or restrictions attaching to the share as the company saw fit.

Directors Contract over 5 years

> **Wright v Atlas Wright (Europe) Ltd (1999) CA**
>
> The plaintiffs sold the entire share capital of a company to the defendant company and agreed that, on their retirement, the defendant company would make annual payments to them 'for life'. The company duly paid the agreed sums for seven years. After that time, the shareholding in the defendant company was again sold. The new directors declined to continue the payments and, when sued by the plaintiffs, the company argued that the agreement for such payments was contrary to s 319 since it could not be terminated by the company and it had not been formally approved by the company in general meeting.
>
> *Held* The Court of Appeal upheld the first instance judgment and determined that s 319 was one of the provisions on company law which was subject to the principle in Re Duomatic Ltd (1969) in that, provided all the then shareholders were apprised of and agreed to the contract, such consent would override the requirement for' the passing of a formal resolution at a meeting.

Directors' powers—Managing Director's remuneration

Craven Ellis v Canons Ltd [1936] 2 KB, CA

The plaintiff had been purportedly appointed managing director of the defendant company by an agreement which set out a rate of remuneration payable but was in actual fact void as the directors of the company were not qualified to act as such under the articles. The company now relied on this want of authority in the plaintiff's appointment in its refusal to pay him for the services of managing director which he had already rendered to the company.

Held Despite the fact that his appointment as managing director was void the plaintiff was still entitled to payment on a *quantum meruit* basis.

Directors—unauthorised remuneration

Guinness plc v Saunders [1990] 1 All ER 652, HL

In 1986 Guinness plc launched a contested takeover bid for the Distillers brewing group. During the course of its bid Guinness formed an executive committee of its directors Mr Roux, Mr Saunders and Mr Ward known as 'the war cabinet'. Mr Ward was a US lawyer and all three were members of the board of directors of Guinness plc. A Jersey-based company owned by Mr Ward provided consultancy advice to Guinness during the bid and was paid a fee of £5.2 million. This fee had, allegedly, been agreed by the war cabinet, but not by the main board of Guinness. Indeed, the main board of directors was not appraised of this payment at all. Guinness sought repayment of this fee on the grounds that the failure to disclose to the board the payment to one of the directors was a breach of fiduciary duty on the part of Mr Ward. He in turn tried to argue that it was remuneration which he was entitled to under Guinness plc's articles of association.

Held The House of Lords held that the contract to pay Mr Ward was void and he was not entitled to keep this sum. Guinness' articles of association did not empower the 'war cabinet' to approve this payment as special remuneration. Neither could Mr Ward rely on another of Guinness' articles which entitled a director acting in another professional capacity to be remunerated as such for work undertaken in that capacity. Mr Ward had no other general right to remuneration and, unless he could point to some provision in Guinness' articles entitling him to this sum as special remuneration, then he must be presumed to have acted gratuitously on Guinness' behalf.

Directors—level of skill

Dorchester Finance Co Ltd v Stebbings (1977)

S, P and H were directors of the plaintiff company. S and P were chartered accountants and H had considerable accounting experience. The management of the company was left to S, with P and H fulfilling roles as non-executive directors. As neither P nor H visited the company frequently, they often left signed cheques in blank to be used by S at some later date. Losses were incurred when unsecured loans were made which turned out to be unrecoverable. The plaintiff company brought an action against S, P and H alleging negligence in the management of the company's affairs.

Held Foster J decided that all three were liable in negligence. A director in carrying out his duties was required to exhibit such a degree of skill as may reasonably be expected from a person of his knowledge and experience. No distinction was to be drawn between executive and non-executive directors. The court rejected the argument that non-executive directors could rely on the competence and diligence of the auditors and do nothing themselves, whether they had accounting experience or not.

Director—level of skill—reliance on others

Norman v Theodore Goddard (1991)

Q was a chartered surveyor with no knowledge of company law or offshore financial matters who was appointed as a director of LB Investments (LBI). B, a partner in Theodore Goddard, suggested that, for tax reasons, substantial sums held in cash by LBI should be invested in an offshore company. B made assurances to Q as to the profitability, availability and security of the funds. The offshore company was in fact controlled by B who stole the money transferred to it by LBI. Theodore Goddard sought a contribution from Q on the basis that he had acted in breach of his duty of care as a director of LBI.

Held Q was not in breach of duty and the claim of Theodore Goddard thus failed. The test of a director's duty was accurately stated in s 214(4) of the Insolvency Act 1986. The relevant test was what could be expected of a person in the position of director carrying out those functions. A director was entitled to trust persons in positions of responsibility until there was reason to distrust them.

Directors' Duties—Conflict of Duty and Interest

<u>Aberdeen Railway Co v Blaikie Bros (1854) HL</u>

The appellant company agreed to buy goods from the respondent partnership. Blaikie was a member of the respondent partnership and was also a director of the appellant company. The company refused to honour the contract and the partnership sought its enforcement.

Held The House of Lords decided that the company was entitled to avoid the contract. There was a clear conflict between Blaikie's duty to secure for the company the lowest possible price, and his interest as a member of the partnership to make the greatest profit, and in such circumstances a contract was unenforceable against the company. Lord Cranworth stated: 'So strictly is this principle adhered to, that no question is allowed to be raised as to the fairness or unfairness of a contract so entered into.'

Directors' Duties—Best Interests of Company, not themselves

<u>Heron International Ltd v Lord Grade (1983) CA</u>

The directors of the target company of a proposed takeover were faced with two competing bids. The articles of the company gave the directors the power to choose which bid to accept. The directors, for a number of reasons, chose the lower bid. The plaintiffs, suing as representatives of the shareholders in the defendant company, sought an injunction to prevent the transfer.

Held The directors were under a fiduciary obligation to exercise the power to register a proposed transfer in the interests of both the company and the shareholders. The Court of Appeal decided that: 'Where directors have decided that it is in the best interests of a company that the company be taken over and there are two or more bidders the only duty of directors…is to obtain the best price.' In considering rival bids in a takeover the interests of the company were the interests of the current shareholders. The injunction was therefore granted.

Directors—account for profit

> **Industrial Development Consultants Ltd v Cooley [1972] 2 All ER 162**
>
> The defendant was the managing director of the plaintiff company and had formerly been an architect with the West Midlands Gas Board. He entered into negotiations on behalf of the company with the Eastern Gas Board. Eastern Gas informed the defendant that it would enter into the contract with him personally but not with the company. The defendant resigned as managing director of the company (on the pretext of ill health) in order to take up the Gas Board contract. The company sued for the profit made.
>
> *Held* The defendant was liable for all benefits accruing under the contract, even though the plaintiff company had lost no corporate opportunity. Whilst managing director of the plaintiff company, a fiduciary relationship existed between himself and the company, and he was therefore under a duty to disclose all information revealed to him in the course of his dealings with the Gas Board. The defendant's actions had put his personal interest in direct conflict with the interests of the company, and this constituted a breach of his fiduciary duty for which he was accountable.

Director—disqualification

> **Re Barings plc (No 5) [2000] 1 BCLC 523, CA**
>
> The Court of Appeal, in upholding the disqualification order against a senior director of one of the Barings' group of companies, agreed with the following comments of Jonathan Parker J, the first instance judge:
>
> Directors have, both collectively and individually, a continuing duty to acquire and maintain a sufficient knowledge and understanding of the company's business to enable them properly to discharge their duties as directors.
>
> Whilst directors are entitled (subject to the articles of association of the company) to delegate particular functions to those below them in the management chain, and to trust their competence and integrity to a reasonable extent, the exercise of the power of delegation does not absolve a director from the duty to supervise the discharge of the delegated functions.
>
> No rule of universal application can be formulated as to the duty referred to in (ii) above. The extent of the duty, and the question whether it has been discharged, must depend on the facts of each particular case, including the director's role in the management of the company.

12—More Revision

Shares—nature of

Bradbury v English Sewing Cotton Co Ltd (1923) HL

The House of Lords examined the nature of shares and said that a share is a fractional part of the share capital. Shares are also the individual property of all the members but this does not mean that all the members as a group own the share capital. The share capital is something different from all the shares aggregated. The share capital belongs to the company.

Liquidation—fraudulent trading

Re William Leitch Brothers (No 1) (1932)

The company was incorporated in December 1926. By the end of 1929 the company was in serious financial difficulties, and by 30 March 1930 the company was unable to pay its debts. William Leitch, a director of the firm, knew that the company owed £6,500 and would not be able to pay it. However, he proceeded to borrow a further £6,000.. In June of that year, the company was wound up and the liquidator wanted the court to find Mr Leitch personally liable for the debts of the company.

Held Mr Leitch was found guilty of fraudulent trading. The test should be subjective, that is, what was the knowledge of the particular director at the time? In other words, the court is not concerned with the question of what a ,reasonable director would have believed had he been in the same position.

Fraudulent trading—meaning

> ### Re Patrick & Lyon Ltd (1933)
>
> The case concerned the meaning of s 275 of the CA 1929 (now s213 IA 1986) which provided that:
>
> If in the course of the winding up of a company it appears that any business of the company has been carried on with intent to defraud creditors of the company or...for any fraudulent purpose, the court, on the application of...the liquidator or any creditor or contributory...may declare that any of the directors...of the company who were knowingly parties to the carrying on of the business in manner aforesaid shall be personally responsible, without any limitation of liability, for all or any of the debts of the company as the court may direct.
>
> That section was the forerunner of the modern s 216 of the IA 1986 and so what the court had to say then is still of relevance today.
>
> *Held* The phrases 'intent to defraud' and 'fraudulent purpose' implied that actual dishonesty must be present as an element rather than fraud in the equitable sense. Maugham J said:
>
> [These] words connote actual dishonesty involving, according to current notions of fair trading among commercial men, real moral blame. No judge, I think, has ever been willing to define 'fraud' and I am attempting no definition.

Director's duty of skill

> ### Norman v Theodore Goddard (1991)
>
> For facts, see 6.2 above. Hoffman J, in discussing a company director's common law duty of care and skill, said:
>
> ...a director performing active duties on behalf of the company need not exhibit a greater degree of skill than may reasonably be expected from a person undertaking those duties. A director who undertakes the management of the company's properties is expected to have reasonable skill in property management, but not in offshore tax avoidance. It may be that in considering what a director ought reasonably to have known or inferred, one should also take into account the knowledge, skill and experience which he actually had in addition to that which a person carrying out his functions should be expected to have...
>
> He went on to approve s214(4) of the IA 1986 as being an accurate statement of the extent of a director's duty of care and skill.

Fraudulent trading—company secretary not liable

> **Re Maidstone Buildings Provisions Ltd (1971)**
>
> Mr Penney was the secretary for the company and not a director. Debts were incurred by the company when it was evident the company was insolvent.
>
> *Held* The person concerned must take an active part in the fraudulent trading to be liable under this section. The fact that the secretary of the company warned the other directors that they should stop trading was not enough to render those directors liable for fraudulent trading.

Wrongful trading—meaning

> **Re Produce Marketing Consortium Ltd (No 2) (1989)**
>
> Two directors were running a fruit importing business and continued to do so when they ought to have known that there was no chance of the company remaining solvent.
>
> *Held* They were liable under s 214 for wrongful trading. Although the two directors did not know that the company was in a grave financial situation and about to become insolvent, Knox J stated that that was immaterial. Under s 214 there is a objective test and the directors will be judged not just on what information they had but any information that, 'given reasonable diligence and an appropriate level of general knowledge, skill and experience, was ascertainable'.

Wrongful trading—disregard to CA requirements

> **Re DKG Contractors Ltd (1990)**
>
> Two directors of a groundwork company were consistently failing to have any regard to the Companies Acts, although they were never dishonest. The company then collapsed.
>
> *Held* The directors were guilty of wrongful trading and had to contribute £500,000 towards the company's debts.

Debenture—nature of

> **Levy v Abercorris Slate and Slab Co (1887)**
>
> The plaintiff's claim against the defendant was based upon an instrument that the defendant argued was void under the Bills of Sale Act (1878) Amendment Act 1882 whereas the plaintiff argued that it was a 'debenture' and therefore exempt from the strictures of that legislation. The court was therefore required to pronounce on the definition of 'debenture'.
>
> *Held* Chitty J said that a debenture was a document which either created a debt or acknowledged it so that any document which fulfilled either of those conditions was a 'debenture'.

Debenture—nature of—example

> **British India Steam Navigation Co v IRC (1881)**
>
> The company had issued instruments whereby the company promised to pay the holder of such an instrument £100 on 30 November 1882 and 5% interest half-yearly. The instruments were not under seal and in order to avoid a higher rate of stamp duty the company argued that they were not debentures but rather promissory notes.
>
> *Held* The court disagreed. However, the court declined to ascribe a precise definition to the term debenture but made it clear it was capable of encompassing many different forms of instrument and an instrument not being under seal was no bar to its being a debenture.

Debenture—floating charge—nature of

> **Re Yorkshire Woolcombers Association Ltd (1903) CA**
>
> Romer LJ said that a floating charge had three key characteristics:
>
> It is a charge on a class of assets of the company which includes present and future assets.
>
> The composition of the class is not fixed—it changes from time to time in the ordinary course of the company's business.
>
> The charge contemplates that the company is free to carry on business normally and deal with the assets subject to it in the ordinary course of that business until such time as the chargeholders enforce the charge—so it 'floats' in suspense until that time.

Retention of title

Aluminium Industrie Vaassen BV v Romalpa Aluminium Ltd (1976) CA

A Dutch company supplied aluminium foil to an English company. The contract between them contained a retention of title clause, which stated that legal title to the foil did not pass to the English company until full payment had been made. Anything made from the foil was to be held by the company as bailees and was to be kept separately from any other manufactured goods. The company was entitled to deal in the ordinary course of business with any products manufactured, but in such a case the company was acting as the agent of the supplier.

Held The clause was effective. The suppliers could claim any aluminium still in its original form, and they could trace into any proceeds of sale from goods manufactured from their aluminium.

Debenture—date of registration

Re Eric Holmes (1965)

A debenture in favour of Mr Richards was executed by the firm on 5 June. The documentation was sent to the company solicitors, but without a date on it. The solicitors were in a state of disarray at the time because the active partner had been killed. The date on the documentation was filled in as 23 June, which would have been within the 21 day period for registration. Evidently, if the true date of execution was used, the charge had not been registered within time. A certificate was issued by Companies House stating the requirements of the Act had been complied with.

Held The charge was valid. Section 98(2) of the CA 1948 (s401 of the CA 1985) states that a certificate is conclusive evidence that the requirements of the act have been complied with.

Debenture—registration out of time

Re Telomatic (1994)

A charge was created by Barclays Bank over land owned by Telomatic. The charge was dated 4 January, but was not registered at Companies House at that time. The bank realised the charge had not been registered on 4 October and tried three times to procure security for their charge. On 5 October, the Cyprus Bank took a second charge over the property. Barclays Bank then applied to the court to get rectification of the register.

Held Registration out of time was not granted by the court. First, Barclays had misled the court as to, whether the company was to be wound up. Secondly, Barclays had tried to procure security in several ways before attempting to use s 404. Registration out of time will normally be granted, but it was held to be inequitable to do so in this instance.

Debenture—automatic crystallisation of floating charge

Re Brightlife Ltd (1986)

Brightlife Ltd went into creditor's voluntary liquidation owing £200,000, secured by debenture to Norandex, and £70,000 to the Commissioners of Customs and Excise, who are classed as preferential creditors. A clause in the debenture stipulated that the chargee could crystallise the floating charge, if it was believed the security was in jeopardy. The liquidator wanted guidance as to the effectiveness of the clause.

Held The court stated that crystallisation was possible in this instance and consequently the debenture-holder did not have to wait until the preferential creditors were paid. Hoffman J was urged to consider the prejudice to other creditors that the operation of automatic crystallisation clauses could cause. However, he rejected this consideration saying:

I do not think that it is open to the courts to restrict the contractual freedom of parties to a floating charge on such grounds. The floating charge was invented by Victorian lawyers to enable manufacturing and trading companies to raise loan capital on debentures. It could offer the security of a charge over the whole of the company's undertaking without inhibiting its ability to trade. But the mirror image of these advantages was the potential prejudice to the general body of creditors, who might know nothing of the floating charge but find that all the company's assets, including the very goods which they had just delivered on credit, had been swept up by the debenture-holder. The public interest requires a balancing of the advantages to the economy of facilitating the borrowing of money against the possibility of injustice to unsecured creditors. These arguments for and against floating charges are matters for Parliament rather than the courts...

The rule in Foss v Harbottle

> **Foss v Harbottle (1843)**
>
> The two plaintiffs, suing 'on behalf of themselves and all the other members of the corporation, except those who committed the injuries complained and alleged that the defendants, who were the directors and promoters of the company, had, *inter alia,* sold land to the company at an undisclosed profit.
>
> *Held* The individual minority shareholders were not the proper plaintiffs and could not therefore sue. If a wrong had been committed it had been committed against the company and therefore the proper plaintiff was the company. It was not open to individual members to assume to themselves the right of suing in the name of the company. Although this was a rule which could be departed from, it should not be, save for 'reasons of a very urgent character'. In the circumstances, there was nothing to prevent the company from obtaining redress in its corporate character regarding the matters complained of.

Foss v Harbottle exception—benefit of company

> Stein v Blake (1998) CA
>
> The plaintiff owned half the shares in a number of companies. The defendant owned the other half and was sole director of the companies. It was alleged that the defendant had misappropriated assets from the companies and the plaintiff brought a personal claim against the defendant, claiming damages for the loss in value of his shares in the companies which had resulted from the misappropriation of the companies' assets. The companies were subsequently placed into liquidation, but no action was brought by the liquidators against the defendant.
>
> *Held* The plaintiff could not recover from the defendant, as the loss caused to the plaintiff was only a reflection of the companies' loss and the companies were the proper plaintiffs to bring legal proceedings against the defendant. Millet LJ stated:
>
> Directors owe fiduciary duties to their company to preserve and defend its assets and to the shareholders to advise them properly so that they are not induced or compelled to part with their shares at an undervalue. No doubt other fiduciary duties are also owed both to the company and to its shareholders. Shareholders may suffer loss in the event of a breach of either duty, but in the first case the loss consists of a diminution of the value of their shares, is fully reflected in the loss sustained by the company, and is fully compensated by restitution to the company. In the second case the company suffers no loss. Its assets are unaffected…All that is pleaded in the present case is wrongdoing to the company and loss suffered by the company. The only loss alleged to have been suffered by the plaintiff is reflected in the loss sustained by the company.

Winding up—just and equitable

> **Ebrahimi v Westbourne Galleries (1973) HL**
>
> Ebrahimi and Nazar ran a successful carpet business as a partnership which they went on to incorporate. Nazar's son George was brought into the business and shares transferred to him. Friction occurred and Nazar and George excluded Ebrahimi from the business, removing him as a director. The profits of the business were paid out in the form of directors' salaries and not in dividends. Due to his exclusion, Ebrahimi saw none of the profits. He therefore petitioned for the company to be wound up on 'just and equitable' grounds.
>
> *Held* The House of Lords unanimously granted the order for the company to be wound up. Lord Wilberforce defined the concept of 'just and equitable' as:
>
> ...a recognition of the fact that a limited company is more than a mere legal entity, with a personality in law of its own; that...there are individuals, with rights, expectations and obligations *inter se* which are not necessarily submerged in the company structure...It does, as equity always does, enable the court to subject the exercise of legal rights to equitable considerations, that is, of personal character arising between one individual and another, which may make it unjust or inequitable, to insist on legal rights, or to exercise them in a particular way.
>
> His Lordship proceeded to set out some of the situations which he had in mind:

Winding up—prejudicial conduct (dividends not increased)

Sam Weller Ltd (1990)

The petitioners were the owners of around 43% of the issued share capital of a family company. The company was run by Sam Weller. In recent years, the company had become increasingly profitable. However, the dividend declared each year remained as it had done for the last 37 years. The petitioners alleged, *inter alia*, that the failure to approve the payment of larger dividends amounted to unfairly prejudicial conduct. Sam Weller applied to have the petition struck out by reason of the fact that the conduct alleged affected all members equally and could not therefore be unfairly prejudicial to the interests of some part of the members.

Held The application was dismissed because members might have different interests even if their rights as members were effectively the same. Conduct could be unfairly prejudicial within the meaning of s 459 notwithstanding that it affected all the members equally. Where conduct prejudiced all members equally, it could still be held to be unfairly prejudicial to the interests of some part of the members. The payment of low dividends was capable of amounting to conduct unfairly prejudicial to some of the members, including the petitioners.

Winding up—price for shares

Re Bird Precision Bellows Ltd (1984) CA

The petitioners had been directors until removed from office. They alleged that the company was in effect a quasi-partnership. Their removal was their wrongful exclusion from the conduct of the company's business. The petition under s 75 of the CA 1980 alleged that the affairs of the company had been conducted in a manner unfairly prejudicial to them, and requested that the respondents purchase the petitioners' shares.

Held The order was granted and the matter which arose was how to value the petitioners' shares. The court decided that if the sale was being forced because of the unfairly prejudicial conduct of the majority, and the shares had been acquired on the incorporation of a quasi-partnership company in which the petitioners had a legitimate expectation that they would participate, the price should be fixed on a *pro rata* basis. If the petitioners had conducted themselves so as to deserve exclusion from the company's affairs, the price should be discounted as if they had elected to sell their shares. In the instant case, the petitioners had been wrongfully excluded and thus the price should be fixed on a *pro rata* basis. The date for valuation was the date of the order.

Criminal liability—criminal liability—brain or nerve centre

> **Tesco Supermarkets Ltd v Nattrass (1972) HL**
>
> The appellant company was charged with an offence under the trade descriptions legislation of displaying inaccurate price information in one of its stores. The company was convicted and fined but appealed on the basis that the company had not committed the offence—it had in place a management and supervisory system designed to prevent this type of offence and the failure that resulted in the offence being committed was the failure of the store supervisor, which should not be attributed to the company.
>
> *Held* The appeal succeeded. Because the store supervisory manager could not be said to be part of the 'directing mind and will' of the company his acts could not be said to be those of the company. The House of Lords stressed the fictional nature of the corporate legal person and the need to distinguish between:
>
> acts which were actually those of the company; and
>
> acts which were those of an agent or servant of the company but for which the company has some statutory or vicarious liability.
>
> The former category are usually those acts committed by the board of directors or senior management of a company who speak and act for it. They are its 'brain' or its 'nerve centre'.

Criminal liability—an employee who acts for the company

Director General of Fair Trading v Pioneer Concrete (UK) Ltd and Another (In Re Supply of Ready Mixed Concrete (No 2)) (1995) HL

The respondent companies had, at a senior level put in place compliance systems to ensure that no employee breached injunctions restraining contravention of restrictive trade practices legislation. Contrary to the companies' express instructions and without their knowledge, some of the employees went ahead and ignored the injunctions. The companies argued that they should not be vicariously liable for the acts of these employees as they acted without any form of authority and contrary to explicit instructions. The court at first instance disagreed and held the companies to be nonetheless in contempt of court. The Court of Appeal allowed the companies' appeal and the Director General of Fair Trading, who is responsible for the enforcement of restrictive practices legislation, appealed to the House of Lords.

Held The appeal was allowed. Since a company is a fictional person, it can only act through the medium of its agents and the actions of its employees acting in the course of their employment amount to the carrying on of business by the company. Simply because a prohibition at senior level existed, designed to prevent illegal agreements being made, it was not enough to prevent the companies becoming party to such agreements where the prohibition was ignored by the employees. Lord Templeman said that 'an employee who acts for the company within the scope of his employment is the company. Directors may give instructions, top management may exhort, middle management may question and workers may listen attentively. But if a worker makes a defective product or a lower manager accepts or rejects an order, he is the company'.

Civil liability—actual fault or privity

Lennard's Carrying Co Ltd v Asiatic Petroleum Co Ltd (1915) HL

The appellants were ship owners and one of their ships caught fire due to its unseaworthy condition, destroying its cargo. When sued by the cargo owners the appellants relied on the statutory let out in the Merchant Shipping Act 1894 that they would not be liable for damages to cargo owners where the loss occurred without their 'actual fault or privity'. The managing director of the appellant company was in full control of the management of the ship.

Held Because of the position he enjoyed, the acts of the managing director in managing the ship could be seen as the acts of the company. The appellant company was responsible for his acts and defaults and so the company could not escape liability by relying on the statutory defence.

Shareholder's theft from company

> **Attorney General's Reference (No 2 of 1982) CA**
>
> The defendant had been charged with theft from companies of which they were sole directors and shareholders. They had been acquitted following *Tesco Supermarkets v Nattrass*, the sole owners of a company were its directing mind and will and therefore could not be said to steal from it.
>
> *Held* The judge's interpretation of *Tesco Supermarkets* was wrong—that case's reasoning related to the company as perpetrator not victim of offences. Where all the members/directors, even if they are sole controllers of a company, act illegally and dishonestly appropriate that company's property they can be said to be guilty of theft.

13—Ready-Made Companies

Solicitors, accountants, company formation agents and others often hold a stock of ready-made companies for sale to their clients. These suppliers register the companies for this purpose and so as a minimum will have:

subscribed to a memorandum of association;

filed it at Companies House with form 10 (particulars of director(s) and company secretary and registered office) and form 12 (declaration of compliance); and

received a certificate of incorporation.

In addition they might have also filed articles of association, but if they have not done so, Table A will apply. These companies should always be guaranteed not to have traded or have any assets or liabilities.

Putting a ready-made company in order

The buyer of a ready-made company must:

take a transfer of the subscriber share or the right the right to subscribe for it;

appoint a new director and accept the resignation of the supplier's nominee as a director;

appoint a new company secretary and accept the resignation of the supplier's nominee as the company secretary;

change the registered office;

change the name of the company if it is either a name that the supplier want to keep as its "trade" name or it is not a name that the buyer wants; and

adopt articles of association or change the articles.

Table A or the supplier's articles are likely to be unsuitable for the buyer's needs and circumstances, but often, if the company is to have only one member, the buyer may take the view that for practical purposes it does not really matter what the articles say.

Advantages and Disadvantages

The amount of work to be done to put a ready-made company in order is not less and is likely to be more than is required to form a new company. Company formation agents can supply ready-made companies for as little as £100 and sometimes less.

Therefore the initial cost of acquiring a ready-made company is very low. This is an advantage if the buyer does not want to tailor the company to suit his needs and if he can deal with the changes which must be made (transfer of share or subscription right and changes of director, secretary and registered office) without professional help. If these apply, cost can be an advantage. If they do not apply, the combined cost of buying a ready-made company and putting it in order are likely to be more that the cost of forming a new company.

The number of suppliers of ready-made companies shows that they are popular, but when the details of buying one and the formation of a new company are analysed, it seems that the only real advantages of buying a ready-made company are:

it can be available more or less instantly; and

it may be more convenient, if the buyer is too busy (eg setting up a new business, buying a business or negotiating a contract) to have time to form a new company.

NB subscriber shares

The ready-made company will have a member (or sometimes two members), usually a person employed by or otherwise associated with the supplier, who has signed the memorandum undertaking to take a share in the company's capital. Practice varies whether the share is or is not allotted. If the share has been allotted, on the sale of the ready-made company, it must be transferred to the buyer. If it has not been allotted the subscriber must transfer his right to the share to the buyer and be released from his obligation to subscribe for it. Lack of attention to this occasionally leads to confusion about a company's issued capital, which can actually be, eg, 102 shares rather than the intended 100 shares, because the two (nowadays usually one) subscriber shares are counted twice on returns of allotments to Companies House, once on the subscription and again when the new owners allot shares to themselves, in this example allotting 100 shares instead of 98, overlooking the two subscriber shares.

Appendix 1—The Carr Case

TransTec plc Secretary of State for Trade and Industry v Carr and others

[2005] EWHC 1723 (Ch)

Company Directors Disqualification Act 1986, s 8.

C and J (the directors) were the directors of T plc (the company) and the respondents to an application by the claimant Secretary of State for disqualification orders under s 8 of the Company Directors Disqualification Act 1986. A number of other intended respondents gave undertakings in accordance with s 1A of the 1986 Act prior to the issue of proceedings. The Secretary of State's application arose out of allegations that the directors were responsible for the non-disclosure in the company's accounts of the terms of a settlement of a claim for substantial compensation made against the company by Ford. The non-disclosure gave rise to criminal charges on the grounds of dishonesty and C applied for a stay of the disqualification proceedings until after the conclusion of the criminal trial.

He alleged, inter alia, that the preparation of his written evidence in the disqualification proceedings would be impracticable before the criminal trial, as it would seriously jeopardise the preparation of his defence in the criminal proceedings, not least because of the time involved in that exercise.

The application would be dismissed.

If an applicant were able to satisfy the court that a requirement to file his evidence in disqualification proceedings before the start of a criminal trial would materially prejudice the preparation of his defence or carry a real risk of doing so, it would be oppressive and unfair to require him to file his evidence at that stage, as there was an overriding interest in the fair trial of criminal charges.

In the instant case, C had failed on the evidence to make out his contentions.

Accordingly, the court would order the service of C's evidence before the start of the criminal trial.

Malcolm Davis-White QC and Edmund Nourse (instructed by the Treasury Solicitor) for the Secretary of State.

Philip Jones (instructed by Kingsley Napley) for C.

Victoria Ellis Barrister.

Judgment

[2005] EWHC 1723 (Ch)

CHANCERY DIVISION (COMPANIES COURT)

29 JULY 2005

MR JUSTICE DAVID RICHARDS

APPROVED JUDGMENT

I DIRECT THAT PURSUANT TO CPR PD 39A PARA 6.1 NO OFFICIAL SHORTHAND NOTE SHALL BE TAKEN OF THIS JUDGMENT AND THAT COPIES OF THIS VERSION AS HANDED DOWN MAY BE TREATED AS AUTHENTIC.

MR JUSTICE DAVID RICHARDS:

1. These are applications for a stay of proceedings under the Company Directors Disqualification Act 1986 (the 1986 Act). The applications are made by Richard Carr and William Jeffrey who were directors of TransTec Plc and a number of its subsidiaries. They are the two remaining respondents to an application made by the Secretary of State for disqualification orders under section 8 of the 1986 Act. They are also the defendants in a criminal prosecution. Both the disqualification and the criminal proceedings arise out of their alleged conduct as directors of TransTec Plc and certain subsidiaries, and there is a very substantial overlap between the factual allegations in the two cases.

2. Mr Carr and Mr Jeffrey apply for a stay of the disqualification proceedings until after the conclusion of the criminal trial. It is due to begin in the Birmingham Crown Court on 9 January 2006, with an estimated length of 3 months. As will appear, there is no question of a trial of the disqualification proceedings occurring before the criminal trial and the real question for decision is whether Mr Carr and Mr Jeffrey should be required to serve their written evidence in the disqualification proceedings before the commencement of the criminal trial.

3. The procedural steps so far taken in the disqualification case are as follows. Notice of the proposed disqualification proceedings was sent to the intended respondents on 23 August 2004. A number of intended respondents gave undertakings in accordance with Section 1 A of the 1986 Act before issue of the proceedings. The claim form was issued on 11 January 2005 against five respondents, of whom three have since given undertakings. The evidence in support of the application was served shortly after the issue of the claim form. Mr Carr's application for a stay was issued on 7 February 2005, while Mr Jeffrey's application was issued on 25 May 2005.

4. A directions hearing took place on 21 March 2005 and, in the usual course, directions would then have been given for the service of the respondents' evidence in answer to the Secretary of State's evidence, a further round of evidence by the respondents in response to each other's evidence (if they wished to serve any) and evidence in reply from the Secretary of State. No directions were given for service of evidence by Mr Carr in view of his application for a stay, and subsequently the Secretary of State agreed to postpone the service of evidence by Mr Jeffery after the issue of his application for a stay.

5. Mr Carr has been represented on this application by solicitors and counsel. His solicitors, Kingsley Napley, also act for him in the criminal proceedings and have instructed different counsel in those proceedings. Mr Philip Jones, appearing for Mr Carr on this application, has not been instructed to act generally in the disqualification proceedings.

6. Mr Jeffrey now lives in Australia. Like the other respondents, he was notified in August 2004 of the intention to bring disqualification proceedings. He was sent the claim form and supporting evidence in January 2005, as was a lawyer in Australia who was providing some assistance to him. Leave to serve Mr Jeffrey out of the jurisdiction was given on 14 March 2005 and formal service was then effected.

7. Mr Jeffrey's application for a stay was issued on 25 May 2005, supported by a witness statement of David McCluskey, a solicitor employed by Peters & Peters. His firm represents Mr Jeffrey in the criminal proceedings but not in these proceedings. Mr Jeffery did not appear and was not represented on this application. However, the submissions made on behalf of Mr Carr are applicable also to Mr Jeffrey and I have also has regard to the particular points relevant to his position set out by Mr McCluskey in his witness statement.

8. The common area of the criminal and disqualification proceedings concerns what is called "the Ford Claim". A very brief summary of the Secretary of State's case is as follows. TransTec manufactured a cylinder head for Ford in Germany. There were significant production problems and, following a number of default notices, Ford faxed a formal claim of $36 million for compensation on 23 April 1997, relating principally to alleged losses in 1996. The following day, TransTec made a substantial offer of settlement. On 25 April 1997, TransTec's accounts for the year ended 31 December 1996 were signed, without providing for or disclosing Ford's claim. By 18 September 1997, TransTec had agreed a set-

tlement with Ford, under which it agreed to pay $18 million to Ford over three years. The payments were to be made by way of price reductions on future orders placed by Ford. This settlement and the payments and liabilities arising from it were not disclosed in the interim accounts published on 22 September 1997 or in the annual accounts for 1997. Payments pursuant to the settlement were made to Ford in 1998 but were allegedly mischaracterised as assets in the interim and annual accounts for that year. Payments made in 1999 were not accounted for in the annual accounts for 1999. The Secretary of State alleges that Mr Carr and Mr Jeffrey were responsible for the non-disclosure or treatment of the Ford Claim, settlement and payments in the various accounts mentioned above.

9. The charges in the criminal proceedings against both Mr Carr and Mr Jeffrey relate to the alleged non-disclosure or mischaracterisation of the Ford Claim, settlement and payments in the various annual and interim accounts referred to above. The charges are made under section 19 of the Theft Act 1968. In addition, each is charged with offences under section 398A(2) of the Companies Act 1985 in relation to the provision of a letter of representation to TransTec's auditors.

10. The significant difference between the two sets of proceedings is that, while the criminal proceedings involve only offences of dishonesty, the Secretary of State alleges recklessness or negligence as alternatives to deliberate misconduct. There are also allegations in the disqualification proceedings of non-disclosure of the Ford Claim to the Stock Exchange, the board of directors of TransTec and others, which do not feature in the criminal charges.

11. While the criminal proceeding are confined to the Ford Claim, there is a single further allegation against Mr Carr and Mr Jeffrey in the disqualification proceedings, which relates to the accounting treatment in the 1997 accounts of a payment of £400,000 to Rover.

12. Mr Carr and Mr Jeffrey state that they entirely reject the case alleged against them in both proceedings. It appears from answers given by Mr Carr in response to provisional criticisms by the inspectors and from the evidence filed on this application that the areas of substantial dispute relate not so much to the underlying facts but to the nature of the agreement with Ford, whether disclosure was required and whether the accounting treatments were proper, and as to Mr Carr's state of mind in relation to those matters. This does not of course preclude him from mounting a wider challenge but he has not given evidence on this application to suggest that there is a greater area of dispute. Mr Jeffrey did not respond to the inspectors' provisional criticisms but it does not appear from his evidence to the inspectors, or from evidence filed on his behalf in this application, that his position is different from that of Mr Carr.

13. There is a long history to this matter. Administrative receivers of TransTec and its subsidiaries were appointed on 29 December 1999. On 16 February 2000 and 8 March 2000 Mr Carr was interviewed by the administrative receivers. He was accompanied by his solicitor and it is apparent from comments at the start of the first interview that he knew that the Ford Claim would be the focus of the interviews and that the administrative receivers had reporting duties under the 1986 Act. Documents were put to Mr Carr in the course of the interviews and he disclosed that he had certain documents concerning the Ford Claim, which he supplied to them.

14. On 20 January 2000 the Secretary of State appointed inspectors to investigate the affairs of the companies under Section 432 of the Companies Act 1985. In announcing their appointment the Secretary of State stated that he expected the inspectors to concentrate on the Ford Claim and its disclosure, and the reasons for the collapse of the group.

15. Mr Carr was interviewed by the inspectors on 26 September 2000 and 23 October 2000. Amongst other matters, he was questioned about the Ford Claim and the Rover payment. The inspectors presented an interim report on 22 January 2001 which was published a month later. They continued their investigations and interviewed Mr Can for a third time on 30 May 2001. The interview included questions on the Ford Claim and the Rover payment and he was specifically warned about the risk of answering a particular question in the light of possible disqualification, regulatory or criminal proceedings. Provisional criticisms were supplied to Mr Carr in a letter dated 10 July 2001 which referred in part to the Ford Claim and the Rover payment and a response was made by the solicitors then acting for him on 3 August 2001. Further provisional criticisms including some relating to the Ford Claim and the Rover payment were sent in a letter dated 6 August 2001. A 41 page response was sent on his behalf on 6 September 2001. The process of provisional criticisms and responses continued until 15 May 2002.

16. In December 2001, following the receipt of reports from office holders pursuant to the 1986 Act, the Secretary of State sent letters to 39 individuals, including Mr Carr and Mr Jeffrey, referring to the possibility of disqualification proceedings and to the matters under investigation, including the Ford Claim and the Rover payment. The inspectors presented their final report to the Secretary of State in January 2003 and it was published in October 2003. The case made against Mr Can and Mr Jeffrey in the disqualification proceedings is based on the report.

17. On 12 March 2004 Mr Can was interviewed over a period of 41/2 hours by the Serious Fraud Office. A month before the interview he was provided with two files of documents totalling about 500 pages. At the interview he read out an 18 page prepared statement, together with a 34 page annex commenting on the documents provided to him. He sent a 7 page supplemental statement to the Serious Fraud Office on 26 March 2004.

18. By letters dated 23 August 2004 from the Treasury Solicitor, Mr Can and Mr Jeffrey were informed of the decision to institute disqualification proceedings against them and were provided with the proposed allegations of unfitness. The letter contained an offer to supply the supporting witness statement in draft. At the request of Mr Can's solicitors, the draft statement was sent to them on 6 September 2004. The exhibits were not provided but the Treasury Solicitor made clear that they too would be supplied on request. No request was made for them by Mr Can or his solicitors. Mr Jeffrey made no request to see the draft statement or exhibits.

19. On 21 October 2004 Mr Can and Mr Jeffrey were charged with the offences in relation to the Ford Claim. The disqualification proceedings were commenced on 11 January 2005.

20. The proper conduct of civil proceedings, including disqualification proceedings, where there are concurrent criminal proceedings arising out of substantially the same facts, has been considered in a number of authorities. In Secretary of State v Crane [2001] 2 BCLC 222, Ferris J identified a number of relevant principles to be deduced from the authorities, although he made clear that it was not an exhaustive list. On behalf of Mr Can, Mr Jones does not take issue with these principles. They include:

1) There is no principle of law that a claimant in a civil action is to be debarred from pursuing that action in accordance with the normal rules merely because to do so would, or might, result in the defendant having to disclose his defence.

2) The judge in criminal proceedings has extensive powers to control those proceedings in order to ensure a fair trial, and the responsibility for doing justice in the criminal proceedings lies primarily with the criminal court.

3) That is not to say that the civil court has no responsibility in the matter. It has powers, including a power to stay the civil proceedings, which will be exercised if justice so requires, having regard to the concurrent criminal proceedings. Ferris J cited the following statement of Neill LJ in R v Panel on Takeovers and Mergers, ex p Fayed [1992] BCLC 938 at 947:

"It is clear that the court has power to intervene to prevent injustice where the continuation of one set of proceedings may prejudice the fairness of the trial of other proceedings...But it is a power which has to be exercised with great care and only where there is a real risk of serious prejudice which may lead to injustice"

Ferris J observed that while the civil court will clearly strive to avoid a manifest risk of injustice, it should not go out of its way to anticipate the existence of a mere possibility of injustice.

4) The Secretary of State has a public duty to apply for the disqualification of unfit directors. Such proceedings are brought in the public interest and the purpose of a disqualification order is the protection of the public. The public interest in bringing such proceedings to a substantive hearing is particularly strong in those cases where serious misconduct is alleged, as will be the case where there are concurrent disqualification and criminal proceedings arising from the same conduct.

21. On behalf of Mr Carr, Mr Jones does not rest his application for a stay on an argument that Mr Can should be entitled to keep silent on his defence in the disqualification proceedings until after the criminal proceedings or that an unparticularised risk of self-incrimination justifies the deferral of his written evidence until after the criminal trial. The principle that these do not provide grounds for a stay, established in relation to ordinary civil claims by the decisions of

the Court of Appeal in Jefferson Ltd v Bhetcha [1979] 1 WLR 898 and Versailles Trade Finance Ltd v Clough [2001] EWCA Civ 1509, is equally applicable to directors disqualification proceedings: see Secretary of State v Crane, and Re Lighting World Limited, Jibrail v Secretary of State (Jacob J, 20.11.97 unreported).

22. Three grounds are advanced for the stay. First, it is said that it will be impracticable for Mr Can to prepare his defence in both sets of proceedings before the start of the criminal trial in January 2006. An order which required him to serve evidence in the disqualification proceedings would jeopardise the proper preparation of his defence to the criminal charges and would therefore be oppressive and unfair. Secondly, there may be a specific prejudice to each defendant's position in the criminal trial if he has to put in evidence in the disqualification proceedings which the other can then use against him. Thirdly, there may be specific prejudice to their position in the criminal trial if the Secretary of State interviews actual or potential witnesses in the criminal proceedings with a view to the preparation of his evidence in reply. This gives rise to the risk of witness contamination.

23. It would seem that the course which the Secretary of State would propose to adopt in relation to any evidence served by Mr Can and Mr Jeffrey would meet the second and third concerns. As regards the second concern, the Secretary of State proposes that Mr Can and Mr Jeffrey should serve their evidence on him but should not serve it on each other or file it. Neither would therefore have access to the other's evidence, unless the judge in the criminal trial ordered disclosure. It would be for that judge to consider the impact of such an order on the fairness of the criminal trial. As regards the third concern, the Secretary of State would not show the evidence of Mr Can and Mr Jeffrey to any witness or potential witness in the criminal trial, pending the outcome of the trial or further order in the meantime.

24. This therefore leaves the principal ground put forward by Mr Can and Mr Jeffrey for a stay of the disqualification proceedings, that preparation of their written evidence will be impracticable before the criminal trial. As I have mentioned, the criminal trial is set to begin on 9 January 2006, with an estimated length of 3 months. Defence statements in the criminal proceedings must be provided by 12 September 2005.

25. Mr Jones on behalf of Mr Can put his application on two bases. First, it would seriously jeopardise the preparation of his defence in the criminal proceedings or would carry a real risk of doing so, and would therefore be oppressive and unfair. Secondly, whether or not the first basis was accepted, it would be the right exercise of case management powers, given the existence of the parallel criminal proceedings. Mr Davis-White, for the Secretary of State, opposes the application and challenges both of the ways in which it is put.

26. The submission that the refusal of a stay would seriously jeopardise the preparation of Mr Can's defence to the criminal charges requires an examination of the work required for the preparation of his defence and an assessment of the additional burden of preparing evidence in the disqualification proceedings.

27. Evidence on these matters has been given by Stephen Parkinson, a solicitor employed by Kingsley Napley who has conduct of Mr Carr's defence in both the criminal and disqualification proceedings. Mr Parkinson is on secondment from the Government Legal Service and has extensive experience with the Crown Prosecution Service, the Companies Investigation Branch of the Department of Trade and Industry and the Treasury Solicitors Department, where he had a supervisory role in relation to civil cases including disqualification proceedings.

28. The principal material in support of the prosecution case was served in December 2004. It consists of 44 witness statements, of which about half deal with substantive issues, and 5 files of exhibits, including one expert's report. This material was considered in detail by Mr Carr and his legal team in the period from January to April 2005.

29. There is also a voluminous amount of unused material in the possession of the Serious Fraud Office and material in the possession of third parties, which has been notified to the defendants. On 10 March 2005 the Serious Fraud Office served schedules of non-sensitive unused material in its own possession and of third party material. The schedule of unused material runs to 32 pages. In late March 2005 the Serious Fraud Office disclosed four files of unused documents in hard copy form and on 10 May 2005 it provided CD-ROMs containing all the remaining unused material which it held and had scanned into its system. Mr Parkinson explains that the summaries of the contents of documents are not in all cases sufficient to enable an informed decision to be made about inspection.

30. There is a very substantial quantity of third party material. It includes 852 boxes of original documents belonging to TransTec and its subsidiaries, which were provided by the administrative receivers and have been retained under the control of the Secretary of State. Solicitors acting for the Secretary of State have considered the lists of contents of all the boxes and on that basis have read the contents of 528 boxes. They extracted documents relating to all possible disqualification issues, including but not limited to the Ford Claim and Rover payment. The extracted documents amounted to eight files. Inventories, running to some 900 pages, of all 852 boxes have been supplied to the defendants. Mr Parkinson says that the contents of these boxes must be considered for any documents relevant to the defence of the criminal proceedings, in some cases relying on the description in the inventory but in other cases requiring an examination of the documents.

31. There is also a large quantity of company documents collected by the inspectors. There is an inventory which is over 220 pages long. Mr Parkinson makes the same point as regards the accuracy of this inventory as he makes in relation to the inventory to the 852 boxes held by the Secretary of State. The inspectors themselves created subject-matter files, so that those relevant to the Ford Claim and the Rover payment are easily identifiable. It does not of course follow that every document with a bearing on those issues is included in the subject-matter files. Many of these subject-matter files were disclosed by the Serious Fraud Office as part of the unused material, as were all or most of the transcripts of evidence taken by the inspectors. These transcripts are also part of the evidence served in the disqualification proceedings in January 2005. They fill 26 files, although a good part of the evidence is irrelevant to the issues of the Ford Claim and the Rover payment.

32. Employees of Kingsley Napley are summarising the documents identified by Mr Carr, Mr Parkinson and his assistant as potentially relevant. Those summaries will be considered by Mr Carr and his legal team. Mr Parkinson deposes that his firm's experience is that the process of examining unused and third party material, though time-consuming, is necessary. He does not believe that this exercise will be completed before late November 2005.

33. Mr Parkinson explains how Mr Can has to be closely involved in this process and in giving instructions on relevant documents. The final stages in the preparation for the criminal trial will be in the period from October to December 2005. In a witness statement made on 7 February 2005, Mr Parkinson expressed his view that it was not unreasonable to expect that, in order to do justice to his defence, Mr Carr would need to devote all or most of his attention to the criminal case from February onwards, a view which he re-affirmed in his second witness statement dated 19 April 2005. The slippage of the timetable for the provision of unused material meant that more work than expected was concentrated in the period from May 2005.

34. As for preparation for the disqualification proceedings, in his first witness statement Mr Parkinson contemplated that before the start of the criminal trial there would be the process of considering the Secretary of State's evidence, preparing evidence in response, considering each defendant's evidence, serving further evidence in reply and considering experts' evidence. All of this would be extremely time consuming for Mr Can and would divert his attention from the preparation of his defence in the criminal proceedings. Mr Parkinson considered that Mr Can would not be able to devote adequate time to the preparation of his defence in both sets of proceedings. Mr Parkinson draws attention to the fact that the case against Mr Can in the disqualification proceedings occupies some 74 pages of the principal witness statement and that the exhibits comprise the Inspector's report of over 400 pages, three files of documents and three CD-ROMs containing the statements and transcripts of evidence given to the inspectors.

35. Mr Parkinson explains that it will not be possible for counsel acting for Mr Can in the criminal proceedings to prepare his defence to the disqualification proceedings. Their view is that they have neither the time nor the technical expertise to do so. Mr Parkinson says that neither he nor the other legal staff at Kingsley Napley who are working on the defence in the criminal proceedings will be able to spend any time on the defence to the disqualification proceedings. It will therefore be necessary to instruct other counsel and involve additional solicitors.

36. Mr Davis-White, for the Secretary of State, submitted that Mr Can would not be prejudiced in his defence of the criminal proceedings by a requirement to file his evidence in the disqualification proceedings before the start of the criminal case. First, the scope of the work is significantly less than that assessed by Mr Parkinson. Mr Can and Mr Jeffrey

would not see each other's evidence at this stage and would not therefore need to consider a response to it until after the criminal trial. Nor would they need to consider the preparation of experts' reports at this stage. If they wished to interview or adduce statements from persons who were actual or potential prosecution witnesses, that too should properly wait until after the criminal trial. Secondly, as is common ground, there is a substantial factual overlap between the two cases, with no significant dispute on at least part of the primary facts. Thirdly, Mr Carr and Mr Jeffrey are very familiar with the facts relevant to the cases being made against them. Fourthly, it is not suggested that Mr Can could not engage the additional legal assistance required to assist the preparation of his evidence. The legal costs of Mr Can's defence to the criminal charges, which he is paying personally, are estimated at £1.35 million. This is a very large sum, but there is no suggestion in the evidence that he could not afford to engage the additional solicitors and counsel required for the disqualification proceedings.

37. It is for Mr Carr to satisfy the court that a requirement to file his evidence in the disqualification proceedings before the start of the criminal trial would materially prejudice the preparation of his defence to the criminal charges, or carry a real risk of doing so. If the court is satisfied on that issue, then it would in my judgment be oppressive and unfair to require him to file his evidence at this stage. The reason is that it would put at risk a fair trial of the criminal charges and, important as disqualification proceedings are, there is in my view an overriding interest in the fair trial of criminal charges. I do not here consider what the position would be if the prejudice resulted from the defendant's own default, for example in delay on his part in preparation of his defence in either set proceedings. No such default is suggested against Mr Can or Mr Jeffrey.

38. I fully appreciate the substantial burden faced by Mr Can and his legal team in preparing for the criminal proceedings. I do not, however, accept that they will be materially prejudiced in that task by the preparation at this stage of the evidence on behalf of Mr Can in response to the disqualification proceedings. My reasons are as follows. First, while the preparation of Mr Carr's evidence in response to the disqualification proceedings is a significant task, it is not at this stage as comprehensive as Mr Parkinson assumed. Before the conclusion of the criminal trial, it will not involve a consideration of the other respondents' evidence or the taking of statements from actual or potential prosecution witnesses or the preparation of expert evidence.

39. Secondly, the issues in the disqualification proceedings are relatively narrow, focussing on the Ford Claim and the Rover payment. Although the allegations arising out of the Ford Claim cover a period from 1996 to 1999, they are not, for example, a general case of trading whilst insolvent over that period. Thirdly, in consequence, although there is inevitably a vast amount of documentation concerning TransTec and its subsidiaries over that period, most of it is irrelevant to the issues. The same is true of a substantial part of the written and oral evidence taken by the inspectors.

40. Fourthly, so far as the relevant events and documents relating to the Ford Claim are concerned, there is a very substantial, perhaps complete, overlap between the criminal and disqualification proceedings. Mr Can and his legal team for the disqualification proceedings can take full advantage of the work on the documents already being undertaken by himself and his team in the criminal proceedings. Mr Parkinson's evidence shows that there is in progress a comprehensive trawl and examination of the available documentation for relevance to the criminal case.

41. Fifthly, I do not accept that the fact that the evidence in the two proceedings is in different form or that the legal issues in the two proceedings are not identical, or that negligence is alleged in the disqualification proceedings as an alternative to dishonesty, creates a significant difficulty.

42. Sixthly, I do not accept the suggestion that Mr Can has not for some considerable time been familiar with the allegations concerning the Ford Claim and the Rover payment. Over a considerable period, he was engaged in the process of interviews with the inspectors, submitting statements and responding to provisional criticisms. The final Report was published in October 2003 and has been available to him since then. The witness statement in support of the disqualification proceedings was supplied to him in draft in September 2004 and the exhibits were available to him on request. The full evidence was served on him in January 2005.

43. In reaching my conclusion, I have carefully considered the evidence of Mr Parkinson and accorded weight to his assessments. But, as Mr Jones submitted, it is in the end for the court to take a view as to the amount of work involved in meeting the Secretary of State's allegations.

44. I have also paid particular attention to concerns which were at one time expressed by counsel for the Serious Fraud Office and by HH Judge Stanley, the trial judge in the criminal proceedings. In an e-mail sent to the judge on 8 April 2005, leading counsel for the Serious Fraud Office referred to the disqualification proceedings and to the defendants' concern not to be side-tracked by preparing defences to the disqualification proceedings. He said that the prosecution was in principle likely to support, if called on, any application by the defendants to adjourn the disqualification proceedings. The present position of the Serious Fraud Office is set out in a letter dated 21 June 2005 to the Department of Trade and Industry. It explains that the comments in the e-mail of 8 April were made at a time when it was believed that there was a danger of a trial of the disqualification proceedings before the criminal case. As it is now clear that this will not occur and that the Serious Fraud Office's concerns for a fair trial are understood, the Serious Fraud Office is neutral as to the stay application. Specifically as regards the burden of preparing for both sets of proceedings, the Serious Fraud Office stated in a letter dated 8 June 2005 to the Treasury Solicitor:

"Another concern is that the defendants should not be in a position to argue that their criminal trial was unfair on the basis that they had to respond to two sets of proceedings simultaneously. While estimates will differ as to the nature and extent of the work required in order to prepare adequately for each set of proceedings, it seems to us that this is a material consideration. It was suggested at our meeting that the disqualification proceedings might be put on hold after the service of the defendants' evidence in response to the Secretary of State as supported by the Affidavit of John Gardner of the DTI. Depending on the timing of such responses, this might well meet our concern."

45. At a directions hearing in the criminal proceedings on 15 April 2005, HH Judge Stanley heard submissions from counsel for Mr Carr on the difficulties presented by the concurrent disqualification proceedings and was asked to express a view which could be passed on to the court hearing the present application for a stay. Judge Stanley said:

"I can see that so far as the directors' disqualification proceedings are concerned there is a great deal involved in that, and there would be a terrific distraction from proper preparation of the criminal case, which must take priority. I therefore express the view strongly that those proceedings should take second place and that they should not continue at this stage."

46. Those comments must be read in the light of the submissions made to the judge. Counsel said that there were two aspects to their objection to the disqualification proceedings "going ahead before the [criminal] trial". The first was "the general oppression to Mr Carr in having to deal with that difficult and complex matter at a time when he is fully engaged with trying to focus on his defence of this serious criminal charge". As "an indication of the amount of material in the DTI proceedings", reference was made to the 850 boxes of third party material which I have described above. In response to an observation by the judge that disqualification proceedings are much wider ranging, counsel replied that "the material is considerably greater: times ten, as far as we can judge at the moment". Secondly, specific concern was expressed "for direct prejudice arising from some events were the DTI disqualification proceedings to take place this year", particularly the possibility of a co-defendant making use of material emerging in the course of the hearing.

47. The position is a great deal clearer now that it appeared on 15 April 2005. First, there is no question of a hearing before the criminal trial. Secondly, as to the scope of the disqualification proceedings, the common ground with the criminal case is very substantial and the documents on the major issue of the Ford Claim to be considered for the disqualification proceedings are largely the same as those for the criminal trial. Thirdly, the Serious Fraud Office, which supported the position taken by Mr Can, is now neutral as regards the limited question of the preparation of the respondents' written evidence. I have had an opportunity of looking at the issues in detail. As I have explained, I share the concern for a fair trial of the criminal charges, but I have concluded that it will not be jeopardised by a requirement that Mr Can and Mr Jeffrey serve their evidence in the disqualification proceedings before the start of the criminal trial.

48. Mr Jones' alternative submission was that it would be right to stay the proceedings on case management grounds. This involves a balancing of the factors for and against a stay. Mr Jones relied on the following factors as justifying a stay.

First, the preparation of evidence will impose a significant burden on Mr Can in terms of time and cost, which will be entirely wasted if he is convicted at his criminal trial and a disqualification order is made by the criminal court under section 2 of the 1986 Act. In this respect, Mr Jones submitted that disqualification proceedings were essentially different from the civil claims under consideration in <u>Jefferson Ltd v Bhetcha</u> and <u>Re Lighting World Limited, Jibrail v Secretary of State (Jacob J, 20.11.97 unreported)</u>. In those cases, the civil claimants could not obtain their remedy in the criminal proceedings. Secondly, service of the respondents' evidence before the end of this year will not result in a hearing of the disqualification proceedings much earlier than would otherwise be the case. It will be after the criminal trial that they will consider each other's evidence and respond to it, approach witnesses in the criminal trial and consider the question of expert evidence. Until then, the Secretary of State will not be able to approach actual or potential witnesses in the criminal trial for responses to the respondents' evidence. Moreover, the Secretary of State will be bound, and the respondents will wish, to take stock of the evidence at the criminal trial before proceeding with the disqualification application. It would be more sensible and cost effective for all parties if all the first round evidence of the respondents was filed at one time. Thirdly, Mr Carr is prepared to give an undertaking to the court in the terms of a disqualification order which will last until judgment in the disqualification proceedings, thereby protecting the public interest so far as possible. Mr Jeffrey is not offering an undertaking but he is not presently living or working in the UK.

49. While taken together these factors have some force, I accept Mr Davis-White's submission that it would not be right to order a stay of the disqualification proceedings on case management grounds. Such proceedings are brought in the public interest and they serve an important purpose. The public interest is best served by such proceedings being brought to a conclusion as soon as reasonably practicable. While Mr Carr's proposed undertaking is designed to achieve as much as possible of the effect of a disqualification order, Mr Jones accepts that it achieves less than an order. For example, breach of the undertaking would be a civil contempt of court with a maximum penalty of 2 years' imprisonment, while breach of a disqualification order is an offence punishable by a maximum of 5 years' imprisonment. There is no public register on which the undertaking could appear. While Mr Can is willing to give an undertaking to be personally liable for debts as provided by section 15 of the 1986 Act as if a disqualification order had been made, there can be no similar liability imposed on his associates (cf section 15(1)(b)). Moreover, if a respondent is to be prohibited from acting as a director, the public is entitled to know as early as reasonably practicable the grounds on which he has been found unfit.

In my judgment, it is likely that service of the respondents' evidence before the criminal trial will lead to an earlier hearing of the disqualification proceedings. Not only will a significant part of the relevant evidence be prepared earlier than if there is a stay, so saving time at a later stage, but the Secretary of State's advisers will be able to consider and perhaps prepare their response to that evidence. Mr Jones said that there were some substantial areas of factual dispute, but in that case the efficient prosecution of these proceedings will be best served by the identification of those areas earlier rather than later. There may be some witnesses who cannot be approached, but all other work including any necessary examination of documents can proceed. In this way the proceedings will be materially more advanced at the end of the criminal trial than would be the case with a stay.

I have therefore come to the conclusion that there should not be a stay of the disqualification proceedings, but that directions should be given for service of the respondents' evidence before the start of the criminal trial. Such evidence will not be filed, nor will one respondent's evidence be given to the other, until after the end of the criminal trial. The respondents will not be required to serve any evidence from actual or potential witnesses in the criminal case at this stage. Directions for further evidence and any application to adduce expert evidence will be considered after the criminal trial.

Appendix 2—Assets and Share Acquisitions

What is an asset acquisition? Share acquisition?

There are two totally different ways of acquiring a business, by a share acquisition or by an assets acquisition. These two types of transaction have different effects and consequences so it is essential to consider which method will be most beneficial given individual circumstances.

There is a non-exhaustive list of points to consider below.

	asset purchase	share purchase
1.	It is possible to select which assets are acquired and to exclude those which are not required.	All the underlying assets of the company are indirectly acquired by the buyer whether required or not.
2.	The purchaser does not automatically take on any corporate liabilities (other than in respect of employees as referred to below).	All liabilities (including tax and any outstanding litigation) pass with the company. Additional due diligence and, as necessary, warranty and indemnity protection is therefore required.
3.	There are certain areas of statutory protection for the purchaser of goods or land eg LPA 1925 and Sale of Goods Act 1979.	The basic rule of "caveat emptor" applies to a sale of shares with no automatically implied terms.
4.	Each asset must be individually transferred by delivery or documented transfer and necessary consents obtained from mortgagees/chargees.	The only items changing direct ownership are the shares for which only a stock transfer form is required to transfer ownership (subject to stamping and registration). It is unlikely that third party consents to the share transfer will be required.
5.	Employees transfer automatically where there is a transfer of an undertaking as a going concern.	Employment contracts are unaffected.
5a	Pension scheme does not transfer. Buyer must either participate in Vendor's scheme, set up own, use own existing scheme or have no pension scheme.	The target company may be the principal or a participating employer in the scheme with potential liabilities.

	asset purchase	share purchase
6.	Assignments and novations of existing trading agreements are required. Third party consents are often required and renegotiation of terms is a possible threat.	Continuity of arrangements (if no break clauses which operate on a transfer of shares).
7.	Landlord's consent to assignment of any leasehold property may be required.	No leasehold property assignment required (provided lease is in the name of the company being acquired).
8.	Appropriate insurances need to be transferred or it is necessary to arrange fresh cover.	Existing insurances usually remain in place (special attention may be required where company covered by group insurance).
9.	Vendor may suffer balancing charges and gains tax on a disposal ie a potential tax charge on the difference between the actual sale price and the written down value of the assets after deducting capital allowances.	No balancing charge for Vendor but assets in the company pass at tax written down value.
10.	Assets are available as security for raising acquisition funding. No financial assistance problem arises under s151 Companies Act 1985.	Under s151 Companies Act 1985 the company is generally prohibited from directly or indirectly financially assisting the acquisition of its shares, although a formal sanctioning procedure is sometimes available for private companies.
11.	Trading stock disposed of or written down can be a deduction for corporation tax purposes in purchaser's business.	Shares offer no tax relief in form of capital allowances.
12.	Tax losses cannot be carried forward. Past tax liabilities are excluded (including VAT unless VAT registration is specifically assigned).	Past tax losses can often be carried forward. However a buyer acquires the company's whole tax history (including VAT).

	asset purchase	share purchase
13.	VAT not payable where there is a transfer as a going concern.	No VAT on share purchase.
14.	Stamp duty on a conveyance/ transfer of assets such as land, goodwill and book debts is charged at 1%. Exemption if stampable assets are less than £60,000. Mitigation/ avoidance is sometimes possible.	Stamp duty on share transfers charged at 0.5%. No minimum price exemption. Limited scope for mitigation/avoidance as share transfers must be stamped before registration. There is little scope to dispute the allocation of consideration where there is only one asset being transferred (unless there are various classes of shares).
15.	The Inland Revenue may seek to dispute the allocation of consideration between various assets acquired.	
16.	Advertising an asset sale is not generally regulated by Financial Services Act 1986.	Advertising a sale of shares is regulated by Financial Services Act 1986.

Appendix 3—the Cushnie case

R v Cushnie and another 2005] EWCA Crim 962

Conspiracy to defraud—Fraudulent trading

The defendants were engaged in the provision of funds on a short-term basis to small to medium-sized distributors or manufacturers. Between 1989 and 1993, both men were directors of NM, of which the second defendant was financial director. It was alleged that both men had traded fraudulently by transferring funds between the bank accounts of various internal companies so as to give an impression of turnover and of substantial assets. The second defendant pleaded guilty to one count of fraudulent trading and two counts of conspiracy to defraud. The first defendant pleaded not guilty to all three counts and was convicted of one count of conspiracy to defraud. Both men were sentenced to a total of six years' imprisonment, and were disqualified from serving as a company director for a number of years. Both defendants renewed their applications for permission to appeal against sentence and the first defendant renewed his application for permission to appeal against conviction.

The first defendant submitted that, having regard to the way in which the prosecution had presented its case, his conviction was inconsistent with the verdict of not guilty which was returned upon him in relation to the other count of conspiracy to defraud; and that the conviction was unsafe because as against him, the prosecution had put forward the second defendant as a witness of truth, but in a subsequent trial of another man, the prosecution had regarded him as an untruthful witness.

The judge had correctly directed the jury on the separate counts of conspiracy to defraud, and the Crown had been entitled to call the second defendant as a witness of truth.

The verdicts had not been logically inconsistent and the conviction on the second count had not been unsafe. There had been no error in the approach or conclusion reached by the sentencing judge in relation to the first defendant, and therefore, his applications for permission to appeal against conviction and sentence were dismissed. The second defendant's application for permission to appeal against sentence was granted and the appeal was allowed, to the extent that all his sentences would be ordered to run concurrently. In the case of Cushnie the sentence of imprisonment was imposed in respect of the one count of which he was convicted. Clough received a sentence of 12 months imprisonment for the Normandy count, five years imprisonment consecutive for the Versailles fraud and three years imprisonment concurrent for the Traders fraud.

Grounds of Appeal against conviction.

Cushnie seeks leave to appeal against conviction on two grounds—

That, having regard to the way in which the prosecution presented its case, the conviction of him in respect of the Traders fraud is inconsistent with the verdict of not guilty which was returned upon him in relation to the Versailles fraud, and

That the conviction is unsafe because as against Cushnie the prosecution put forward Clough as a witness of truth, but in a subsequent trial of a man named Black the prosecution took a different stance.

The business in which both Cushnie and Clough were engaged was the provision of funds on a short-term basis to small to medium-sized distributors or manufacturers to facilitate their supplies to larger businesses. The Versailles fraud, of which Cushnie was acquitted, related to the activities of Cushnie and Clough as executive directors of Versailles Group Limited (VGL) and its subsidiary company Versailles Trade Finance Limited (VTF) between June 1991 and January 2000.

The two men conspired to defraud trade creditors, banks or lending institutions induced to provide loans, the Stock Exchange and their own shareholders, by dishonestly overstating trading turnover and assets, and by falsifying and concealing accounting documents. VGL and VTF did conduct a genuine business, but a significant part of the money which went into VTF came from wealthy individuals or "Traders" who were willing to pool their resources to finance specific transactions. To accommodate those individuals Versailles Traders Ltd (VTL) was incorporated in March 1992 and, as with the other companies, Cushnie and Clough were executive directors. The prosecution as the Traders fraud in due course described the operation of VTL/TPL.

The position was complicated by the fact that Clough was also operating dishonestly on his own behalf. The Crown accepted that Cushnie did not know that over the years Clough had stolen almost £19 million. Falsely representing those monies loaned or invested by individuals known, as "traders" would be used for the purpose of genuine and specific trading transactions by or on behalf of VTL and/or TPL. In other words the Traders fraud was presented as one aspect of the Versailles fraud.

The judge found that the elements of the agreement were not confused with the overt acts, and continued: "Sub-paragraphs (a) to (e) of count 2 serve a valuable purpose. The judge found the submission difficult, and as he explained: "The deception allegedly perpetrated on the traders differed from that perpetrated on creditors, lenders, the Stock exchange and shareholders in three respects:

The traders did not deal with VTF or Versailles Group. The traders were led to believe that the money, which they paid, would not go to VTF or VG. Money was cross-fired and circulated to give a false impression of trading activity. The same companies were used in the cross-firing operation. Furthermore, the alleged fraud against traders spanned approximately the same period as the defendants' other allegedly fraudulent activities."

As to whether there were two conspiracies or one the judge's conclusion was that either approach was legitimate so count 2 was not defective, but that the task of the jury could be made easier if the Traders fraud were to be presented as a separate count. The prosecution recognised the force of what was said, and prepared a fresh three count indictment in which count 1 (the Normandy Marketing count) was left undisturbed, but count 2 was amended by deleting the reference to traders as one of the victims of the conspiracy, and excising sub-paragraph (e). That count was thus confined to the Versailles fraud. The new count 3 alleged that the three defendants conspired to defraud—

The Trial

The prosecution case at the trial was, of course, that Cushnie was well aware of and a participant in most of the fraudulent activity in which Clough admitted that he had been engaged. There was no need to dwell for long on the distinction between the two counts, because no one suggested that there had not been fraudulent activity, both in relation to the Versailles Group and in relation to the Traders companies, and the live issue was whether the prosecution could show that Cushnie was knowingly involved.

In due course the prosecution decided to offer no further evidence against Lorraine Jones and she was acquitted by direction of the trial judge.

In his summing-up the judge in chapter 1 instructed the jury to consider each of the two counts separately. In chapter 2 he dealt with count 1, the ingredients of the conspiracy to defraud, and the evidence of Clough, which showed that the Versailles fraud had been perpetrated. Similarly in chapter 3 the judge dealt with count 2, where again the issue was whether the Crown had proved that Cushnie had conspired with Clough to carry out the fraud, or whether Clough may have carried it out without Cushnie's knowledge. After the jury had returned their verdicts the judge helpfully spelt out in his sentencing remarks his understanding of the jury's decision, thus we know precisely the basis on which sentence was imposed. The judge said:

"In my judgment the only impact upon count 2 of Mr Cushnie's acquittal on count 1 is in relation to the last three words of sub-paragraph (b). The jury must have been satisfied that funds were being circulated for the purpose of inflating turnover and assets of VTL and TPL. However, the jury were not satisfied that Mr Cushnie's purpose was also to inflate the turnover and assets of VTF. On this basis, the jury were quite entitled to return a verdict of guilty on count 2.

It should be borne in mind that count 1 is primarily focussed on VTF and VG, whereas count 2 is focussed upon VTL and TPL. ."

Mr Jones' submission that the two verdicts indicate that in relation to count 2 there was no meeting of minds adds nothing to the submission already dealt with that paragraphs (a) and (b) were essential elements of the offence, which in the light of the verdicts the judge was not entitled to re-draft or read down.

The submission that count 2 was bad for uncertainty was never advanced at trial, and we are not surprised. Everyone knew precisely what was alleged, and had the submission been made it would have had no prospect of success.

Similarly when the jury returned verdicts there was no reason whatsoever to seek further assistance from the jury. It would have been wholly inappropriate to do so. As the judge demonstrated, he was able to interpret the verdicts in a way, which enabled him to proceed to sentence, and no more was required.

Finally in relation to the first ground of appeal we make three points. First, it is obvious that counts 1 and 2 differ as to those alleged to have been defrauded. Second, the two counts differ as to the means by which the victims are alleged to have been defrauded, in other words as to the nature of the fraud. Where those differences exist we find it difficult to envisage any situation in which it would not have been open to a jury to convict on one count and acquit on the other. The jury might, for example, be satisfied that the defendant agreed with his co-accused to defraud the victims in group A, but not satisfied that he was party to an agreement to defraud the victims in group B. Thirdly, as we pointed out to Mr Jones during the course of argument, it was plainly open to the jury to consider count 2 first, and if the trial judge had advocated that approach he could not possibly have gone on to direct the jury that if they convicted on count 2 they must then convict on count 1.

Ground 2: Clough and the trial of Black.

Mr Jones' second ground of appeal relates to the Crown's attitude to Clough as a witness. Initially, it seems, the Crown was minded to call Clough as a witness for the prosecution first in the trial of Cushnie and Lorraine Jones, and secondly in the subsequent trial of Black, even though the statement of Clough tended to exculpate Black. At a directions hearing in relation to the trial of Black held on 12th February 2004, during the course of the trial of Cushnie, counsel for the Crown said that no final decision had yet been reached as to whether Clough would be called by the Crown in the subsequent trial. After the trial of Cushnie came to an end the Crown decided not to call Clough in the subsequent trial.

Now it is said in the second ground of appeal that the conviction on count 2 is unsafe because the prosecution regarded Clough as an untruthful witness at the trial of Black, and that at the time of Cushnie's trial those acting for the defence of Cushnie did not know that the Crown did not accept what Clough had said in his statement about Black. Mr Jones began his submissions by referring us to this ground of appeal. The Crown was entitled to regard Clough as a man who was truthful and reliable about some matters but not about others. So he was put forward as a witness of truth in the trial of Cushnie and Lorraine Jones, but not in the trial of Black. That did not disadvantage Cushnie in any way. His lawyers knew what Clough was prepared to say. Mr Jones submits that because during the trial of Cushnie the defence did not know what the Crown would later decide they were deprived of the opportunity to submit that the evidence of Clough should be excluded pursuant to section 78 of the Police and Criminal Evidence Act 1984.

Sentence: Cushnie.

In relation to sentence Mr Jones relied upon the grounds of appeal drafted by counsel who appeared at the trial. In those grounds it is submitted that the sentence was passed on a wrong factual basis because it was imposed, at least in part, for an offence of which Cushnie had been acquitted. We reject that submission. The judge then referred to Cushnie's good character, which, he said, "counts for little in the case of a conspiracy to defraud upon this scale over a period of eight years". So he imposed the sentence which Cushnie now seeks leave to appeal. In our judgment there was no error in the approach, or in the conclusion reached by the sentencing judge.

Sentencing Clough.

On behalf of Clough Mr Jonathan Caplan QC, in an attractive submission, made four points. First he submitted that the judge's starting point was too high. For the Versailles fraud, which gave rise to losses exceeding £150 million and involved a massive deception of the London Stock Exchange impacting upon the confidence of investors, the judge took as his starting point the statutory maximum of ten years. Mr Caplan submitted that he should have left room for even more serious cases, and taken account of Clough's role as first lieutenant. In our judgment once fraudulent activity reaches a certain level of gravity a judge is entitled to say that the gravity is such as to justify the statutory maximum even though it is possible to envisage more serious cases, and, as to the role of Clough, the judge was clearly entitled to regard him as bearing full responsibility.

Mr Caplan's second point relates to the pleas tendered by Clough and to his co-operation. The judge did allow for those matters, but Mr Caplan submits that the discount of 50% granted by the judge was insufficient. The judge referred in passing to Clough having been convicted in Jersey in 1966 of offences including false accounting, but it seems clear to us that the judge was doing no more than set the scene.

Mr Caplan's fourth point we found more troublesome. It relates to the consecutive sentence of twelve months imprisonment imposed in relation to count 1, the Normandy count. It was the Crown's case that Normandy was simply the start of the fraudulent activity, which blossomed in the Versailles fraud and in the Traders fraud. In our judgment the right course would have been to order that the sentences in respect of all of three counts be served concurrently. For that reason we granted Clough leave to appeal, and indicated that unless he gave notice of a desire to be present when his appeal is heard we would allow his appeal to the extent of ordering that the sentences imposed upon him, namely 1 year in respect of count 1 (the Normandy count), 5 years in respect of count 2 (the Versailles fraud) and 3 years in respect of count 3 (the Traders fraud) be all served concurrently.

Appendix 4—United Kingdom: Document Destruction in Business

Article by Sally Ramage

Being deeply involved with the figures as accountants can often lead us to miss the importance of the very documents we use to get to the accounts we deal with.

When things go wrong, contemporary documents are of the utmost value. It is to documents that the lawyers look with special care when there is any issue with accounts. Oral testimony alone is less reliable. Documents are the means of tracing a contemporary record going to the thing in issue. That is why no documents should be destroyed.

In certain cases, the destruction of documents is illegal. For example, a company officer who destroys or falsifies a document affecting the company's property or affairs is liable to prosecution under the Companies Act 1985, section 450, unless he can prove that he did not intend to deceive by doing so. Section 450 of the Companies Act states:

"Punishment for destroying, mutilating, etc, company documents."

(1) An officer of a company who

(a) destroys, mutilates or falsifies or is privy to the destruction, mutilation or falsification of a document affecting or relating to the company's property or affairs, or

(b) Makes, or is privy to the making of a false entry in such a document,

Is guilty of an offence, unless he proves that he had no intention to conceal the state of affairs of the company or to defeat the law.

(2) Such a person as above mentioned who fraudulently either parts with, alters or makes an omission in any such document or is privy to fraudulent parting with, fraudulent making of an omission in any such document, is guilty of an offence.

(3) A person guilty of an offence under this section is liable to imprisonment or a fine, or both;

(4) Section 732 (restriction on prosecutions), section 733 (liability of individuals for corporate default) and section 734 (criminal proceedings against unincorporated bodies) apply to an offence under this section.

(5) In this section "document" includes information recorded in any form."

If a dispute has already arisen, it is very dangerous to destroy any documents as was seen in the Australian case of BAT v McCabe, in which the Australian High Court identified that a company, by having a document destruction policy, illustrated that it could manage its own documents.

In the case of Douglas v Hello, the Douglas' objected to their photograph being taken by the magazine "Hello!" During this privacy issue, the Douglas' alleged that Hello had destroyed documents, this interfering with the course of justice. The English court, adopting the reasoning in BAT v McCabe, accepted Hello's document destruction as persuasive authority, having proved the facts. The court, however, could not agree with the Douglas' that this document destruction was indeed an attempt to pervert the course of justice.

In some cases a deliberate decision to destroy documents, if it is extremely likely that a dispute is soon to arise, or after a dispute has arisen could make one liable under the criminal offence of obstructing or perverting the course of justice.

Anyway, missing documents usually leave telltale indications of their existence because they are often referred to in surviving documents. If the case goes to court, one has to list not only documents in one's possession, custody or power, but also those, which were but are no longer.

Destruction of documents can lead to the case being found against you by inference. Such a case was the 1985 case of Infabrics v Jaytex, a case of copyright infringement of prints for shirts It was discovered that after the case commenced, most of the invoices, stock records and similar documents had been destroyed.

The judge said:

"I am not prepared to give the defendants the benefit of any doubt or to draw an inference in their favour where a document, if not destroyed, would have established the matter beyond doubt." It speaks for itself.

A similar case was Logicrose v Southend United Football Club . The judge considered the application to strike out the case. He said that it was not always necessary to strike out such a case if a fair trial was still possible without that document. But if the destroyed documents were key to the case, as in Landauer Ltd v Comins and Co. the case would have to be struck off, since the absence of such documents was going to impede the case.

Companies should have document retention policies and should not be haphazard as to what they keep and what they decide not to keep. It used to be the case that we could look to the Limitation Act 1980 for how long we should keep files, most professions keeping papers for at least six years. But the recent case of Brocklesby v Armitage makes it possible now for someone to bring a case in respect of say, a bad piece of accounting advice, long after the six year limit. There is no excuse for destroying documents, especially as case after case illustrates that the Limitation Act is not a simple matter. Just recently, in the judgment on 18th March 2005 In Re Loftus (deceased), it was held that the twelve year limitation period in respect of any claim to the personal estate of a deceased person, ran, not from the date of death, but from the date of the executor's year: the time during which a personal representative was not bound to distribute.

What are the documents that the Companies Act mentions in section 450? Well, documents can include text messages and emails. In Guinness v Saunders [1986], Mr Saunders was charged with destroying a jottings book, some correspondence, some pages from an address book and a 1986 diary, among other things. They were seen to be documents. In this case the judge said:

"Section 450 is the part of the heavy artillery of the Companies Act. It carries a maximum of a seven year sentence."

The judge went on to decide that Mr Saunders' diary, etc. were documents as per section 450.

He went on to say:

"Those words 'affecting or relating to the company's property or affairs' show that the embargo against destruction goes beyond the formal documents that are the company's documents, to the officer's private documents, provided they affect or relate to the company's property or affairs. In my judgement, the ordinary literal construction of the word 'document' is the correct one, it being the intention of the legislature to forbid all unjustifiable destruction of documents or other less formal documents, whether the company's documents or not, and whether in the company's possession or not. The onus is then on the defendant to show that he had no intention to conceal the state of affairs of the company or to defeat the law."

No other Companies Act offence carries a higher maximum sentence…This section (450) is also unusual in that it places the burden of making out the statutory defence on the defence. Under this section, the prosecution need merely prove that the documents destroyed affected or related to the company's property or affairs.

In any case, even if documents are alleged to have disappeared, they can be re-constructed and retrieved. For example, a lawyer had lost email that was critical to the case and needed it to recover this to prove that an exchange of emails had taken place. There were no back-ups of the system. Forensic examination recovered the metadata of the file as well as that of the operating system and this supported the claim.

It couldn't have been stated more clearly. More recent cases in the United States, especially since the Sarbanes Oxley Act, illustrate what a dim view the US Federal court takes of destruction of documents.

Nowadays with advanced technology at our hands, it would be wise to preserve files using scanners and other electronic storage means rather than destroy them. A written policy on document destruction and retention, to be applied consistently, is a wise move.

Appendix 5—Directors' Pensions

(DIRECTORS CAN FORFEIT THEIR PENSIONS)

See Pensions Act 1995

'Assignment, forfeiture, bankruptcy etc

91 Inalienability of occupational pension

(1) Subject to subsection (5), where a person is entitled [to a pension under an occupational pension scheme or has a right to a future pension under such a scheme]—

(a) The entitlement or right cannot be assigned, commuted or surrendered,

(b) The entitlement or right cannot be charged or a lien exercised in respect of it, and

(c) No set-off can be exercised in respect of it,

And an agreement to affect any of those things is unenforceable.

(2) Where by virtue of this section a person's entitlement [to a pension under an occupational pension scheme, or right to a future pension under such a scheme,] cannot, apart from subsection (5), be assigned, no order can be made by any court the effect of which would be that he would be restrained from receiving that pension.

(3) Where a bankruptcy order is made against a person, any entitlement or right of his which by virtue of this section cannot, apart from subsection (5), be assigned is excluded from his estate for the purposes of Parts VIII to XI of the Insolvency Act 1986 or the Bankruptcy (Scotland) Act 1985.

(4) Subsection (2) does not prevent the making of—

(a) An attachment of earnings order under the Attachment of Earnings Act 1971, or

(b) An income payments order under the Insolvency Act 1986.

(5) In the case of a person ("the person in question") who is entitled [to a pension under an occupational pension scheme, or has a right to a future pension under such a scheme], subsection (1) does not apply to any of the following, or any agreement to effect any of the following—

(a) an assignment in favour of the person in question's widow, widower or dependant,

(b) a surrender, at the option of the person in question, for the purpose of—

(i) providing benefits for that person's widow, widower or dependant, or

(ii) acquiring for the person in question entitlement to further benefits under the scheme,

(c) a commutation—

(i) of the person in question's benefit on or after retirement or in exceptional circumstances of serious ill health,

(ii) in prescribed circumstances, of any benefit for that person's widow, widower or dependant, or

(iii) in other prescribed circumstances,

(d) subject to subsection (6), a charge or lien on, or set-off against, the person in question's entitlement, or [right,](except to the extent that it includes transfer credits other than prescribed transfer credits) for the purpose of enabling the employer to obtain the discharge by him of some monetary obligation due to the employer and arising out of a criminal, negligent or fraudulent act or omission by him,

(e) subject to subsection (6), except in prescribed circumstances a charge or lien on, or set-off against, the person in question's entitlement, or [right], for the purpose of discharging some monetary obligation due from the person in question to the scheme and—

(i) arising out of a criminal, negligent or fraudulent act or omission by him, or

(ii) in the case of a trust scheme of which the person in question is a trustee, arising out of a breach of trust by him.

(6) Where a charge, lien or set-off is exercisable by virtue of subsection (5)(d) or (e)—

(a) its amount must not exceed the amount of the monetary obligation in question, or (if less) the value (determined in the prescribed manner) of the person in question's entitlement or accrued right, and

(b) the person in question must be given a certificate showing the amount of the charge, lien or set-off and its effect on his benefits under the scheme, and where there is a dispute as to its amount, the charge, lien or set-off must not be exercised unless the obligation in question has become enforceable under an order of a competent court or in consequence of an award of an arbitrator or, in Scotland, an arbiter to be appointed (failing agreement between the parties) by the sheriff.

(7) This section is subject to section 159 of the Pension Schemes Act 1993 (inalienability of guaranteed minimum pension and protected rights payments).

92 Forfeiture, etc

(1) Subject to the provisions of this section and section 93, an entitlement [to a pension under an occupational pension scheme or a right to a future pension under such a scheme] cannot be forfeited.

(2) Subsection (1) does not prevent forfeiture by reference to—

(a) a transaction or purported transaction which under section 91 is of no effect, or

(b) the bankruptcy of the person entitled to the pension or whose right to it has accrued, whether or not that event occurred before or after the pension became payable.

(3) Where such forfeiture as is mentioned in subsection (2) occurs, any pension which was, or would but for the forfeiture have become, payable may, if the trustees or managers of the scheme so determine, be paid to all or any of the following—

(a) the member of the scheme to or in respect of whom the pension was, or would have become, payable,

(b) the spouse, widow or widower of the member,

(c) any dependant of the member, and

(d) any other person falling within a prescribed class.

(4) Subsection (1) does not prevent forfeiture by reference to the [pensioner, or prospective pensioner], having been convicted of one or more offences—

(a) which are committed before the pension becomes payable, and

(b) which are—

(i) offences of treason,

(ii) offences under the Official Secrets Acts 1911 to 1989 for which the person has been sentenced on the same occasion to a term of imprisonment of, or to two or more consecutive terms amounting in the aggregate to, at least 10 years, or

(iii) prescribed offences.

(5) Subsection (1) does not prevent forfeiture by reference to a failure by any person to make a claim for pension—

(a) where the forfeiture is in reliance on any enactment relating to the limitation of actions, or

(b) where the claim is not made within six years of the date on which the pension becomes due.

(6) Subsection (1) does not prevent forfeiture in prescribed circumstances.

(7) In this section and section 93, references to forfeiture include any manner of deprivation or suspension.

(1) Subject to subsection (2), section 92(1) does not prevent forfeiture of a person's entitlement [to a pension under an occupational pension scheme or right to a future due to the employer and arising out of a criminal, negligent or fraudulent act or omission by the person. pension under such a scheme] by reference to the person having incurred some monetary obligation

(2) A person's entitlement or [right] may be forfeited by reason of subsection (1) to the extent only that it does not exceed the amount of the monetary obligation in question, or (if less) the value (determined in the prescribed manner) of the person's entitlement.

(3) Such forfeiture as is mentioned in subsection (1) must not take effect where there is a dispute as to the amount of the monetary obligation in question, unless the obligation has become enforceable under an order of a competent court or in consequence of an award of an arbitrator or, in Scotland, an arbiter to be appointed (failing agreement between the parties) by the sheriff.

(4) Where a person's entitlement or [right] is forfeited by reason of subsection (1), the person must be given a certificate showing the amount forfeited and the effect of the forfeiture on his benefits under the scheme.

(5) Where such forfeiture as is mentioned in subsection (1) occurs, an amount not exceeding the amount forfeited may, if the trustees or managers of the scheme so determine, be paid to the employer.

(a) Charge or lien on or set-off against transfer credits

For the purposes of section 91(5)(d) of the 1995 Act (charge or a lien or set-off against transfer credits by employer) the prescribed transfer credits are those transfer credits attributable to employment with the same employer or an associated employer and the benefits of which could have been charged or a lien or set-off exercised in respect of such benefits under the occupational pension scheme from which the transfer was made.

(b) Charge or lien on or set-off against an occupational pension For the purposes of section 91(5)(e) of the 1995 Act (charge or lien or set-off against entitlement or accrued right to a pension for the purpose of discharging some monetary obligation to the scheme) the prescribed circumstance is where a monetary obligation arises out of a breach of trust by the person in question and the court has relieved him wholly or partly from personal liability under section 61 of the Trustee Act 1925 or section 32 of the Trusts (Scotland) Act 1921.

(c) Pay-ability of pension where forfeiture occurs

For the purposes of section 92(3)(d) of the 1995 Act (class of persons to whom a forfeited pension may be paid) the prescribed class is any person (other than a person mentioned in section 92(3)(a) to (c)) to whom, under the rules of the scheme, the pension was or could have been paid.

6 Forfeiture of occupational pension

(1) For the purposes of section 92(6) of the 1995 Act (a pension under an occupational pension scheme cannot be forfeited except in prescribed circumstances) the prescribed circumstances are where—

> (a) a pension is payable to a member's widow or widower, dependant or any other person who is nominated under the scheme rules by the member and that person is convicted of the offence of murder or manslaughter of that member or any other offence of which unlawful killing of that member is an element;

> (b) a person in respect of whom a pension is or would have been payable has caused a monetary loss to the scheme as a result of—
>
>> a criminal, negligent or fraudulent act or omission by him,
>>
>> or in the case of a trust scheme of which the person is a trustee, a breach of trust by him.

> (c) in the case of a public service pension scheme—

the member is convicted of an offence committed in connection with his service as a public servant, and

(ii) a Minister of the Crown certifies that the commission of that offence has been gravely injurious to the interests of the State or is liable to lead to serious loss of confidence in the public service;

> (d) in the case of the Armed Forces Pension Scheme—
>
>> the member is convicted of an offence committed in connection with his service as a member of the Armed Forces, and
>>
>> the Secretary of State considers that offence to have been gravely injurious to the defence, security or other interests of the State

(2) For the purposes of paragraph (1)(a) unlawful killing shall include the case of a person who has unlawfully aided, abetted, counselled or procured the death of a person.

(3) A person's entitlement or accrued right to a pension may be forfeited under paragraph (1)(b) to the extent only that it does not exceed the amount of the monetary loss to the scheme, or (if less) the value of the person's entitlement or accrued right under the scheme.

7 Modification of section 91 of the 1995 Act in respect of public service pension schemes and the Armed Forces Pension Scheme

Section 91(5)(d) of the 1995 Act shall have effect in its application to public service pension schemes and the Armed Forces Pension Scheme with the omission of the words "and arising out of a criminal, negligent or fraudulent act or omission by him".

8 Exemptions from the inalienability and forfeiture provisions

(1) If a scheme is one the trustees of which have made…a loan in respect of which the conditions of regulation 6(8) of the Occupational Pension Schemes (Investment) Regulations 1996 are met (investments to which the restrictions do not apply), [section 91(1)] of the 1995 Act shall not apply to the extent that it would [prevent enforcement of the security referred to in sub-paragraph (b) of that regulation 6(8)].

[(1A) If a scheme is one the trustees of which have given or wish to give security in respect of which the conditions of regulation 6(8A) of the Occupational Pension Schemes (Investment) Regulations 1996 are met (investments to which restrictions do not apply), section 91(1) of the 1995 Act shall not apply to the extent that it would prevent that security being given or enforced.]

> (2) Section 91(1)(a) of the 1995 Act shall not apply to that part of an occupational pension scheme under which there is an entitlement or an accrued right to a lump sum retirement benefit and the Inland Revenue have granted a concession, in accordance with a statement issued on 11th October 1996, to a member in respect of that lump sum retirement benefit.

> (3) Subject to paragraph (4), section 91(2) of the 1995 Act shall not apply in relation to schemes which are not approved schemes.

Paragraph (3) shall not apply to public service pension schemes and the Armed Forces Pension Scheme.

> (5) Section 92(4)(a) of the 1995 Act (forfeiture) shall not apply in relation to public service pension schemes.

UK Statutes, Limited Liability Partnerships Act 2000 (2000 c 12)

Appendix 6—Limited Liability Partnerships Act 2000

An Act to make provision for limited liability partnerships.

1 Limited liability partnerships

(1) There shall be a new form of legal entity to be known as a limited liability partnership.

(2) **A limited liability partnership is a body corporate** (with legal personality separate from that of its members) which is formed by being incorporated under this Act; and—

(a) in the following provisions of this Act (except in the phrase "oversea limited liability partnership"), and

(b) in any other enactment (except where provision is made to the contrary or the context otherwise requires),

references to a limited liability partnership are to such a body corporate.

(1) **A limited liability partnership has unlimited capacity.**

(2) The members of a limited liability partnership have such liability to contribute to its assets in the event of its being wound up as is provided for by virtue of this Act.

(3) Accordingly, except as far as otherwise provided by this Act or any other enactment, the law relating to partnerships does not apply to a limited liability partnership.

(4) The Schedule (which makes provision about the names and registered offices of limited liability partnerships) has effect.

2 Incorporation document etc

(1) For a limited liability partnership to be incorporated—

(a) two or more persons associated for carrying on a lawful business with a view to profit must have subscribed their names to an incorporation document,

(b) there must have been delivered to the registrar either the incorporation document or a copy authenticated in a manner approved by him, and

(c) there must have been so delivered a statement in a form approved by the registrar, made by either a solicitor engaged in the formation of the limited liability partnership or anyone who subscribed his name to the incorporation document, that the requirement imposed by paragraph (a) has been complied with.

(2) The incorporation document must—

(a) be in a form approved by the registrar (or as near to such a form as circumstances allow),

(b) state the name of the limited liability partnership,

(c) state whether the registered office of the limited liability partnership is to be situated in England and Wales, in Wales or in Scotland,

(d) state the address of that registered office,

(e) state the name and address of each of the persons who are to be members of the limited liability partnership on incorporation, and

(f) either specify which of those persons are to be designated members or state that every person who from time to time is a member of the limited liability partnership is a designated member.

(2A) *Where a confidentiality order, made under section 723B of the Companies Act 1985 as applied to a limited liability partnerships, is in force in respect of any individual named as a member of a limited liability partnership under subsection (2) that subsection shall have effect as if the reference to the address of the individual were a reference to the address for the time being notified by him under the Limited Liability Partnerships (Particulars of Usual Residential Address) (Confidentiality Orders) Regulations 2002 to any limited liability partnership of which he is a member or if he is not such a member either the address specified in his application for a confidentiality order or the address last notified by him under such a confidentiality order as the case may be.*

(2B) Where the incorporation document or a copy of such delivered under this section includes an address specified in reliance on subsection (2A) there shall be delivered with it or the copy of it a statement in a form approved by the registrar containing particulars of the usual residential address of the member whose address is so specified.]

False Statements

(1) **If a person makes a false statement** under subsection (1) (c) which he—

(a) knows to be false, or

(b) does not believe to be true,

he commits an offence.

(4) A person guilty of an offence under subsection (3) is liable—

(a) on summary conviction, to imprisonment for a period not exceeding six months or a fine not exceeding the statutory maximum, or to both, or

(b) on conviction on indictment, to imprisonment for a period not exceeding two years or a fine, or to both.

(1) When the requirements imposed by paragraphs (b) and (c) of subsection (1) of section 2 have been complied with, the registrar shall retain the incorporation document or copy delivered to him and, unless the requirement imposed by paragraph (a) of that subsection has not been complied with, he shall—

(a) register the incorporation document or copy, and

(b) give a certificate that the limited liability partnership is incorporated by the name specified in the incorporation document.

(2) The registrar may accept the statement delivered under paragraph (c) of subsection (1) of section 2 as sufficient evidence that the requirement imposed by paragraph (a) of that subsection has been complied with.

(3) The certificate shall either be signed by the registrar or be authenticated by his official seal.

(4) The certificate is conclusive evidence that the requirements of section 2 are complied with and that the limited liability partnership is incorporated by the name specified in the incorporation document.

4 Members

(1) On the incorporation of a limited liability partnership its members are the persons who subscribed their names to the incorporation document (other than any who have died or been dissolved).

(2) Any other person may become a member of a limited liability partnership by and in accordance with an agreement with the existing members.

(3) A person may cease to be a member of a limited liability partnership (as well as by death or dissolution) in accordance with an agreement with the other members or, in the absence of agreement with the other members as to cessation of membership, by giving reasonable notice to the other members.

A member of a limited liability partnership shall not be regarded for any purpose as employed by the limited liability partnership unless, if he and the other members were partners in a partnership, he would be regarded for that purpose as employed by the partnership.

5 Relationship of members etc

(1) Except as far as otherwise provided by this Act or any other enactment, the mutual rights and duties of the members of a limited liability partnership, and the mutual rights and duties of a limited liability partnership and its members, shall be governed—

(a) by agreement between the members, or between the limited liability partnership and its members, or

(b) in the absence of agreement as to any matter, by any provision made in relation to that matter by regulations under section 15(c).

(2) An agreement made before the incorporation of a limited liability partnership between the persons who subscribe their names to the incorporation document may impose obligations on the limited liability partnership (to take effect at any time after its incorporation).

6 Members as agents

(1) Every member of a limited liability partnership is the agent of the limited liability partnership.

(2) But a limited liability partnership is not bound by anything done by a member in dealing with a person if—

(a) the member in fact has no authority to act for the limited liability partnership by doing that thing, and

(b) the person knows that he has no authority or does not know or believe him to be a member of the limited liability partnership.

(3) Where a person has ceased to be a member of a limited liability partnership, the former member is to be regarded (in relation to any person dealing with the limited liability partnership) as still being a member of the limited liability partnership unless—

(a) the person has notice that the former member has ceased to be a member of the limited liability partnership, or

(b) notice that the former member has ceased to be a member of the limited liability partnership has been delivered to the registrar.

(4) Where a member of a limited liability partnership is liable to any person (other than another member of the limited liability partnership) as a result of a wrongful act or omission of his in the course of the business of the limited liability partnership or with its authority, the limited liability partnership is liable to the same extent as the member.

7 Ex-members

(1) This section applies where a member of a limited liability partnership has either ceased to be a member or—has died,

(b) has become bankrupt or had his estate sequestrated or has been wound up,

(c) has granted a trust deed for the benefit of his creditors, or

(d) has assigned the whole or any part of his share in the limited liability partnership (absolutely or by way of charge or security).

(2) In such an event the former member or—

(a) his personal representative,

(b) his trustee in bankruptcy or permanent or interim trustee (within the meaning of the Bankruptcy (Scotland) Act 1985) or liquidator,

(c) his trustee under the trust deed for the benefit of his creditors, or

(d) his assignee,

may not interfere in the management or administration of any business or affairs of the limited liability partnership.

(3) But subsection (2) does not affect any right to receive an amount from the limited liability partnership in that event.

SI 2000/3316, art 2.

8 Designated members

(1) If the incorporation document specifies who are to be designated members—

(a) they are designated members on incorporation, and

(b) any member may become a designated member by and in accordance with an agreement with the other members, and a member may cease to be a designated member in accordance with an agreement with the other members.

(2) But if there would otherwise be no designated members, or only one, every member is a designated member.

(3) If the incorporation document states that every person who from time to time is a member of the limited liability partnership is a designated member, every member is a designated member.

(4) A limited liability partnership may at any time deliver to the registrar—

(a) notice that specified members are to be designated members, or

(b) notice that every person who from time to time is a member of the limited liability partnership is a designated member, and, once it is delivered, subsection (1) (apart from paragraph (a)) and subsection (2), or subsection (3), shall have effect as if that were stated in the incorporation document.

(5) A notice delivered under subsection (4)—

(a) shall be in a form approved by the registrar, and

(b) shall be signed by a designated member of the limited liability partnership or authenticated in a manner approved by the registrar.

(6) A person ceases to be a designated member if he ceases to be a member.

9 Registration of membership changes

(1) A limited liability partnership must ensure that—

(a) where a person becomes or ceases to be a member or designated member, notice is delivered to the registrar within fourteen days, and

(b) where there is any change in the name or address of a member, notice is delivered to the registrar within 28 days.

(2) Where all the members from time to time of a limited liability partnership are designated members, subsection (1)(a) does not require notice that a person has become or ceased to be a designated member as well as a member.

(3) A notice delivered under subsection (1)—

(a) shall be in a form approved by the registrar, and

(b) shall be signed by a designated member of the limited liability partnership or authenticated in a manner approved by the registrar, and, if it relates to a person becoming a member or designated member, shall contain a statement that he consents to becoming a member or designated member signed by him or authenticated in a manner approved by the registrar.

[(3A) Where a confidentiality order under section 723B of the Companies Act 1985 as applied to limited liability partnerships is made in respect of an existing member, the limited liability partnership must ensure that there is delivered within 28 days to the registrar notice in a form approved by the registrar containing the address for the time being notified to it by the member under the Limited Liability Partnerships (Particulars of Usual Residential Address) (Confidentiality Orders) Regulations 2002.

(3B) Where such a confidentiality order is in force in respect of a member the requirement in subsection (1)(b) to notify a change in the address of a member shall be read in relation to that member as a requirement to deliver to the registrar, within 28 days, notice of—

(a) any change in the usual residential address of that member; and

(b) any change in the address for the time being notified to the limited liability partnership by the member under the Limited Liability Partnerships (Particulars of Usual Residential Address) (Confidentiality Orders) Regulations 2002,

and the registrar may approve different forms for the notification of each kind of address.]

(4) If a limited liability partnership fails to comply with subsection (1), the partnership and every designated member commits an offence.

(5) But it is a defence for a designated member charged with an offence under subsection (4) to prove that he took all reasonable steps for securing that subsection (1) was complied with.

(6) A person guilty of an offence under subsection (4) is liable on summary conviction to a fine not exceeding level 5 on the standard scale.

10 Income tax and chargeable gains

(1) and (2) omitted.

(3) The amount subscribed by a member of a limited liability partnership is the amount which he has contributed to the limited liability partnership as capital, less so much of that amount (if any) as—

(a) he has previously, directly or indirectly, drawn out or received back,

(b) he so draws out or receives back during the period of five years beginning with the relevant time,

(c) he is or may be entitled so to draw out or receive back at any time when he is a member of the limited liability partnership, or

(d) he is or may be entitled to require another person to reimburse to him.

(4) The amount of the liability of a member of a limited liability partnership on a winding up is the amount which—

(a) he is liable to contribute to the assets of the limited liability partnership in the event of its being wound up, and

(b) he remains liable so to contribute for the period of at least five years beginning with the relevant time (or until it is wound up, if that happens before the end of that period).

11 Carry forward of unrelieved losses

(1) Where amounts relating to a trade carried on by a member of a limited liability partnership are, in any one or more chargeable periods, prevented from being given or allowed by section 117 or 118 as it applies otherwise than by virtue of this section (his "total unrelieved loss"), subsection (2) applies in each subsequent chargeable period in which—

(a) he carries on the trade as a member of the limited liability partnership, and

(b) any of his total unrelieved loss remains outstanding.

(2) Sections 380, 381, 393A(1) and 403 (and sections 117 and 118 as they apply in relation to those sections) shall have effect in the subsequent chargeable period as if—

(a) any loss sustained or incurred by the member in the trade in that chargeable period were increased by an amount equal to so much of his total unrelieved loss as remains outstanding in that period, or

(b) (if no loss is so sustained or incurred) a loss of that amount were so sustained or incurred.

(3) To ascertain whether any (and, if so, how much) of a member's total unrelieved loss remains outstanding in the subsequent chargeable period, deduct from the amount of his total unrelieved loss the aggregate of—

(a) any relief given under any provision of the Tax Acts (otherwise than as a result of subsection (2)) in respect of his total unrelieved loss in that or any previous chargeable period, and

(b) any amount given or allowed in respect of his total unrelieved loss as a result of subsection (2) in any previous chargeable period (or which would have been so given or allowed had a claim been made)."

(2) In section 362(2)(a) of that Act (loan to buy into partnership), after "partner" insert "in a limited partnership registered under the Limited Partnerships Act 1907".

(3) In the Taxation of Chargeable Gains Act 1992, after section 59 insert—

"59A Limited liability partnerships

(1) Where a limited liability partnership carries on a trade or business with a view to profit—

(a) assets held by the limited liability partnership shall be treated for the purposes of tax in respect of chargeable gains as held by its members as partners, and

(b) any dealings by the limited liability partnership shall be treated for those purposes as dealings by its members in partnership (and not by the limited liability partnership as such), and tax in respect of chargeable gains accruing to the members of the limited liability partnership on the disposal of any of its assets shall be assessed and charged on them separately.

(2) Where subsection (1) ceases to apply in relation to a limited liability partnership with the effect that tax is assessed and charged—

(a) on the limited liability partnership (as a company) in respect of chargeable gains accruing on the disposal of any of its assets, and

(b) on the members in respect of chargeable gains accruing on the disposal of any of their capital interests in the limited liability partnership, it shall be assessed and charged on the limited liability partnership as if subsection (1) had never applied in relation to it.

(3) Neither the commencement of the application of subsection (1) nor the cessation of its application in relation to a limited liability partnership is to be taken as giving rise to the disposal of any assets by it or any of its members."

(4)

(1) Where, immediately before the time of cessation of trade, a member of a limited liability partnership holds an asset, or an interest in an asset, acquired by him for a consideration treated as reduced under section 152 or 153, he shall be treated as if a chargeable gain equal to the amount of the reduction accrued to him immediately before that time.

(2) Where, as a result of section 154(2), a chargeable gain on the disposal of an asset, or an interest in an asset, by a member of a limited liability partnership has not accrued before the time of cessation of trade, the member shall be treated as if the chargeable gain accrued immediately before that time.

(3) In this section "the time of cessation of trade", in relation to a limited liability partnership, means the time when section 59A(1) ceases to apply in relation to the limited liability partnership."

11 Inheritance tax

For the purposes of this Act and any other enactments relating to inheritance tax—

(a) property to which a limited liability partnership is entitled, or which it occupies or uses, shall be treated as property to which its members are entitled, or which they occupy or use, as partners,

(b) any business carried on by a limited liability partnership shall be treated as carried on in partnership by its members,

(c) incorporation, change in membership or dissolution of a limited liability partnership shall be treated as formation, alteration or dissolution of a partnership, and

(d) any transfer of value made by or to a limited liability partnership shall be treated as made by or to its members in partnership (and not by or to the limited liability partnership as such)."

12 Stamp duty

(1) Stamp duty shall not be chargeable on an instrument by which property is conveyed or transferred by a person to a limited liability partnership in connection with its incorporation within the period of one year beginning with the date of incorporation if the following two conditions are satisfied.

(2) The first condition is that at the relevant time the person—

(a) is a partner in a partnership comprised of all the persons who are or are to be members of the limited liability partnership (and no-one else), or

(b) holds the property conveyed or transferred as nominee or bare trustee for one or more of the partners in such a partnership.

(3) The second condition is that—

(a) the proportions of the property conveyed or transferred to which the persons mentioned in subsection (2)(a) are entitled immediately after the conveyance or transfer are the same as those to which they were entitled at the relevant time, or

(b) none of the differences in those proportions has arisen as part of a scheme or arrangement of which the main purpose, or one of the main purposes, is avoidance of liability to any duty or tax.

(4) For the purposes of subsection (2) a person holds property as bare trustee for a partner if the partner has the exclusive right (subject only to satisfying any outstanding charge, lien or other right of the trustee to resort to the property for payment of duty, taxes, costs or other outgoings) to direct how the property shall be dealt with.

(5) In this section "the relevant time" means—

(a) if the person who conveyed or transferred the property to the limited liability partnership acquired the property after its incorporation, immediately after he acquired the property, and

(b) in any other case, immediately before its incorporation.

(6) An instrument in respect of which stamp duty is not chargeable by virtue of subsection (1) shall not be taken to be duly stamped unless—

(a) it has, in accordance with section 12 of the Stamp Act 1891, been stamped with a particular stamp denoting that it is not chargeable with any duty or that it is duly stamped, or

(b) it is stamped with the duty to which it would be liable apart from that subsection.

13 Class 4 national insurance contributions

Where income tax is (or would be) charged on a member of a limited liability partnership in respect of profits or gains arising from the carrying on of a trade or profession by the limited liability partnership, Class 4 contributions shall be payable by him if they would be payable were the trade or profession carried on in partnership by the members.

14 Insolvency and winding up

(1) Regulations shall make provision about the insolvency and winding up of limited liability partnerships by applying or incorporating, with such modifications as appear appropriate, Parts I to IV, VI and VII of the Insolvency Act 1986.

(2) Regulations may make other provision about the insolvency and winding up of limited liability partnerships, and provision about the insolvency and winding up of oversea limited liability partnerships, by—

(a) applying or incorporating, with such modifications as appear appropriate, any law relating to the insolvency or winding up of companies or other corporations which would not otherwise have effect in relation to them, or

(b) providing for any law relating to the insolvency or winding up of companies or other corporations which would otherwise have effect in relation to them not to apply to them or to apply to them with such modifications as appear appropriate.

(3) In this Act "overseas limited liability partnership" means a body incorporated or otherwise established outside Great Britain and having such connection with Great Britain, and such other features, as regulations may prescribe.

15 Application of company law etc

Regulations may make provision about limited liability partnerships and overseas limited liability partnerships (not being provision about insolvency or winding up) by—

(a) applying or incorporating, with such modifications as appear appropriate, any law relating to companies or other corporations which would not otherwise have effect in relation to them,

(b) providing for any law relating to companies or other corporations which would otherwise have effect in relation to them not to apply to them or to apply to them with such modifications as appear appropriate, or

(c) applying or incorporating, with such modifications as appear appropriate, any law relating to partnerships.

(2) The regulations may, in particular, make amendments and repeals affecting companies or other corporations or partnerships.

17 General

(1) In this Act "regulations" means regulations made by the Secretary of State by statutory instrument.

(2) Regulations under this Act may in particular—

(a) make provisions for dealing with non-compliance with any of the regulations (including the creation of criminal offences),

(b) impose fees (which shall be paid into the Consolidated Fund), and

(c) provide for the exercise of functions by persons prescribed by the regulations.

(3) Regulations under this Act may—

(a) contain any appropriate consequential, incidental, supplementary or transitional provisions or savings, and

(b) make different provision for different purposes.

(4) No regulations to which this subsection applies shall be made unless a draft of the statutory instrument containing the regulations (whether or not together with other provisions) has been laid before, and approved by a resolution of, each House of Parliament.

(5) Subsection (4) applies to—

(a) regulations under section 14(2) not consisting entirely of the application or incorporation (with or without modifications) of provisions contained in or made under the Insolvency Act 1986,

(b) regulations under section 15 not consisting entirely of the application or incorporation (with or without modifications) of provisions contained in or made under Part I, Chapter VIII of Part V, Part VII, Parts XI to XIII, Parts XVI to XVIII, Part XX or Parts XXIV to XXVI of the Companies Act 1985,

(c) regulations under section 14 or 15 making provision about overseas limited liability partnerships, and

(d) regulations under section 16.

(6) A statutory instrument containing regulations under this Act shall (unless a draft of it has been approved by a resolution of each House of Parliament) be subject to annulment in pursuance of a resolution of either House of Parliament.

18 Interpretation

In this Act—

"address", in relation to a member of a limited liability partnership, means—

(a) if an individual, his usual residential address, and

(b) if a corporation or Scottish firm, its registered or principal office,

"business" includes every trade, profession and occupation,

"designated member" shall be construed in accordance with section 8,

"enactment" includes subordinate legislation (within the meaning of the Interpretation Act 1978),

"incorporation document" shall be construed in accordance with section 2,

"limited liability partnership" has the meaning given by section 1(2),

"member" shall be construed in accordance with section 4,

"modifications" includes additions and omissions,

"name", in relation to a member of a limited liability partnership, means—

(a) if an individual, his forename and surname (or, in the case of a peer or other person usually known by a title, his title instead of or in addition to either or both his forename and surname), and

(b) if a corporation or Scottish firm, its corporate or firm name,

"overseas limited liability partnership" has the meaning given by section 14(3),

"the registrar" means—

(a) if the registered office of the limited liability partnership is, or is to be, situated in England and Wales or in Wales, the registrar or other officer performing under the Companies Act 1985 the duty of registration of companies in England and Wales, and

(b) if its registered office is, or is to be, situated in Scotland, the registrar or other officer performing under that Act the duty of registration of companies in Scotland, and

"regulations" has the meaning given by section 17(1).

19 Commencement, extent and short title

(1) The preceding provisions of this Act shall come into force on such day as the Secretary of State may by order made by statutory instrument appoint; and different days may be appointed for different purposes.

(2) The Secretary of State may by order made by statutory instrument make any transitional provisions and savings which appear appropriate in connection with the coming into force of any provision of this Act.

(3) For the purposes of the Scotland Act 1998 this Act shall be taken to be a pre-commencement enactment within the meaning of that Act.

(4) Apart from sections 10 to 13 (and this section), this Act does not extend to Northern Ireland.

This Act may be cited as the Limited Liability Partnerships Act 2000.

Limited Liability Partnerships Act 2000

In section 714(1) of the Companies Act 1985 (index of names), after paragraph (d) insert—

"(da)

limited liability partnerships incorporated under the Limited Liability Partnerships Act 2000."

Name to indicate status

2

(1) **The name of a limited liability partnership must end with—**

(a) the expression "limited liability partnership", or

(b) the abbreviation "llp" or "LLP".

(2) But if the incorporation document for a limited liability partnership states that the registered office is to be situated in Wales, its name must end with—

(a) one of the expressions "limited liability partnership" and *"partneriaeth atebolrwydd cyfyngedig"*, or

(b) *one of the abbreviations "llp", "LLP", "pac" and "PAC".*

Registration of names

3

(1) A limited liability partnership shall not be registered by a name—

(a) which includes, otherwise than at the end of the name, either of the expressions "limited liability partnership" and "partneriaeth atebolrwydd cyfyngedig" or any of the abbreviations "llp", "LLP", "pac" and "PAC",

(b) which is the same as a name appearing in the index kept under section 714(1) of the Companies Act 1985,

(c) the use of which by the limited liability partnership would in the opinion of the Secretary of State constitute a criminal offence, or

(d) which in the opinion of the Secretary of State is offensive.

(2) Except with the approval of the Secretary of State, a limited liability partnership shall not be registered by a name which—

(a) in the opinion of the Secretary of State would be likely to give the impression that it is connected in any way with Her Majesty's Government or with any local authority, or

(b) includes any word or expression for the time being specified in regulations under section 29 of the Companies Act 1985 (names needing approval),

and in paragraph (a) "local authority" means any local authority within the meaning of the Local Government Act 1972 or the Local Government etc (Scotland) Act 1994, the Common Council of the City of London or the Council of the Isles of Scilly.

Change of name

4 A limited liability partnership may change its name at any time.

(2) Where a limited liability partnership has been registered by a name which—

(a) is the same as or, in the opinion of the Secretary of State, too like a name appearing at the time of registration in the index kept under section 714(1) of the Companies Act 1985, or

is the same as or, in the opinion of the Secretary of State, too like a name which should have appeared in the index at that time, the Secretary of State may within twelve months of that time in writing direct the limited liability partnership to change its name within such period as he may specify.

(3) If it appears to the Secretary of State—

(a) that misleading information has been given for the purpose of the registration of a limited liability partnership by a particular name, or

that undertakings or assurances have been given for that purpose and have not been fulfilled, he may, within five years of the date of its registration by that name, in writing direct the limited liability partnership to change its name within such period as he may specify.

(4) If in the Secretary of State's opinion the name by which a limited liability partnership is registered gives so misleading an indication of the nature of its activities as to be likely to cause harm to the public, he may in writing direct the limited liability partnership to change its name within such period as he may specify.

(5) But the limited liability partnership may, within three weeks from the date of the direction apply to the court to set it aside and the court may set the direction aside or confirm it and, if it confirms it, shall specify the period within which it must be complied with.

(6) In sub-paragraph (5) "the court" means—

(a) if the registered office of the limited liability partnership is situated in England and Wales or in Wales, the High Court, and

(b) if it is situated in Scotland, the Court of Session.

(7) Where a direction has been given under sub-paragraph (2), (3) or (4) specifying a period within which a limited liability partnership is to change its name, the Secretary of State may at any time before that period ends extend it by a further direction in writing.

(8) If a limited liability partnership fails to comply with a direction under this paragraph—

(a) the limited liability partnership, and

(b) any designated member in default, commits an offence.

(9) A person guilty of an offence under sub-paragraph (8) is liable on summary conviction to a fine not exceeding level 3 on the standard scale.

5. Notification of change of name

(1) Where a limited liability partnership changes its name it shall deliver notice of the change to the registrar.

(2) A notice delivered under sub-paragraph (1)—

(a) shall be in a form approved by the registrar, and

(b) shall be signed by a designated member of the limited liability partnership or authenticated in a manner approved by the registrar.

(3) Where the registrar receives a notice under sub-paragraph (2) he shall (unless the new name is one by which a limited liability partnership may not be registered)—

(a) enter the new name in the index kept under section 714(1) of the Companies Act 1985, and

(b) issue a certificate of the change of name.

(4) The change of name has effect from the date on which the certificate is issued.

6. Effect of change of name

A change of name by a limited liability partnership does not—

(a) affect any of its rights or duties,

(b) render defective any legal proceedings by or against it,

and any legal proceedings that might have been commenced or continued against it by its former name may be commenced or continued against it by its new name.

7 Improper use of "limited liability partnership" etc

(1) If any person carries on a business under a name or title which includes as the last words—

(a) the expression "limited liability partnership" or "partneriaeth atebolrwydd cyfyngedig", or

(b) any contraction or imitation of either of those expressions,

that person, unless a limited liability partnership or overseas limited liability partnership, commits an offence.

(2) A person guilty of an offence under sub-paragraph (1) is liable on summary conviction to a fine not exceeding level 3 on the standard scale.

8. Similarity of names

In determining for the purposes of this Part whether one name is the same as another there are to be disregarded—

(1) the definite article as the first word of the name,

(2) any of the following (or their Welsh equivalents or abbreviations of them or their Welsh equivalents) at the end of the name—

"limited liability partnership",

"company",

"and company",

"company limited",

"and company limited",

"limited",

"unlimited",

"public limited company",…

"investment company with variable capital", and

"open-ended investment company", and]

(3) type and case of letters, accents, spaces between letters and punctuation marks,

and "and" and "&" are to be taken as the same.

Date in force: 1 December 2001 (being the date on which the Financial Services and Markets Act 2000, s 19, came into force): see SI 2001/3538, art 2(1) andSI 2001/1228, reg 1(2)(c).

Part II

Registered Offices

9. Situation of registered office

(1) A limited liability partnership shall—

(a)

at all times have a registered office situated in England and Wales or in Wales, or

(b)

at all times have a registered office situated in Scotland, to which communications and notices may be addressed.

(2) On the incorporation of a limited liability partnership the situation of its registered office shall be that stated in the incorporation document.

(3) Where the registered office of a limited liability partnership is situated in Wales, but the incorporation document does not state that it is to be situated in Wales (as opposed to England and Wales), the limited liability partnership may deliver notice to the registrar stating that its registered office is to be situated in Wales.

(4) A notice delivered under sub-paragraph (3)—

(a) shall be in a form approved by the registrar, and

(b) shall be signed by a designated member of the limited liability partnership or authenticated in a manner approved by the registrar.

10. Change of registered office

(1) A limited liability partnership may change its registered office by delivering notice of the change to the registrar.

(2) A notice delivered under sub-paragraph (1)—

(a) shall be in a form approved by the registrar, and

(b) shall be signed by a designated member of the limited liability partnership or authenticated in a manner approved by the registrar.

Appendix 7—the Guinness Case

Guinness plc v Saunders and another [1988] BCLC 43

Director—Breach of fiduciary duty—Right of company to recover money allegedly illegally received by the director—Failure of director to disclose his interest in a contract with the company—Exercise of discretion by court to exonerate director for breach of duty—Companies Act 1985, ss 317 and 727

W was a director of the plaintiff company which had made a take-over bid for another company. MAC, a Jersey company, submitted an invoice for £5·2m for services connected with the bid and this sum was duly paid. It was admitted by W that the payment to MAC was received for and on behalf of W in return for his professional services in connection with the take-over bid. W claimed that the payment was made pursuant to an oral agreement between him and the plaintiff company. The plaintiff company denied the existence of the agreement and claimed that even had it been made it was made in breach of W's duty as a director in that it was not disclosed in accordance with either s 317 of the Companies Act 1985 or the company's articles of association. In the present proceedings the plaintiff company by a summons under RSC Ord 14, or alternatively by a motion for judgment on admissions under RSC Ord 27, r 3, applied for summary judgment that W held the £5·2m as a constructive trustee for the plaintiff company and was bound to return it to the company. By way of defence W alleged that he had made proper disclosure by disclosing his interest to a committee of the board of the plaintiff company and also claimed that if he was held accountable for the money then he should (a) be excused under s 727 of the 1985 Act, (b) be entitled to set off his counter-claim for his services, or (c) that the plaintiff company should be obliged as a condition of recovery to give him equitable compensation for his services.

Held—As W had failed to allege in his pleadings or in evidence that he had made a full disclosure of his interest in connection with the payment of the £5·2m to MAC, he must be taken to have impliedly admitted that no such disclosure had been made and the defence that disclosure had been made to a committee of the board could not constitute compliance with s 317 which required disclosure to the full board and not to a committee of the board to which this statutory function could not be delegated. Although the articles of the plaintiff company specifically entitled a director in certain circumstances to retain profits from contracts entered into with the company this only applied where there had been full disclosure as was required by the company's articles and s 317 of the 1985 Act. Accordingly as full disclosure had not been made as was required by s 317 and the plaintiff company's articles of association, W was therefore obliged to account to the company for the £5·2m. In addition W could not set off his cross claims whether arising by way of quantum meruit or equitable compensation as these cross-claims did not impugn the title of the plaintiff company to the £5·2m which the plaintiff company was claiming on the grounds that it belonged to it and on the broader ground that a director

[

Guinness plc applied for summary judgment to recover £5·2m alleged to have been unlawfully received from Guinness by the second defendant, Thomas Joseph Ward. By a summons dated 15 May 1987 Guinness applied for an order under RSC Ord 14 for final judgment in the action against Mr Ward for the relief claimed against him in the statement of claim. By a notice of motion dated 1 July 1987 Guinness sought an order that judgment be entered in the action for Guinness against Mr Ward for the relief claimed against him in the statement of claim on the admissions contained in the second defendant's defence and in his affidavits sworn on 1 and 9 April 1987 pursuant to RSC Ord 27, r 3. The facts are set out in the judgment of Sir Nicolas Browne-Wilkinson V-C.

Said SIR NICOLAS BROWNE-WILKINSON V-C:-

"This is an application by the plaintiff, Guinness plc, against the second defendant, Mr Ward, for summary judgment to recover £5·2m alleged to have been unlawfully received from Guinness by Mr Ward, a director of Guinness. Mr Saunders, the first defendant, is not concerned in this application. The application is made in two ways: first, by a summons under RSC Ord 14; second, by a motion for judgment on admissions under RSC Ord 27, r 3. The background facts surrounding the claim are complicated and are set out at some length in the judgment I gave on 15 April 1987 on a motion for interim relief. For the purposes of this judgment I can summarise them quite shortly. At all material times Mr Ward was a director of Guinness. In January 1986 Guinness launched a takeover bid for Distillers plc. The bid was fiercely fought. The bid was conducted on behalf of Guinness largely by three of its directors, the chief executive Mr Saunders, Mr Roux and Mr Ward. In May 1986 a Jersey company MAC submitted an invoice for £5·2m for services rendered in connection with the bid. On 23 May 1986 £5·2m was paid by Guinness to MAC. Although Guinness say that they were not, at the time, aware of the connection between the payment to MAC and Mr Ward, Guinness now allege, and Mr Ward admits, that the £5·2m was received for and on behalf of Mr Ward. Mr Ward and Mr Saunders allege an oral agreement ('the agreement') made between Mr Ward and Mr Saunders (on behalf of Guinness) that Mr Ward should receive £5·2m as remuneration for his non-legal services and advice in connection with the bid, such payment being in addition to substantial payments to be made to Mr Ward's law firm for legal services connected with the bid. Guinness deny the existence of the agreement, but claim that, even if the agreement was made, it was made in breach of fiduciary duty by Mr Ward in that it was not disclosed to the directors of Guinness as required by s 317 of the Companies Act 1985 and art 100(A) of Guinness' articles. Guinness therefore claims on that ground alone that Mr Ward holds the £5·2m or the assets now representing it as a constructive trustee and is bound to repay to Guinness the balance not now traceable. On the motion for interim relief I made certain orders as a result of which the solicitors for Mr Ward hold a substantial sum of money and various rights of action which are traceable as being the assets now representing part of the £5·2m. Many of the allegations of fact made by Guinness against Mr Saunders and Mr Ward are strongly denied. On these applications I am not invited to make [any findings as to the truth or otherwise of those allegations. The applications are made on the basis that, even if all that Mr Ward alleges is true, he still has no defence to Guinness' claim to recover the £5·2m. Section 317 provides, so far as material, as follows:

'(1) It is the duty of a director of a company who is in any way, whether directly or indirectly, interested in a contract or proposed contract with the company to declare the nature of his interest at a meeting of the directors of the company…

(7) A director who fails to comply with this section is liable to a fine…

(9) Nothing in this section prejudices the operation of any rule of law restricting directors of a company from having an interest in contracts with the company.'

Article 100 of Guinness' articles of association reads:

'(A) A Director who is in any way, whether directly or indirectly, interested in a contract or proposed contract with the Company shall declare the nature of his interest at a meeting of the Directors in accordance with the Statutes…

(C) A Director may hold any other office or place of profit under the Company (other than the office of Auditor) in conjunction with his office of Director for such period and on such terms (as to remuneration and otherwise) as the Board may determine and no Director or intending Director shall be disqualified by his office from contracting with the Company either with regard to his tenure of any such other office or place of profit or as vendor, purchaser or otherwise, nor shall any such contract, or any contract or arrangement entered into by or on behalf of the Company in which any Director is in any way interested, be liable to be avoided, nor shall any Director so contracting or being so interested (unless otherwise agreed between him and the Company) be liable to account to the Company for any profit realised by any such contract or arrangement, by reason of such Director holding that office or of the fiduciary relationship thereby established.

(D) Any Director may act by himself or his firm in a professional capacity for the Company and any company in which the Company is interested, and he or his firm shall be entitled to remuneration for professional services as if he were not a Director…'

I turn to consider the relevant parts of the pleadings. The statement of claim (as amended) pleads that Mr Ward was a director, that he caused the invoice for £5·2m to be presented by MAC and that MAC received the £5·2m for and on behalf of Mr Ward. This is all admitted by Mr Ward in his defence. Paragraphs 7 and 8 of the statement of claim then allege:

'7. By reason of his position as a Director of the Plaintiff, the Second Defendant owed a duty to disclose his interest in the said payment to the Plaintiff before the said payment was made…

8. In breach of the said fiduciary duties owed by each of the Defendants

[1988] BCLC 43 at 47

the said payment was made without the Second Defendant's interest therein being disclosed to the Plaintiff…'

These allegations are either not admitted or are denied by Mr Ward's defence. Paragraph 9 of the statement of claim then refers to the fact that Mr Ward and Mr Saunders allege an agreement as to Mr Ward's remuneration: para 7 of the defence admits and avers the existence of the agreement. Paragraph 10(A) of the statement of claim reads as follows:

'10(A) If, which is not admitted, the Second Defendant did provide business consulting services to the Plaintiff in respect of the said bid and the First and Second Defendants made the agreement in February 1986 referred to above and/or the First Defendant approved the said payment as remuneration for such services, the First and Second Defendants acted in breach of their said fiduciary duties in causing and/or permitting and/or approving the said payment and, in the case of the Second Defendant, receiving the same through MAC…

Particulars

(i) Neither the alleged agreement nor the said payment and the Second Defendant's interest therein was disclosed to the Plaintiff whether to the General Meeting or the Board of Directors as it should have been by each of the Defendants by reason of the Second Defendant's said interest therein.'

Mr Ward pleads to para 10A of the statement of claim in para 14A of the defence. It contains a general denial of breach of duty and then continues:

'…the Second Defendant will say with regard to paragraph 10A: (i) so far as concerns disclosure, the Second Defendant will rely on the matters set out in paragraph 11 above.'

Paragraph 11 of the defence contains no positive allegation of a disclosure to a meeting of the full board. It relies on a disclosure to Guinness 'by its Board, and for this purpose being the Committee of' the directors. Paragraphs 11 and 12 of the statement of claim allege that in the circumstances Mr Ward is liable to account and holds the £5·2m as constructive trustee. Mr Ward denies this. Pausing at that juncture, it seems to me that on the pleadings the matter stands thus. Mr Ward admits receipt of the £5·2m which he alleges was received pursuant to the agreement. He denies any duty to disclose either the agreement or his interest under it but alleges that if such duty does exist it was discharged by disclosure to the duly authorised committee of the directors consisting of Mr Saunders, Mr Roux and himself. There is no allegation in the defence that the agreement was disclosed to a 'meeting of the directors' as opposed to a committee of the directors. The defence raises three further points which are relevant. It alleges that if Mr Ward is accountable for the £5·2m as claimed (i) he acted honestly and reasonably and in all the circumstances should be excused from liability under s 727 of the 1985 Act; (ii) that he is entitled to set off his counter claim to be paid for his services on a quantum meruit; (iii) that Guinness is not entitled in equity to recover the £5·2m from Mr Ward without giving him equitable compensation for the valuable services he has rendered to Guinness. Counsel for Mr Ward (Mr Curry QC), took a preliminary point. He submitted that Guinness could not proceed for summary judgment under Ord 14 since the statement of claim contains an allegation against Mr Ward of fraudulent misrepresentation. Order 14, r 1 (2) (b) excludes from those actions to which Ord 14 applies 'an action which includes a claim by the plaintiff based on an allegation of fraud'. There was considerable argument on this point. Counsel for Guinness (Mr Oliver QC), contended that procedure by way of Ord 14 was permissible since, even though there was an allegation of fraud which could have given rise to a common law claim for damages for deceit under Derry v Peek (1889) 14 App Cas 337, [1886-90] All ER Rep 1, no such claim for damages is based on the allegation of fraud. The allegation of fraudulent misrepresentation is made as part of the factual basis on which the only claim (ie a claim for equitable relief) is based. I do not find it necessary to decide this point since in my judgment I can *fully deal with the matter on the motion for judgment on admissions. Three questions arise: (1) Has Mr Ward admitted, expressly or impliedly, that there was no disclosure of the alleged agreement for remuneration to a full meeting of the directors of Guinness so as to permit a judgment to be given under Ord 27, r 3? (2) If so, it being admitted that Mr Ward, a director, has received £5·2m from Guinness without disclosure of the agreement to a full meeting of directors, is Guinness entitled to judgment against Ward for repayment of the £5·2m? (3) If so, is Guinness prevented from recovering judgment on admissions by the claims to be relieved from liability under s 727 of the 1985 Act for a quantum meruit or for equitable compensation?*

(1) Is there an admission?

Under Ord 27, r 3 an admission does not have to be contained in the pleadings: it can be made 'otherwise'. Nor need the admission be express: an implied admission is sufficient provided that it is clear: see The Supreme Court Practice 1985, vol 1, para 27/3/1. The defence does not expressly admit the allegation in para 10A of the statement of claim that Mr Ward was in breach of fiduciary duty in failing to disclose the agreement to the directors. On the other hand, para 10A is not denied. Paragraph 14A of the defence denies any breach of fiduciary duty, but so far as disclosure of the agreement is concerned relies only on those matters pleaded in para 11 of the defence. Paragraph 11 of the defence only pleads that, if there was a duty of disclosure, it was discharged not by a disclosure to a meeting of the full board but by disclosure to a duly authorised committee of the board. If Mr Ward were going to allege disclosure of the agreement to a meeting of the full board he would have had to plead it. On the motion for interim relief, evidence was sworn that there had been no disclosure to a meeting of the full board. Mr Ward swore two affidavits, in neither of which did he allege such disclosure. The motion was conducted throughout on the basis that there had been no such disclosure: the argument as to disclosure put forward on behalf of Mr Ward was based entirely on the proposition that the disclosure to Mr Saunders, Mr Roux and Mr Ward as a duly authorised committee of the directors, was a sufficient disclosure.

Again, on the present application, the argument has proceeded wholly on the footing that there was no such disclosure. Counsel (Mr Curry QC) has not on Mr Ward's behalf admitted that there was no such disclosure. However he accepts that it is open to me to hold that there is an implied admission that there was no such disclosure. At least since the opening of the motion for interim relief, it has been clear that disclosure to a meeting of the full board of Guinness would provide a complete answer to this part of Guinness' claim. In my judgment, Mr Ward's failure to allege such disclosure, either in the pleadings or in evidence, and the way in which the case has been conducted throughout is only consistent with an implied admission that there was no such disclosure.

(2) Is Guinness entitled to judgment?

Given (a) the mandatory requirement of s 317 of the 1985 Act that any agreement for remuneration must be disclosed to a meeting of the directors; (b) the implied admission that there was no disclosure to a meeting of the full board and (c) the admission of the receipt of £5·2m on the basis that it was remuneration payable under the agreement not so disclosed, what answer has Mr Ward to Guinness' claim? Mr Ward has put forward two defences. First, on the motion for interim relief he argued the defence expressly pleaded viz that the alleged disclosure to a duly authorised committee of the directors was sufficient. In the judgment on the motion for interim relief I ruled that this was not a good defence since, whatever the articles of Guinness provide as to delegation by the board to committees, the articles could not authorise a delegation of the statutory function of receiving disclosures under s 317 of the 1985 Act. Counsel for Mr Ward has not sought to pursue that defence on this application for judgment. The defence relied on by counsel on this application runs as follows. Guinness seek to make Mr Ward liable on the basis that, as a director, he was in a fiduciary position and has received a benefit from the company, ie the £5·2m. On ordinary basic principles Mr Ward would normally be accountable for such benefits. But such accountability is not an invariable rule: a director can be authorised by the articles to enter into transactions with the company from which he makes a personal profit for which he is not accountable. So far I agree with Counsel's submission. Then, says counsel, article 100(C) and (D) expressly authorise a director to enter into contracts with the company without being accountable for any profit. So, says counsel, even if there is a breach by a director of his duty to make proper disclosure in accordance with s 317 of the 1985 Act and art 100(A), the director is still entitled under art 100(C) and (D) to retain any benefit received by him under that contract. Section 317 does not impose a separate statutory duty to account for profits from contracts in which the directors interests have not been disclosed: the only statutory penalty is the fine imposed by s 317(7). I have no hesitation in rejecting this argument which is contrary to both principle and authority. I accept that s 317 does not, by itself, impose a statutory liability to account separate from the liability to account under the general equitable principle. But it does impose a statutory duty to disclose. A director who fails to make disclosure as required by this section is not only liable to a fine: he is also in breach of his duty to the company. It is against that background that art 100(C) and (D) have to be construed. Even though art 100(C) and (D) do not in express terms refer to the statutory duty to disclose, art 100(A) does.

I find it impossible to construe (C) and (D) as authorising the retention of profits from contracts which in breach of the duty imposed by (A) and s 317 have not been disclosed. The whole of art 100 is dealing with contracts in which a director has an interest and starts by reaffirming the statutory duty of disclosure. By necessary implication the provisions permitting retention of profits by directors can only apply to those contracts which have been properly entered into without any breach of duty. This conclusion is supported by the decision in Hely-Hutchinson v Brayhead Ltd [1967] 3 All ER 98, [1968] 1 QB 549. In that case the plaintiff, a director of the defendant company, had agreed at the request of the defendant company to advance monies to P Ltd (a company in which both the plaintiff and the defendant company were beneficially interested) on being indemnified by the defendant company against any loss. No disclosure of the indemnity agreement was made to the board of the defendant company. The plaintiff, having lost the monies advanced to the P company, sued on the indemnity. He was met with the defence that as he had not disclosed his interests to the defendant company the indemnity contract was void. The Court of Appeal held that a contract with a director whose interest was not disclosed was not void but voidable by the company and that in the circumstance of that case it was too late for the company to avoid the contract. It is to be noted that the plaintiff in that case had made not a profit but a loss on the contract which he had failed to disclose. The Court of Appeal held that the effect of a breach of the statutory predecessor of s 317 of the 1985 Act (s 199 of the Companies Act 1948) was to make the contract voidable and the director accountable for any profit made by him on the usual equitable principles: see [1967] 3 All ER 98 at 103-104, 105-106, [1968] 1 QB 549 at 585-586, 589-590, per Lord Denning MR and Lord Wilberforce. Counsel for Mr Ward seeks to distinguish the case on the fact that the relevant article in that case was different from Guinness' art 100 in an important respect: a director's right to retain profits from contracts with the company was made expressly conditional on disclosure by the director of his interest. But in my judgment that does not affect the general statement of principle by Lord Denning MR (before he started to consider the effect of the relevant article) ([1967] 3 All ER 98 at 103, [1968] 1 QB 549 at 585):

'It seems to me that when a director fails to disclose his interest, the effect is the same as non-disclosure in contracts uberrimae fidei, or nondisclosure by a promoter who sells to the company property in which he is interested (see Re Cape Breton Co. (1884) 26 ChD 221; affd (1885) 29 ChD 795; Burland v Earle [1902] AC 83). Non-disclosure does not render the contract void or a nullity. It renders the contract voidable at the instance of the company and makes the director accountable for any secret profit which he has made.'

In my judgment art 100(C) and (D) on their true construction do not permit Mr Ward to retain any profit from a secret agreement with the company of which the disclosure required by s 317 of the 1985 Act and art 100(A) has not been made. Accordingly, on the admissions made by Mr Ward, there is no answer to Guinness' claim and, subject to questions of set-off, Guinness is entitled to judgment.

[Set-off and s 727

Mr Ward claims that, even if otherwise liable to repay the £5·2m, he is entitled at law to payment on a quantum meruit for the services he rendered. Alternatively, he says that under equitable principles in taking the account of the profit for which he is liable as a fiduciary he should be compensated for the services he has rendered: see Boardman v Phipps [1966] 3 All ER 721, [1967] 2 AC 46. Without hearing all the evidence, it is impossible to say whether or not such claims are valid or, if so, the amount to which Mr Ward will be held entitled. Therefore, says Mr Ward, no judgment can be entered which will require immediate repayment to Guinness of the £5·2m since he is entitled to set off his cross-claims against Guinness' claim. Since the cross-claims are not quantified, any set-off would have to be an equitable set-off. In Federal Commerce and Navigation Co Ltd v Molena Alpha Inc, The Nanfri, The Benfri, The Lorfri [1978] 3 All ER 1066 at 1078, [1978] QB 927 at 974 Lord Denning MR said this of equitable set-off:

We have no longer to ask ourselves: what would the courts of common law or the courts of equity have done before the Supreme Court of Judicature Act 1873? We have to ask ourselves: what should we do now so as to ensure fair dealing between the parties? This question must be asked in each case as it arises for decision; and then, from case to case, we shall build up a series of *precedents to guide those who come after us. But one thing is quite clear: it is not every cross-claim which can be deducted. It is only cross-claims that arise out of the same transaction or are closely connected with it. And it is only cross-claims which go directly to impeach the plaintiff's demands, that is, so closely connected with his demands that it would be manifestly unjust to allow him to enforce payment without taking into account the cross-claim.*

The reference to equitable set-off applying to cross-claims which impeach the plaintiff's demand reflect older authorities on equitable set-off. The question therefore is whether the alleged cross-claim impugns Guinness' title to recover the £5·2m and whether, in all the circumstances, it would be just to permit a set-off. In my judgment Mr Ward's cross-claims whether by way of quantum meruit or equitable compensation do not impugn Guinness' title to recover the £5·2m. That money has at all times been Guinness' money. From the date of its receipt by or on behalf of Mr Ward, he has held it on a constructive trust for Guinness. Guinness is now entitled to a judgment to recover its own property. The fact that, arising out of the same transaction, Mr Ward may be entitled to remuneration for his services in no way impugns Guinness' right to recover its property from Mr Ward. The case is quite different to <u>Boardman v Phipps</u> where, in taking the account of profits made by the defendant, the equitable compensation was directed to be deducted from the amount of profits, the only order for payment being as to the ultimate balance on the taking of the account. In that case, the defendants had not received any trust property: their accountability arose simply from their unauthorised use of an opportunity to make a profit, which opportunity belonged to the trust. They had not received trust money as such in the way that Mr Ward in this case has received £5·2m of Guinness' money which has at all times, in equity, remained Guinness' money. On wider principles, in my judgment it would be unfortunate if a director who has secretly received remuneration without proper authority is entitled to retain such remuneration until a possibly groundless claim on a quantum meruit has been determined. The first duty of directors and other fiduciaries who have procured that they receive money or property belonging to the company or their beneficiaries without due authorisation should be to repay what has wrongfully been abstracted. Their claim to receive some compensation on a basis different to that on which they took the money should stand as a cross-claim, not as a set-off. Similar considerations apply to the claim for relief under s 727 of the 1985 Act.

That section (which corresponds to s 61 of the Trustee Act 1925) permits the court to relieve a director from liability for breach of duty or breach of trust if he has acted honestly and reasonably and in all the circumstances ought fairly to be excused. It is clear that if the court exercises its discretion, the effect is to extinguish pro tanto any liability on the director to repay. The question therefore is whether it is impossible to obtain summary judgment for immediate repayment of the company's moneys wrongfully received by a director if he puts forward a claim for relief under s 727. There is authority on the statutory predecessor of s 61 of the 1925 Act (s 3 of the Judicial Trustee Act 1896) that a trustee who has retained part of the trust estate cannot be relieved from liability: Re Clark (1920) 150 LT 94. The case is inadequately reported and I have considerable doubt whether there is any absolute bar on relief in such circumstances, although relief must be improbable. But in the present case I do not think there is any possibility of relief under s 727.

Quite apart from the fact that Mr Ward has been and is wrongfully in possession of Guinness' money, the only basis on which he claims relief under the section is that he ought to receive remuneration or compensation for the valuable services he says he has rendered, ie relief is claimed on exactly the same grounds as those on which he has counterclaimed for a quantum meruit or equitable compensation. A judgment against him on the claim would not prevent him from pursuing such counterclaim. In my judgment in the circumstances of this case there is no possibility that if the case went to a full trial the court would exercise its jurisdiction under s 727. If Mr Ward's counterclaim succeeds, he would not require to be relieved under s 727: if the counterclaim does not succeed, Mr Ward would not have demonstrated any grounds for relief under the section. Therefore the claim under s 727 is not a bar to Guinness obtaining judgment on their claim. I will therefore give Guinness judgment on their claim against Mr Ward.

Order accordingly."

Appendix 8—Business Names Act 1985

An Act to consolidate certain enactments relating to the names under which persons may carry on business in Great Britain

1. Persons subject to this Act

(1) This Act applies to any person who has a place of business in Great Britain and who carries on business in Great Britain under a name which—

(a) in the case of a partnership, does not consist of the surnames of all partners who are individuals and the corporate names of all partners who are bodies corporate without any addition other than an addition permitted by this Act;

(b) in the case of an individual, does not consist of his surname without any addition other than one so permitted;

(c) in the case of a company, being a company which is capable of being wound up under the Companies Act 1985, does not consist of its corporate name without any addition other than one so permitted;

(d) in the case of a limited liability partnership, does not consist of its corporate name without any addition other than one so permitted].

(2) The following are permitted additions for the purposes of subsection (1):

(a) in the case of a partnership, the forenames of individual partners or the initials of those forenames or, where two or more individual partners have the same surname, the addition of "s" at the end of that surname; or

(b) in the case of an individual, his forename or its initial;

(c) in any case, any addition merely indicating that the business is carried on in succession to a former owner of the business.

2. Prohibition of use of certain business names

(1) Subject to the following subsections, a person to whom this Act applies shall not, without the written approval of the Secretary of State, carry on business in Great Britain under a name which—(a) would be likely to give the impression that the business is connected with Her Majesty's Government[, with any part of the Scottish Administration,] or with any local authority; or

(b) includes any word or expression for the time being specified in regulations made under this Act.

(2) Subsection (1) does not apply to the carrying on of a business by a person—

(a) to whom the business has been transferred on or after 26th February 1982; and

(b) who carries on the business under the name which was its lawful business name immediately before that transfer, during the period of 12 months beginning with the date of that transfer.

(3) Subsection (1) does not apply to the carrying on of a business by a person who—

(a) carried on that business immediately before 26th February 1982; and

(b) continues to carry it on under the name which immediately before that date was its lawful business name.

(4) A person who contravenes subsection (1) is guilty of an offence.

3. Words and expressions requiring Secretary of State's approval

(1) The Secretary of State may by regulations—

(a) specify words or expressions for the use of which as or as part of a business name his approval is required by section 2(1)(b); and

(b) in relation to any such word or expression, specify a Government department or other body as the relevant body for purposes of the following subsection.

(2) Where a person to whom this Act applies proposes to carry on a business under a name which is or includes any such word or expression, and a Government department or other body is specified under subsection

(1)(b) in relation to that word or expression, that person shall—

(a) request (in writing) the relevant body to indicate whether (and if so why) it has any objections to the proposal; and

(b) submit to the Secretary of State a statement that such a request has been made and a copy of any response received from the relevant body.

3. Disclosure required of persons using business names

(1) A person to whom this Act applies shall—

(a) [subject to subsections (3) and (3A)], state in legible characters on all business letters, written orders for goods or services to be supplied to the business, invoices and receipts issued in the course of the business and written demands for payment of debts arising in the course of the business—

(i) in the case of a partnership, the name of each partner,

(ii) in the case of an individual, his name.

(iii) in the case of a company, its corporate name…

(iiia) In the case of a limited liability partnership, its corporate name and the name of each member, and

(iv) in relation to each person so named, an address in Great Britain at which service of any document relating in any way to the business will be effective; and

(b) in any premises where the business is carried on and to which the customers of the business or suppliers of any goods or services to the business have access, display in a prominent position so that it may easily be read by such customers or suppliers a notice containing such names and addresses.

(2) A person to whom this Act applies shall secure that the names and addresses required by subsection (1)(a) to be stated on his business letters, or which would have been so required but for [subsection (3) or

(3A)], are immediately given, by written notice to any person with whom anything is done or discussed in the course of the business and who asks for such names and addresses.

(3) Subsection (1)(a) does not apply in relation to any document issued by a partnership of more than 20 persons which maintains at its principal place of business a list of the names of all the partners if—

(a) none of the names of the partners appears in the document otherwise than in the text or as a signatory; and

(b) the document states in legible characters the address of the partnership's principal place of business and that the list of the partners' names is open to inspection at that place.

(3A) Subsection (1)(a) does not apply in relation to any document issued by a limited liability partnership with more than 20 members which maintains at its principal place of business a list of the names of all the members if—

(a) none of the names of the members appears in the document otherwise than in the text or as a signatory; and

(b) the document states in legible characters the address of the principal place of business of the limited liability partnership and that the list of the members' names is open to inspection at that place.]

(4) Where a partnership maintains a list of the partners' names for purposes of subsection (3), any person may inspect the list during office hours.

(4A) Where a limited liability partnership maintains a list of the members' names for the purposes of subsection (3A), any person may inspect the list during office hours.]

(5) The Secretary of State may by regulations require notices under subsection (1)(b) or (2) to be displayed or given in a specified form.

(6) A person who without reasonable excuse contravenes subsection (1) or

(2), or any regulations made under subsection (5), is guilty of an offence.

(7) Where an inspection required by a person in accordance with subsection (4) [or (4A)] is refused, any partner of the partnership concerned[, or any member of the limited liability partnership concerned,] who without reasonable excuse refused that inspection, or permitted it to be refused, is guilty of an offence.

4 Civil remedies for breach of s 4

(1) Any legal proceedings brought by a person to whom this Act applies to enforce a right arising out of a contract made in the course of a business in respect of which he was, at the time the contract was made, in breach of subsection (1) or (2) of section 4 shall be dismissed if the defendant (or, in Scotland, the defender) to the proceedings shows—

(a) that he has a claim against the plaintiff (pursuer) arising out of that contract which he has been unable to pursue by reason of the latter's breach of section 4(1) or (2), or

(b) that he has suffered some financial loss in connection with the contract by reason of the plaintiff's (pursuer's) breach of section 4(1) or (2), unless the court before which the proceedings are brought is satisfied that it is just and equitable to permit the proceedings to continue.

(2) This section is without prejudice to the right of any person to enforce such rights as he may have against another person in any proceedings brought by that person.

Derivation

This section derived from the Companies Act 1981, s 30.

6 Regulations

(1) Regulations under this Act shall be made by statutory instrument and may contain such transitional provisions and savings as the Secretary of State thinks appropriate, and may make different provision for different cases or classes of case.

(2) In the case of regulations made under section 3, the statutory instrument containing them shall be laid before Parliament after the regulations are made and shall cease to have effect at the end of the period of 28 days beginning with the day on which they were made (but without prejudice to anything previously done by virtue of them or to the

making of new regulations) unless during that period they are approved by a resolution of each House of Parliament.

In reckoning this period of 28 days, no account is to be taken of any time during which Parliament is dissolved or prorogued, or during which both Houses are adjourned for more than 4 days.

(3) In the case of regulations made under section 4, the statutory instrument containing them is subject to annulment in pursuance of a resolution of either House of Parliament.

5 Offences

(1) Offences under this Act are punishable on summary conviction.

(2) A person guilty of an offence under this Act is liable to a fine not exceeding one-fifth of the statutory maximum.

(3) If after a person has been convicted summarily of an offence under section 2 or 4(6) the original contravention is continued, he is liable on a second or subsequent summary conviction of the offence to a fine not exceeding one-fiftieth of the statutory maximum for each day on which the contravention is continued (instead of to the penalty which may be imposed on the first conviction of the offence).

(4) Where an offence under section 2 or 4(6) or (7) committed by a body corporate is proved to have been committed with the consent or connivance of, or to be attributable to any neglect on the part of, any director, manager, secretary or other similar officer of the body corporate, or any person who was purporting to act in any such capacity, he as well as the body corporate is guilty of the offence and liable to be proceeded against and punished accordingly.

(5) Where the affairs of a body corporate are managed by its members, subsection (4) applies in relation to the acts and defaults of a member in connection with his functions of management as if he were a director of the body corporate.

Interpretation

(1) The following definitions apply for purposes of this Act—

"business" includes a profession;

"initial" includes any recognised abbreviation of a name;

"lawful business name", in relation to a business, means a name under which the business was carried on without contravening section 2(1) of this Act or section 2 of the Registration of Business Names Act 1916;

"local authority" means any local authority within the meaning of the Local Government Act 1972 or the Local Government (Scotland) Act 1973, the Common Council of the City of London or the Council of the Isles of Scilly;

"partnership" includes a foreign partnership;

and "surname", in relation to a peer or person usually known by a British title different from his surname, means the title by which he is known.

(2) Any expression used in this Act and also in the Companies Act 1985 has the same meaning in this Act as in that.

This Act comes into force on 1st July 1985.

Appendix 9—Company Law Reform Bill

PART X

CAPACITY OF COMPANY AND POWER OF DIRECTORS TO BIND IT

X1 Statement of company's objects

X2 A company's capacity

X3 Power of directors to bind the company

X4 Constitutional limitations: transactions involving directors or their associates

X5 Constitutional limitations: companies that are charities

Company Law Reform Bill

Part X—Capacity of company and power of directors to bind it

PART X

CAPACITY OF COMPANY AND POWER OF DIRECTORS TO BIND IT

X1 **Statement of company's objects**

(1) Unless a company's articles specifically restrict the objects of the company, its objects are unrestricted.

(2) Where a company alters its articles so as to add, remove or alter a statement of the company's objects—

(a) it must give notice to the registrar,

(b) on receipt of the notice, the registrar shall register it, and

(c) the alteration is not effective until entry of that notice on the register.

(3) Any such alteration does not affect any rights or obligations of the company or render defective any legal proceedings by or against it.

(4) In the case of a company that is a charity, the provisions of this section have effect subject to the provisions of the Charities Act 1993 (c. 10).

X2 **A company's capacity**

(1) The validity of an act done by a company shall not be called into question on the ground of lack of capacity by reason of anything in the company's constitution.

(2) This section has effect subject to section X5 (companies that are charities).

X3 Power of directors to bind the company

(1) In favour of a person dealing with a company in good faith, the power of the directors to bind the company, or authorise others to do so, is deemed to be free of any limitation under the company's constitution.

(2) For this purpose—

(a) a person "deals with" a company if he is a party to any transaction or other act to which the company is a party,

(b) a person dealing with a company—

(i) is not bound to enquire as to any limitation on the powers of the directors to bind the company or authorise others to do so,

(ii) is presumed to have acted in good faith unless the contrary is proved, and

(iii) is not to be regarded as acting in bad faith by reason only of his knowing that an act is beyond the powers of the directors under the company's constitution.

Company Law Reform Bill

Part X—Capacity of company and power of directors to bind it

2

(3) The references above to limitations on the directors' powers under the company's constitution include limitations deriving—

(a) from a resolution of the company or of any class of shareholders, or (b) from any agreement between the members of the company or of any class of shareholders.

(4) This section does not affect any right of a member of the company to bring proceedings to restrain the doing of an action that is beyond the powers of the directors. But no such proceedings lie in respect of an act to be done in fulfilment of a legal obligation arising from a previous act of the company.

(5) This section does not affect any liability incurred by the directors, or any other person, by reason of the directors' exceeding their powers.

(6) This section has effect subject to—

section X4 (transactions with directors or their associates), and

section X5 (companies that are charities).

X4 Constitutional limitations: transactions involving directors or their associates

(1) This section applies to a transaction if or to the extent that its validity depends on section X3 (power of directors deemed to be free of limitations under company's constitution in favour of person dealing with company in good faith).

Nothing in this section shall be read as excluding the operation of any other enactment or rule of law by virtue of which the transaction may be called in question or any liability to the company may arise.

(2) Where—

(a) a company enters into such a transaction, and

(b) the parties to the transaction include—

(i) a director of the company or of its holding company, or

(ii) a person connected with such a director or a body corporate with whom such a director is associated, the transaction is voidable at the instance of the company

(3) Whether or not it is avoided, any such party to the transaction as is mentioned in subsection (2)(b)(i) or (ii), and any director of the company who authorised the transaction, is liable—

(a) to account to the company for any gain he has made directly or indirectly by the transaction, and

(b) to indemnify the company for any loss or damage resulting from the transaction.

(4) The transaction ceases to be voidable if—

(a) restitution of any money or other asset which was the subject-matter of the transaction is no longer possible, or

(b) the company is indemnified for any loss or damage resulting from the transaction, or

(c) rights acquired bona fide for value and without actual notice of the directors' exceeding their powers by a person who is not party to the transaction would be affected by the avoidance, or

(d) the transaction is affirmed by the company.

Company Law Reform Bill

Part X—Capacity of company and power of directors to bind it

3

(5) A person other than a director of the company is not liable under subsection (3) if he shows that at the time the transaction was entered into he did not know that the directors were exceeding their powers.

(6) Nothing in the preceding provisions of this section affects the rights of any party to the transaction not within subsection (2)(b)(i) or (ii), but the court may, on the application of the company or any such party, make such order affirming, severing or setting aside the transaction, on such terms, as appear to the court to be just.

(7) In this section—

(a) "transaction" includes any act; and

(b) the references to a person connected with a director, and to a body corporate with which a director is associated, have the same meaning as in Part 15 (directors).

X5 Constitutional limitations: companies that are charities

(1) Sections X2 and X3 (company's capacity and power of directors to bind company) do not apply to the acts of a company that is a charity except in favour of a person who—

(a) does not know at the time the act is done that the company is a charity, or

(b) gives full consideration in money or money's worth in relation to the act in question and does not know (as the case may be)—

(i) that the act is not permitted by the company's constitution or,

(ii) that the act is beyond the powers of the directors.

(2) Where a company that is a charity purports to transfer or grant an interest in property, the fact that (as the case may be)—

(a) the act was not permitted by the company's constitution, or

(b) the directors in connection with the act exceeded any limitation on their powers under the company's constitution, does not affect the title of a person who subsequently acquires the property or any interest in it for full consideration without actual notice of any such circumstances affecting the validity of the company's act.

(3) In any proceedings arising out of subsection (1) or (2) the burden of proving—

(a) that a person knew that the company was a charity, or

(b) that a person knew that an act was not permitted by the company's constitution or was beyond the powers of the directors, lies on the person asserting that fact.

(4) Where a company registered in England and Wales or Northern Ireland is a charity the affirmation of a transaction to which section X4 applies (transactions with directors or their associates) is ineffective without the prior written consent of the Charity Commissioners.

Appendix 10—*Buchler and another v Talbot and others (the Leyland Daf case)*

The House of Lords overruled the High Court and the Court of Appeal in the recent case of Re Leyland Daf Ltd (sub nom Buchler v Talbot). In doing so, the House of Lords ruled that liquidators' expenses were not to be paid out of property subject to a floating charge which had crystallised and held that Re Barleycorn Enterprises Ltd (1970) ("Barleycorn") had been wrongly decided in the Court of Appeal.

Leyland Daf Limited ("Leyland Daf") granted a mortgage debenture in favour of a Dutch entity Stichting Ofasec ("Ofasec") in March 1992. This was to secure money lent to the group of companies headed by DAF NV, of which Leyland Daf was a member. The mortgage debenture contained fixed and floating charges over Leyland Daf's assets.

The following year, DAF NV group found itself in financial difficulty and Ofasec, in exercise of its powers under the mortgage debenture, appointed receivers to Leyland Daf, crystallising its floating charge into a fixed charge. The receivers realised the assets subject to the security, paying preferential creditors, as well as making interim payments to Ofasec. In 1996, Leyland Daf entered creditors' voluntary liquidation with a shortfall of funds to pay the full amount of liquidation costs and expenses. The question for the House of Lords was whether these should be paid out of realisations made by the receivers from the assets in priority to amounts owed to the chargeholder, Ofasec. Lord Millett, Lord Nicholls and Lord Hoffman gave concurring speeches, with which Lord Rodger and Lord Walker agreed.

As readers will be aware, on insolvency creditors of a company are paid out in the following order of priority: holders of fixed charges rank first, followed by the so-called "preferential creditors", then floating chargeholders and finally unsecured creditors. However, this was not always the case: when the category of preferential debts was created by statute in the late nineteenth century, they were a category of unsecured debts which ranked behind the claims of floating chargeholders. It soon became apparent that the law needed to change, as there would often be no surplus to pay preferential creditors after payment was made to floating chargeholders. Section 2 of the Preferential Payments in Bankruptcy (Amendment) Act 1897 (the "1897 Act") addressed this issue, providing as follows:

"In the winding up of any company...the debts mentioned in section one of the Preferential Payments in Bankruptcy Act, 1888, shall, so far as the assets of the company available for payment of general creditors may be insufficient to meet them, have priority over the claims of holders of debentures or debenture stock under any floating charge created by such company, and shall be paid accordingly out of any property comprised in or subject to such charge."

Where a company was not being wound up and a debenture holder appointed a receiver or took possession of property subject to a floating charge, section 3 of the 1897 Act provided that "the debts mentioned in section one of the said Preferential Payments Act shall be paid forthwith out of any assets coming to the hands of the receiver, or other person taking possession as aforesaid, in priority to any claim for principal or interest in respect of such debentures". Section 2 of the 1897 Act referred to preferential debts only. There was nothing to suggest that liquidation expenses should be discharged from assets subject to a debenture and nor were there any grounds for implying that this had been Parliament's intention. Whilst the statutes mentioned above had since been amended and replaced—so that the relevant provisions were currently to be found in sections 40 and 175 of the Insolvency Act 1986—their meaning had not changed.

Lord Nicholls made a distinction between a company's charged assets and its noncharged assets in the context of distributing a company's assets to creditors. He held that in the distribution of non-charged assets of the company, liquidation expenses ranked ahead of the preferential debts. However, the charged assets belonged to the debenture holders to the extent of the amounts secured. Whilst the charged assets might be eroded to the extent of the claims of preferential creditors,

"*...According a like priority in respect of liquidation expenses would represent a potentially major additional incursion into the proprietary interests of debenture holders.*" Lord Nicholls' distinction between distribution of a company's charged and non-charged assets was further developed in the speeches of Lord Hoffmann and Lord Millett. Lord Hoffmann held that there were two separate funds from which the different categories of creditor would be paid. The charged assets would be realised and funds paid to the debenture holder, subject to the company's equity of redemption. This was the so-called "debenture holder's fund". The non-charged assets—the so-called "company's fund"—would be held in trust for unsecured creditors. Each fund would bear its own costs so that the expenses of administrative receivership would be paid out of the debenture holder's fund and the expenses of the winding up would be paid out of the company's fund. Neither fund would bear the costs of administering the other,

"*...And in particular the assets comprised in the floating charge are not required to bear the costs and expenses of the winding up as well as those of the receivership.*" Lord Millett set out the two distinct funds and order of priority of payments as follows:

1. *Assets subject to a floating charge....*

(i) the costs of preserving and realising the assets;

(ii) the receiver's remuneration and the proper costs and expenses of the receivership;

(iii) the debts which are preferential in the receivership;

(iv) the principal and interest secured by the floating charge;

(v) the company.

2. *The company's free assets....*

(i) the costs of preserving and realising the assets;

(ii) the liquidator's remuneration and the proper costs and expenses of the winding up;

(iii) the debts which are preferential in the winding up;

(iv) the charge holder to the extent that the preferential debts have been paid out of assets subject to the floating charge;

(v) the general body of creditors."

In Barleycorn, the Court of Appeal had held that the costs of winding up a company were payable from property subject to a floating charge which had crystallised, in priority to the floating chargeholder. However, this was wrong, due to a misreading of the word "assets" to include not only a company's free assets but also those subject to a floating charge. The decision ignores the proprietary interest of the debenture holder in the debenture holder's fund and treats it and the company's fund as a single massed fund in which there is a single order of priorities. In holding that the Barleycorn decision was wrong, the House of Lords has clarified the position for all of a company's creditors, but this is of course particularly good news for floating chargeholders.

Appendix 14—Disqualification of Directors

<u>Buchler and another v Talbot and others</u> 2004] UKHL 9

Companies—Winding up—Liquidator—Charged assets—Costs and expenses of winding up company—Insolvency Act 1986, ss 40, <u>175</u>.

Lord Nicholls said :-

"[;1] In England and Wales floating charges are a judge-made, or judge-approved, type of security. They originated in the early days of the development of company law in the 1870s. They are a means whereby a financier, typically a bank, provides a company with money on the security of the company's assets which continue to be used and turned over in the ordinary course of business until, when certain events happen, the charge 'crystallises' into a fixed charge on the assets then within its scope. Notable among crystallising events are the appointment of a receiver by the charge holder or the company being wound up.

[2] Over the years floating charges have played an invaluable role in the development of business. They bridge a gap between businessmen and financiers. Businessmen need money but may have insufficient fixed assets to offer as security. Financiers have money but want security for any loans they make. They wish to rank ahead of the company's unsecured creditors if the business does not prosper. They wish to minimise their risks by having a charge over whatever assets a company may acquire in the course of carrying on its trade. Floating charges have provided a legal mechanism by which in these circumstances capital and business enterprise can be harnessed.

[3] Typically a floating charge extends to substantially all the assets of a company. On its face this gives a charge holder a high degree of control over the assets and fortunes of a company. At times this has been seen to work unsatisfactorily. The security afforded by a floating charge on the assets of a business, and the charge holder's ability to enforce his security, should not always be allowed to prevail. More than once Parliament has intervened to correct perceived imbalance between the rights and interests of charge holders and the rights and interests of other persons. The most recent intervention was in the Enterprise Act 2002.

[4] This appeal concerns the proper interpretation of a legislative intervention made in the early days of the history of floating charges. The issue is whether, when a company is being wound up, the costs and expenses incurred by the liquidator rank ahead of the claims of the holder of a charge which at its inception was a floating charge. The answer turns on the proper interpretation of what is now s 175(2)(b) of the Insolvency Act 1986.

The failure of the Leyland DAF group

[5] The issue arises in the winding up of Leyland Daf Ltd, one of the companies in a group headed by DAF NV. The facts are set out lucidly in the opinion of my noble and learned friend Lord Millett. I need do no more than mention the salient features in the broadest terms. In March 1992 Leyland Daf Ltd granted a mortgage debenture to Stichting Ofasec, a Dutch foundation, to secure money loaned to the group. The debenture created fixed and floating charges over the assets of Leyland Daf Ltd in the accustomed fashion. Early in 1993 the DAF NV group collapsed. Ofasec appointed receivers under the mortgage debenture, whereupon the floating charge crystallised into a fixed charge.

[6] The receivers proceeded to realise the assets comprised in the charges. They paid the receivership preferential creditors, totalling £8m. They made substantial interim distributions to Ofasec, the debenture holder. The receivers now hold, from realisations and interest, £72m. Litigation in the Netherlands, which is still continuing, has raised the prospect that these proceeds will be insufficient to meet the claims of those entitled to share in the debenture security.

[7] Leyland Daf Ltd went into creditors' voluntary winding up on 24 July 1996. The liquidators estimate that, excluding intra-group claims, the debts owing to unsecured creditors amount to £125m. Liquidators' realisations amount to £1.5m but estimated liquidation costs and expenses far exceed this amount. They total £10m. The question raised by this appeal, stated shortly, is whether the liquidation costs and expenses should be paid out of amounts realised by the charged assets in priority to the claims of the debenture holder.

The legislation

[8] The relevant law starts with the statutory creation of a class of preferential debts in the 19th century. The Companies Act 1883, s 4, made provision that to a defined extent unpaid wages and salaries of clerks, servants, labourers and workmen should be paid before all other debts in the distribution of the assets of a company being wound up under the Companies Acts 1862 and 1867. They were to rank equally among themselves and be paid in full unless the assets of the company were insufficient to meet them. Then they would abate rateably: s 5. Subject to retaining the amount needed 'for the costs of administration or otherwise' the liquidator was to discharge these preferential debts 'forthwith' as and when assets come into the liquidator's hands: s 6.

[9] In 1888 the scope of preferential debts was widened to include rates and taxes falling due, in short, within a period of twelve months preceding the commencement of the winding up: see s 1 of the Preferential Payments in Bankruptcy Act 1888.

[10] These successive statutory provisions did not affect the proprietary rights of chargees. The secured claims of debenture holders are pursued, not in the winding up, but by enforcement of the debenture holders' proprietary rights as chargees of the assets in question: In Re David Lloyd & Co (1877) 6 Ch D 339. Thus under the Acts of 1883 and 1888 the preferential debts continued to rank behind the claims of debenture holders under a floating charge created by the company. The legislation gave preferential creditors a limited degree of priority in the winding up of a company, but their status remained that of unsecured creditors. As such, along with other unsecured creditors they could lay no claim to assets charged to a debenture holder unless and until all payments secured by the debenture had been made.

[11] In practice this meant that unpaid workers, although accorded priority in a winding up, often received nothing. The debenture holder, by virtue of his (crystallised) floating charge, scooped the pool. There was no surplus available for distribution among unsecured creditors, preferential or otherwise.

[12] The law in this regard was changed by the Preferential Payments in Bankruptcy (Amendment) Act 1897. Section 2 of this Act, 'the 1897 Act', is of prime importance on this appeal. Section 2 provided:

'In the winding up of any company under the Companies Act, 1862, and the Acts amending the same, the debts mentioned in section one of the Preferential Payments in Bankruptcy Act, 1888, shall, so far as the assets of the company available for payment of general creditors may be insufficient to meet them, have priority over the claims of holders of debentures or debenture stock under any floating charge created by such company, and shall be paid accordingly out of any property comprised in or subject to such charge.'

[13] The 1897 Act made corresponding provision for what should happen if a debenture holder appointed a receiver or took possession of property comprised in a floating charge when the company was not being wound up. Section 3 provided that in such a case 'the debts mentioned in section one of the said Preferential Payments Act shall be paid forthwith out of any assets coming to the hands of the receiver, or other person taking possession as aforesaid, in priority to any claim for principal or interest in respect of such debentures'.

[14] To my mind the effect of s 2 admits of no doubt or ambiguity in the relevant respect. Thenceforth preferential debts as defined in the 1888 Act were to be paid out of the property comprised in a floating charge so far as the non-charged assets were insufficient to discharge those debts. The proprietary rights of a debenture holder were, to that extent, bitten into. That was the object and effect of the provision.

[15] I can see nothing in this provision to suggest that, additionally, liquidation expenses as such were thenceforth to be discharged out of the charged property. These expenses are not mentioned in s 2. The priority accorded by s 2 over the holder of a floating charge was confined to the 'debts' mentioned in s 1 of the 1888 Act. The language is unequivocal.

[16] Nor is there any ground for implying such an additional incursion into the debenture holders' rights in respect of their charged property. In distribution of non-charged assets of the company liquidation expenses rank ahead of the claims of preferential creditors. But, unlike the non-charged assets, the charged assets belong to the debenture holders to the extent of the amounts secured. There is nothing inherently surprising in Parliament deciding that in future the proprietary interests of a debenture holder in his fund, that is, the charged assets, shall be eroded to the extent of the claims of preferential creditors without making any similar incursion in respect of liquidation expenses. The fact that liquidation expenses enjoy priority over the claims of preferential creditors in a winding up is not of itself a reason

for according to liquidation expenses the like priority in respect of charged assets. As vividly illustrated by the facts in the present case, according a like priority in respect of liquidation expenses would represent a potentially major additional incursion into the proprietary interests of debenture holders.

[17] *This additional incursion, for which the liquidators contend on this appeal, would not be confined to cases where the company being wound up has preferential creditors. Trading companies usually do have preferential creditors when they go into liquidation. But the argument advanced by the liquidators on this appeal is that s 2 of the 1897 Act, concerned as it is with according priority to preferential creditors, had the additional effect of encroaching upon the proprietary interests of debenture holders in the charged assets in respect of liquidation expenses in all cases, that is, whether or not there existed preferential debts. I can see nothing in the language or context of this section to justify the court so interpreting this section.*

[18] *A prominent feature of Mr Snowden's submissions was that when enacting s 2 of the 1897 Act Parliament must have intended that the liquidator should be paid costs and expenses incurred by him in discharging the statutory obligation imposed by that section. It is implicit in this statutory provision, he submitted, that these costs and expenses, necessarily incurred in achieving the statutory objective, would themselves be payable out of the charged assets ahead of the claims of debenture holders.*

[19] *There is force in this submission. When interpreting statutes courts seek to further the expressed intention of Parliament by having due regard to the practicalities involved in implementing that intention. Thus, costs incurred by liquidators in realising charged assets are payable ahead of the debenture holder's claims: In Re Regents Canal Ironworks Co (1875) 3 Ch D 411, 427, per James LJ. Likewise, as it seems to me, if there are no uncharged assets and the liquidator reasonably incurs costs and expenses in identifying preferential creditors and paying them pursuant to the statutory obligation: those administrative costs and expenses, which are likely to be modest in amount, will be payable ahead of the debenture holder, just as much as they would be if the debenture holder himself, or a receiver appointed by him, had incurred costs and expenses in discharging this statutory duty.*

[20] *Building on this base Mr Snowden submitted that s 2 had a wider effect. Although s 2 did not expressly refer to liquidation expenses, the inclusion of charged assets '[i]n the winding up' of a company under s 2 necessarily also had the effect of subjecting the charged assets to payment of the costs and expenses of the liquidator incurred in the winding up. I do not agree. Costs and expenses incurred in discharging the particular duty imposed by s 2 of the 1897 Act, or its modern equivalent, are one matter, the liquidation costs and expenses as a whole are quite another. Mr Snowden's foundation stone does not form an adequate base for the purpose for which he seeks to use it.*

[21] *Successive consolidating statutes of 1908, 1929 and 1948 reproduced the effect of these provisions of the Acts of 1888 and 1897 without relevant amendment in intervening amending legislation. There were changes in the definition of preferential debts but these are not material to the purpose in hand. There were also changes in lay-out and minor changes in language. As already noted the 1883 Act, replaced by the 1888 Act, and the 1897 Act effected two separate changes in the law regarding preferential debts when a company was in course of being wound up: preferential debts were given priority over other unsecured debts and, additionally, over debenture holder's claims under a floating charge. In the Companies (Consolidation) Act 1908 these two distinct changes were telescoped into a single section. This format has been retained ever since. The current statutory provision is s 175 of the Insolvency Act 1986:*

'1) In a winding up the company's preferential debts (within the meaning given by section 386 in Part XII) shall be paid in priority to all other debts.

(2) Preferential debts—

(a) rank equally among themselves after the expenses of the winding up and shall be paid in full, unless the assets are insufficient to meet them, in which case they abate in equal proportions; and

(b) so far as the assets of the company available for payment of general creditors are insufficient to meet them, have priority over the claims of holders of debentures secured by, or holders of, any floating charge created by the company, and shall be paid accordingly out of any property comprised in or subject to that charge.'

[22] *In this Act a floating charge means a charge which 'as created' was a floating charge: s 251. This was a change introduced by the Insolvency Act 1985, s 108(3) and Sch 6, para 15. This change in the law fills a loophole mentioned by Hoffmann J in In Re Brightlife [1987] Ch 200, [1986] 3 All ER 673, 211. This change does not affect the point now under consideration.*

[23] Section 75(1) and (2)(a) of the Insolvency Act 1986 derives indirectly from s 1 of the 1888 Act. The phrase 'after the expenses of the winding up' is the modern equivalent of 'the costs of administration or otherwise' in s 1(3) of the 1888 Act and 'costs and expenses of the winding up' in s 209(3) of the 1908 Act. Section 175(2)(b) derives indirectly from s 2 of the 1897 Act, reproduced as s 209(2)(b) in the 1908 Act. There is no reason to suppose that the change in lay-out from the earlier statutes, or that these and other minor linguistic changes, were intended to achieve a different result from that obtaining under the Acts of 1888 and 1897. On the contrary, in my view the telescoped provisions of s 175 of the Insolvency Act 1986 are, for the purpose in hand, apt to produce the same result as s 2 of the 1897 Act.

The Barleycorn decision

[24] In the courts below Rimer J and the Court of Appeal, comprising Peter Gibson, Chadwick and Longmore L JJ, reached the contrary decision: see [2001] 1 BCLC 419, [2002] 1 BCLC 511. They were bound to do so, by the decision of the Court of Appeal in In Re Barleycorn Enterprises Ltd [1970] Ch 465, [1970] 2 All ER 155. In that case the issue now under consideration arose in the context of the relevant section of the Companies Act 1948, s 319. The Court of Appeal, comprising Lord Denning MR and Sachs and Phillimore L JJ, held that from 1897 the property comprised in a floating charge forms part of the 'assets' of a company for the purposes of paying (1) costs and expenses of winding up as well as (2) preferential debts. For the reasons given above I respectfully disagree with limb (1) of this proposition.

[25] I would allow this appeal.

LORD HOFFMANN:

My Lords,

[26] The reasoning of the Court of Appeal in this case goes as follows. The expenses of winding-up are payable out of an insolvent company's funds in priority to the claims of unsecured creditors, whether preferential or otherwise. The claims of preferential creditors, so far as unpaid out the company's funds, are payable out of the debenture-holder's funds. It therefore follows that the expenses of winding up are payable out of the debenture-holder's funds.

[27] I find this hard to follow. If A has priority over B in respect of payment out of the proceeds of Blackacre and B has priority over C in respect of payment out of the proceeds of Whiteacre, why does it follow that A has any right to payment out of Whiteacre? But that was the reasoning of the Court of Appeal in In Re Barleycorn Enterprises Ltd [1970] Ch 465, which was not merely followed but endorsed by the Court of Appeal in this case.

[28] The winding up of a company is a form of collective execution by all its creditors against all its available assets. The resolution or order for winding up divests the company of the beneficial interest in its assets. They become a fund which the company thereafter holds in trust to discharge its liabilities: Ayerst (Inspector of Taxes) v C & K (Construction) Ltd [1976] AC 167, [1975] 2 All ER 537, 50 TC 651. It is a special kind of trust because neither the creditors nor anyone else have a proprietary beneficial interest in the fund. The creditors have only a right to have the assets administered by the liquidator in accordance with the provisions of the Insolvency Act 1986: see In Re Calgary and Edmonton Land Co Ltd (In liquidation) [1975] 1 All ER 1046, [1975] 1 WLR 355, 359. But the trust applies only to the company's property. It does not affect the proprietary interests of others.

[29] When a floating charge crystallises, it becomes a fixed charge attaching to all the assets of the company which fall within its terms. Thereafter the assets subject to the floating charge form a separate fund in which the debenture holder has a proprietary interest. For the purposes of paying off the secured debt, it is his fund. The company has only an equity of redemption; the right to retransfer of the assets when the debt secured by the floating charge has been paid off. It is this equity of redemption which forms part of the fund held on trust for the company's creditors which arises upon a winding up.

[30] Putting aside any fixed charges, the position is therefore that if a company is in both administrative receivership and liquidation, its former assets are comprised in two quite separate funds. Those which were subject to the floating charge ("the debenture-holder's fund") belong beneficially to the debenture-holder. The company has only an equity of redemption. Those which were not subject to the floating charge ("the company's fund") are held in trust for unsecured creditors. In the usual case in which the whole of the company's assets and undertaking are subject to the floating charge, the company's fund will consist only of the equity of redemption in the debenture-holder's fund.

[31] In principle, each fund bears its own costs. The expenses of the administrative receivership are borne by the debenture-holder's fund. The expenses of winding up are borne by the company's fund. The debenture-holder has no interest in the winding up and the unsecured creditors have no interest in the administrative receivership. So there is no reason why either group should contribute to the expenses of the other. Occasionally (for example, if no receiver has been appointed) a liquidator will realise an asset forming part of the debenture-holder's fund. As the debenture-holder is entitled to the proceeds, it is right that he should pay the cost of realisation: see In Re Regent's Canal Ironworks Company (1875) 3 Ch App 411. But the debenture-holder has no liability for the general costs of the winding up.

[32] The general rule is that unsecured creditors are entitled to share pari passu in the company's fund. But the Companies Act 1883 introduced (by analogy with the law of bankruptcy) the concept of preferential debts, to be paid out of the company's fund in priority to other unsecured creditors. Section 1 of the Preferential Payments in Bankruptcy Act 1888 listed these claims and said that "in the distribution of the assets of any company being wound up under the Companies Act 1862" they should be paid in priority to all other debts.

[33] Section of the Preferential Payments in Bankruptcy (Amendment) Act 1897 extended the rights of preferential creditors by giving them a claim on the debenture-holder's fund:

"In the winding up of any company…[preferential debts] shall, so far as the assets of the company available for payment of general creditors may be insufficient to meet them, have priority over the claims of holders of debentures or debenture stock under any floating charge created by such company, and shall be paid accordingly out of any property comprised in or subject to such charge."

[34] The provisions of the 1888 and 1897 Acts have since been consolidated and reproduced in successive Companies Acts and are now contained in s 175 of the Insolvency Act 1986. But there is nothing to suggest that any of these consolidating Acts was intended to alter the effect of the original Acts. So the question is whether the 1897 Act changed the rule that the costs of winding up are payable out of the company's fund and not out of the debenture-holder's fund.

[35] The 1897 Act is not a particularly sophisticated piece of legislation. It says that if preferential creditors have not been paid out of the company's fund, they shall be entitled to resort to the debenture-holder's fund. It has absolutely nothing to say about the costs of the winding up. And there is no reason why it should have impliedly changed the law on this point.

[36] The contrary reasoning of the Court of Appeal in In Re Barleycorn Enterprises Ltd [1970] Ch 465, [1970] 2 All ER 155, [1970] 2 WLR 898 is best exemplified by a quotation from the judgment of Phillimore LJ, at p 476:

"Mr Wooton's submission [for the debenture-holder]…was that if there were…assets not covered by some floating charge…then the proper order for payment would be: first, the costs of the winding up; secondly, the preferential debts; and thirdly, the floating charge. On the other hand if there were no free assets and everything was covered by the floating charge, then the order would be: first, the preferential debts; secondly the floating charge; and, thirdly, the costs of the winding up…I find it very difficult to defend the logic which would make the order of priority as between costs and preferential debts dependent upon whether or not there was a floating charge."

[37] This passage is, with all respect, a complete muddle. It amounts to saying that the judge cannot see the logic of making the question of which fund should bear the costs depend upon whether they were incurred in connection with that fund. It ignores the proprietary interest of the debenture holder in the debenture holder's fund and treats it and the company's fund as a single massed fund in which there is a single order of priorities. But there is nothing in the 1897 Act or any subsequent legislation which can have brought about the radical change of depriving the debenture-holder of his proprietary interest in the debenture-holder's fund and giving him instead a preferential claim (after the expenses of winding up and the preferential creditors but before the unsecured creditors) in a single amalgamated fund.

[38] For these reasons and those of my noble and learned friend Lord Millett, I think that In re Barleycorn Enterprises Ltd [1970] Ch 465 was wrongly decided and I would allow the appeal.

LORD MILLETT:

My Lords,

[39] The question in this appeal, as formulated by the parties, is whether the expenses incurred by a liquidator in winding up an insolvent company are payable out of the assets comprised in a crystallised floating charge in priority to the claims of the charge holder. The question assumes importance only where, as is unfortunately often the case, the company has insufficient uncharged (or "free") assets to meet the costs

of the winding up. The Judge (Rimer J) and the Court of Appeal (Peter Gibson, Chadwick and Longmore LJJ) held that in such circumstances they are so payable.

[40] In reaching this decision the Court of Appeal, as they were bound to do, followed the reasoning of the Court of Appeal (Lord Denning MR, Sachs and Phillimore LJJ) in In re Barleycorn Enterprises Ltd, Mathias and Davies (a Firm) v Down [1970] Ch 465. In that case the charge did not crystallise until the company was ordered to be wound up and no receiver was ever appointed, so that the assets in question, though subject to the floating charge, remained under the control of the liquidator. The Court of Appeal decided that in such a case the expenses of the winding up are payable out of the assets subject to the charge in priority to both the preferential creditors and the claims of the charge holder. In the present case the charge holder appointed receivers who collected and realised the assets subject to the floating charge and paid the preferential creditors before the commencement of the winding up. The earlier decision is thus technically distinguishable; but it cannot sensibly be distinguished, for its rationale applies as much to the one situation as to the other. The question for the House, therefore, is whether Barleycorn was rightly decided.

[41] As formulated, the question appears to be concerned with priorities. But the real question is whether the expenses of a winding up are payable out of charged assets at all. If they are, there is no doubt that they are payable in priority to the claims of the charge holder. If they are not, questions of priority do not arise.

The facts

[42] The facts are not in dispute. They are set out in full in the judgment of Rimer J reported at [2001] BCLC 419 at pp 420-422 and may be briefly summarised. The company in liquidation is Leyland Daf Limited ("the Company"), an English company and a member of a Dutch group of companies. In 1992 the company issued debentures which contained a floating charge over the whole or substantially the whole of its undertaking. In the following year the group collapsed and the charge holder appointed joint administrative receivers ("the receivers"). On their appointment the floating charge crystallised into a fixed charge. The receivers proceeded to realise the assets comprised in the charge and paid the debts (amounting to some £8m) which were preferential in the receivership. They also made interim distributions of some £110m to the charge holder towards satisfying the secured indebtedness. At the time of the hearing before Rimer J the receivers still held some £61m derived from the assets that were subject to the charge. That figure has since increased (with interest and other realisations) to some £72m.

[43] On 24 July 1996, that is to say more than three years after the Receivers' appointment, the company went into creditors' voluntary liquidation and the respondents ("the liquidators") were appointed joint liquidators.

[44] Liquidation expenses to date, including the liquidators' remuneration and corporation tax, amount to over £9.5m before VAT and interest on overdue accounts. This figure does not include any provision for future costs of the liquidation, which are unquantifiable but are said to be likely to exceed £1m. The liquidators have been able to realise only some £1.4m. Furthermore proceedings are still pending in the Netherlands which may have the result that the charged assets are insufficient to meet the claims of the secured creditors. There are thus likely to be insufficient free assets to meet the expenses of the liquidation, and unless the charged assets are available to pay them in priority to the claims of the charge holder there will be nothing with which to pay the greater part of the costs of winding up the Company.

[45] In these circumstances the liquidators have sought and obtained from the courts below a declaration that the liquidation expenses are payable out of the charged assets in the receivers' hands in priority to the claims of the secured creditors.

[46] Two matters should be mentioned at this point. First, the liquidators make no claim to money which was distributed by the receivers to the charge holder before the commencement of the winding up. Secondly, the present proceedings raise a question of principle. They are not concerned with the propriety or proper amount of any particular sum claimed to be an expense of the liquidation.

The current statutory provisions

[47] The question turns on the proper construction of ss 40(2) and 175(2)(b) of the Insolvency Act 1986 ("the 1986 Act"); although of these only s 40 is strictly applicable. Sections 40 and 175 of the 1986 Act are in the following terms:

"40. (1) The following applies, in the case of a company, where a receiver is appointed on behalf of the holders of any debentures of the company secured by a charge which, as created, was a floating charge.

(2) If the company is not at the time in course of being wound up, its preferential debts (within the meaning given to that expression by section 386 in Part XII) shall be paid out of the assets coming to the hands of the receiver in priority to any claims for principal or interest in respect of the debentures.

(3) Payments made under this section shall be recouped, as far as may be, out of the assets of the company available for payment of general creditors.

175. (1) In a winding up, the company's preferential debts (within the meaning given by section 386 in Part XII) shall be paid in priority to all other debts.

(2) Preferential debts (a) rank equally among themselves after the expenses of the winding up and shall be paid in full, unless the assets are insufficient to meet them, in which case they abate in equal proportions; and

(b) so far as the assets of the company available for payment of general creditors are insufficient to meet them, have priority over the claims of holders of debentures secured by, or holders of, any floating charge created by the company, and shall be paid accordingly out of any property comprised in or subject to that charge.

[48] *Section 40 is contained in Part III of the Act which forms part of a group of sections headed "Provisions applicable to every receivership." It contains no reference to the expenses of the winding up, which would be out of place in a section dealing with receivership. Section 175 is contained in Part IV of the Act and forms part of a group of sections headed "Provisions of general application in winding up." Subsection (2)(a) contains a reference to the expenses of the winding up but only to confirm their priority over the preferential debts when these are being paid in the winding up. Both sections are concerned exclusively with the priority of preferential debts, one in a receivership, where they are given priority to the claims of the charge holder, and the other in a winding up, where they are postponed to the expenses of the winding up but are given priority to the claims of the charge holder.*

[49] *The relevant statutory provisions have a long history, having been introduced in two stages towards the end of the 19th Century and successively re-enacted in later Acts in substantially similar terms. At the first stage a class of unsecured debts was given priority in a winding up. At the second stage such debts were made payable so far as necessary out of the assets comprised in a floating charge (but not out of the assets comprised in a fixed charge) in priority to the claims of the holder of the charge.*

[50] *Provision for the preferential payment of wages and salaries due to certain classes of employees was introduced in personal bankruptcy in 1825 and was extended to the winding up of companies by the Companies Act 1883 ("the 1883 Act"). Section 4 of the 1883 Act provided that*

in the distribution of the assets of any company being wound up under the Companies Acts 1862 or 1867"

certain categories of debts should be paid in priority to others. Section 5 provided that such debts should rank equally among themselves and be paid in full unless there were insufficient assets to meet them, in which case they should abate in equal proportions among themselves. Section 6 made it clear that payment of the costs and expenses of the winding up took priority over the preferential debts. These sections were re-enacted in the like terms by s 1 of the Preferential Payments in Bankruptcy Act 1888 ("the 1888 Act").

[51] *Bankruptcy and companies liquidation are concerned with the realisation and distribution of the insolvent's free assets among the unsecured creditors. They are not concerned with assets which have been charged to creditors as security, whether by way of fixed or floating charge. Secured creditors can resort to their security for the discharge of their debts outside the bankruptcy or winding up. Assets subject to a charge belong to the charge holder to the extent of the amounts secured by them; only the equity of redemption remains the property of the chargor and falls within the scope of the chargor's bankruptcy or winding up. As James LJ observed in In re Regents Canal Ironworks Co, Ex p Grissell [1877] 3 Ch. D. 411, 427 charge holders are creditors*

to whom the [charged] property belong[s] with a specific right to the property for the purpose of paying their debts. Such a creditor is a person who is to be considered as entirely outside the company, who is merely seeking to enforce a claim, not against the company, but to his own property.

[52] *The 1883 and 1888 Acts were concerned with the distribution of "the assets of any company being wound up". They were not concerned with assets to the extent to which they belonged to secured creditors, and accordingly did not affect assets over which the company had given a*

charge whether fixed or floating. Preferential creditors were thus given priority over other unsecured creditors in the distribution of the company's free assets, but like them were postponed to the expenses of the winding up and had no right to be paid out of any charged assets.

[53] After several successive re-enactments these provisions are now reproduced in ss 175(1) and (2)(a) of the 1986 Act where the language has been modernised but (save for the definition of "a floating charge") without effecting any change of substance. Section 175(1) opens with the words "In a winding up" and like their predecessors subsections (1) and (2)(a) are concerned with the distribution of the assets in a winding up, that is to say with the distribution of the company's free assets after the costs and expenses of the winding up have been paid or provided for.

[54] It would clearly have been inappropriate to allow unsecured but preferential debts to be paid out of assets charged by way of fixed charge in priority to the claims of the holder of the charge. This would have been an unwarranted interference with the property rights of the charge holder. By making it very difficult for businesses to raise money on the security of their assets it would also have been contrary to the interests of both lenders and borrowers. But the development of the floating charge, which enabled a company to grant a charge over the whole or substantially the whole of its undertaking, and which was still of recent origin in 1883, changed the picture. The existence of a floating charge deprived the preferential creditors of much of the benefit which the 1883 and 1888 Acts were intended to give them. It enabled the charge holder to withdraw all or most of the assets of an insolvent company from the scope of the winding up and leave the liquidator with little more than an empty shell and nothing with which to pay preferential debts. Accordingly the Preferential Payments in Bankruptcy (Amendment) Act 1897 ("the 1897 Amendment Act") made the preferential debts payable if and so far as necessary out of the proceeds of a floating charge in priority to the debt secured by the charge.

[55] The 1897 Amendment Act did not affect the operation of the 1888 Act in any relevant respect. The 1888 Act continued to govern the payment of preferential debts out of the assets comprised in the winding up. What the 1897 Amendment Act did was to allow the preferential creditors recourse if necessary to a further source for payment of their debts, viz the assets comprised in a floating charge. Section 2 applied in a winding up (whether or not there was also a receivership). Section 3 applied in a receivership (but only if the company was not in the course of being wound up at the relevant date).

[56] Section of the 1897 Amendment Act provided that in the winding up of a company the preferential debts should, so far as the assets of the company available for payment of general creditors were insufficient to meet them, have priority over the claims of holders of any floating charge and be paid accordingly out of the property comprised in such charge. This later became s 319(5) of the Companies Act 1948 ("the 1948 Act") and is now s 175(2)(b) of the 1986 Act.

[57] It is necessary to appreciate what s 2 of the 1897 Amendment Act and its successors did and, even more importantly, what they did not do. They applied in the winding up of a company where the assets available for payment of general creditors were insufficient to meet the preferential debts in full. So the assets available for payment of general creditors in a winding up remained the primary source of payment of the preferential debts. Such assets do not include charged assets, which are not available for payment of the general body of creditors until the claims of the charge holder have been satisfied. They are what remains of the company's free assets after the expenses of the winding up have been paid or provided for. The greater such expenses the less that is left for the general creditors and consequently the less that is available for the preferential creditors. So far as there were insufficient assets after the expenses of the winding up had been paid or provided for to enable the preferential debts to be paid in full, s 2 of the 1897 Amendment Act and its successors made them payable out of the assets subject to the floating charge.

[58] But s 2 and its successors did not authorise any of the costs and expenses of the winding up to be paid out of the assets subject to the floating charge, nor was there any reason for them to do so. Of course, if there were insufficient free assets to meet the expenses of the winding up in full, there would be nothing left to meet the preferential debts, and the whole of those debts would fall to be paid out of the assets comprised in the floating charge. There would also be nothing with which to pay the balance of the expenses of the winding up. Like the debts due to the ordinary unsecured creditors these would remain unpaid. But so they would before 1897: James LJ had already drawn attention to the fact that those who render services to an insolvent company or person frequently find that they have to go without payment, a result which did not strike him as unjust: see the Regents Canal case 3 Ch D 411, 426. If this was a hardship, it was not one which the 1897 Amendment Act was intended to remedy. Its purpose was to provide a secondary fund for the payment of the preferential debts, not to relieve liquidators by making new provision for the payment of the costs of a winding up at the expense of the holder of a floating charge.

[59] Section of the 1897 Amendment Act applied if, and only if, (i) a receiver was appointed under a floating charge; or (ii) possession was taken by or on behalf of the charge holder of any property comprised in such a charge; and (iii) the company was not at the time in course

of being wound up. In such a case preferential debts were made payable out of any assets coming to the hands of the receiver or charge holder in priority to any principal and interest secured by the charge. The section also provided that any payments to preferential creditors should be recouped as far as might be out of the assets available for general creditors.

[60] Section is now reproduced partly in s 40 of the 1986 Act (where a receiver is appointed) and partly in s 196 of the Companies Act 1985 as substituted by Sch 13 Pt 1 of the 1986 Act (where possession of any of the charged assets is taken by or on behalf of the charge holder).

[61] The effect of ss 2 and 3 of the 1897 Amendment Act taken together was to make the company's free assets the primary source for the payment of preferential debts but only after the costs of winding up the company had been paid or provided for. To the extent that such free assets were insufficient to pay the preferential debts in full, the balance of such debts (but not unpaid liquidation expenses) was payable out of the assets comprised in the charge in priority to the principal and interest secured by the charge. Any such payment would reduce the amount available for the discharge of the debt secured by the charge and might leave it partly or wholly unpaid. The receiver's duty (or that of the charge holder who had taken possession of the charged assets) was to pay the preferential debts "forthwith"; and it was possible that they would be paid out of the assets comprised in the charge even though it later appeared that there were free assets available out of which they ought to have been paid. In such circumstances the charge holder, to the extent that the secured debt was not discharged, was entitled to recoup such payments by participating in the distribution of the company's free assets in the winding up after the expenses of the winding up had been paid or provided for.

The costs of realisation

[62] In considering the incidence of the costs and expenses of the winding up it must be borne in mind that there are two distinct funds: (i) the proceeds of the free assets which belong to the company and are administered by the liquidator in a winding up and (ii) the proceeds of the assets comprised in a floating charge which belong to the charge holder to the extent of the security and are administered by the receiver. In principle, and save to the extent, if any, that statute may make provision to the contrary, the costs of administering each fund are borne by the fund in question. In principle, therefore, the expenses of a winding up are borne by the assets comprised in the winding up, that is to say the company's free assets, and the expenses of a receivership are borne by the assets comprised in the floating charge.

[63] The costs of realising a particular property, however, must be distinguished from the general expenses of the winding up or receivership. The costs of realisation are deductible from the proceeds of the property realised, whether it is realised by the liquidator or the receiver, for it is only the net proceeds of the property which are comprised in the winding up or receivership as the case may be. Costs incurred in preserving an asset are treated in the same manner. The costs of preserving or realising assets comprised in a floating charge, if incurred by the liquidator, may therefore be recouped by him out of the charged assets in priority to the claims of the charge holder: see the Regents Canal case 3 Ch D 411, 427.

In re Barleycorn Enterprises Ltd

[64] These principles were well understood before Barleycorn [1970] Ch 465, but they were subverted by the decision of the Court of Appeal in that case, which decided for the first time that the costs of winding up a company were payable out of property comprised in a floating charge (which had crystallised when the company was ordered to be wound up) in priority to the claims of the holder of the charge.

[65] The case concerned a company which went into compulsory liquidation after having granted its bank a floating charge over the whole of its undertaking. At the date of the winding up order its assets amounted to £4,744. Preferential debts amounted to £5,161; the debt secured by the floating charge amounted to £6,972, of which £3,000 represented money advanced for wages and was included in the figure of £5,161.

[66] On any view the preferential debts exhausted all the assets. There was nothing left for the general body of unsecured creditors or for the bank as the holder of a floating charge. There was no advantage to be gained by appointing a receiver or taking possession of the charged assets and the bank did not do so. The Official Receiver instructed a firm of chartered accountants to prepare a statement of affairs for the purpose of the winding up. This was a proper expense of the winding up, and the question (as formulated by Lord Denning MR) was whether it ranked behind the preferential debts and the claims of the bank, or whether it came first. The Court of Appeal held that it came first and was payable in priority to the preferential debts.

[67] It may be observed in passing that this ruling was exclusively at the expense of the preferential creditors. On any view the bank was due to receive nothing by virtue of its security. The Court of Appeal's decision had the result that a statute passed for the benefit of the company's workers could well benefit the liquidator (by enabling him to recoup his expenses of administering one fund by taking them out of another for the administration of which he was not responsible) without benefiting the workers at all. A curiosity of the case is that there would have been no answer to the accountants' claim if they had persuaded the bank to release its security, which was worthless. But the bank would no doubt have refused to do so, since it was also the largest single preferred creditor.

[68] Lord Denning MR, with whose judgment Sachs and Phillimore LJJ agreed, acknowledged, at p 473, that in the 1883 Act the word "assets" meant only the company's free assets, and that "in those days" when a floating charge crystallised on a winding up the property comprised in the charge did not belong to the company but to the charge holder. If the floating charge covered all the property of the company the charge holder took it all, subject only to the costs of realising it. But, he said, in 1888 and 1897 Parliament began to use the word "assets" in a different sense to include not only the free assets but also all those assets which were subject to the floating charge. It used the words in this new sense in the statute which created, for the first time, preferred payments in a winding up.

[69] Although it does not affect his reasoning, Lord Denning's chronology was at fault and his references to 1888 and the 1888 Act were a slip. Preferential payments were created for the first time in corporate insolvency by the 1883 Act, not the 1888 Act; and if Parliament gave such payments priority over the floating charge it was by the 1897 Amendment Act, not by the 1888 Act which merely re-enacted the 1883 Act. But nothing turns on this.

[70] Lord Denning acknowledged that it was "unusual" (a better word might have been "unprecedented" or even "heretical") to interpret a later statute as changing the meaning of a word in an earlier one without changing the word itself but, he said, this was necessary in order to make sense of the legislation as a whole. He cited the then current s 319 of the 1948 Act and emphasised the word "assets" in subss (5)(a) (now s 175(2)(a) of the 1986 Act) and (6) (repealed by the 1986 Act and replaced by the insertion of the words "after the expenses of the winding up" in s 175 (2)(a)). He contrasted the word "assets" with the expression "the assets of the company available for payment of general creditors" in subsection (5)(b) (now s 175(2)(b) of the 1986 Act). These passages, he said, showed that since 1897 the holder of a floating charge could no longer sweep up all the company's property for his own benefit. The costs and expenses of the winding up had to be paid before the charge holder took any of it. Accordingly, he ruled, the order of payment was: (i) the costs of the winding up; (ii) the preferential payments; (iii) the bank as holder of the floating charge; (iv) the unsecured creditors.

[71] This is certainly the correct order of payment out of the company's free assets. These fall to be administered by the liquidator in the winding up and unless otherwise provided the costs of administering them are payable out of them in priority to the claims of creditors. But there was nothing in the 1897 Amendment Act or s 319 of the Companies Act 1948 to make them payable out of the charged assets.

[72] With all respect to Lord Denning, I think that his reasoning was based upon a misreading of s 319. He recognised that the "assets of the company available for payment of general creditors" means the company's free assets; they cannot possibly include assets which have been charged in favour of a third party and which are consequently not available for payment of general creditors. By contrasting this expression with the use of the word "assets" alone in subsections (5)(a) and (6) he evidently reasoned that the latter expression included the charged assets also.

[73] In the context of a winding up the most natural meaning of the words "the assets" is "the assets of the company being wound up", that is to say its free assets. Once the words are extended to include assets charged in favour of a third party by way of security it is difficult to see why they include assets subject to a floating charge but not a fixed charge. But in fact a close analysis of s 319 shows that the word "assets" in subsections (5)(a) and (6) means the company's free assets.

[74] Subsection (5)(a) explains how the preferential debts are to rank among themselves. It is ancillary to sub-s (1), which directs that in a winding up certain classes of debts are to be paid in priority to all other debts. This carries the necessary implication that they are payable out of the same fund, for unless the debts are competing with one another for payment out of the same fund there can be no question of priority between them. The "other debts" of the company are payable exclusively out of its free assets; and a direction that preferential debts must be paid in full in priority to them unless "the assets" are insufficient to meet them is a direction to pay them in full in priority to the other debts unless the assets out of which they are both payable, ie the free assets, are insufficient to meet them.

[75] Subsection (6) was also ancillary to sub-s (1) and was purely procedural. It was concerned with timing of payment and proof of debt. It was in the following terms:

"(6) Subject to the retention of such sums as may be necessary for the costs and expenses of the winding up, the foregoing debts shall be discharged forthwith so far as the assets are sufficient to meet them, and in the case of the debts to which priority is given by paragraph (e) of subsection (1) of this section formal proof thereof shall not be required except in so far as is otherwise provided by general rules."

The first part of the subsection down to the words "so far as the assets are sufficient to meet them" provided for immediate payment of the preferential debts. It was taken almost verbatim from s 6 of the 1883 Act, which did not authorise payment of such debts out of assets comprised in a floating charge, and where, as Lord Denning accepted, at p 473, the words "the assets" meant the company's free assets. The last part of the subsection, which dispensed with the need for formal proof of certain preferential debts, was added by the Companies Act 1929. The subsection was re-enacted by s 614 of the Companies Act 1985 and then repealed and replaced by the insertion of the words "after the expenses of the winding up" in s 175(2)(a) of the 1986 Act which, it will be remembered, is the current re-enactment of the 1883 Act which gave the preferential debts priority in the distribution of the company's free assets.

[76] The statutory history alone is sufficient to demonstrate that "the assets" in s 319(6) meant the company's free assets and did not include the assets comprised in a floating charge. But this is also borne out by the language of the subsection itself. The "foregoing debts" which are to be discharged forthwith "so far as the assets are sufficient to meet them" are the preferential debts which subsection (1) has directed shall be payable "in priority to all other debts". The "other debts" are the debts of the company as at the date of the winding up which are payable out of the company's free assets alone. They do not include the costs and expenses of the winding up itself, which retain their priority over the debts whether preferential or not. In directing that the preferential debts should be paid "forthwith", therefore, it was necessary to preserve the priority of the costs and expenses of the winding up by authorising the liquidator to retain sufficient sums to meet the anticipated costs and expenses of the winding up before paying the preferential debts.

[77] Accordingly s 319 provided that preferential debts should (i) be paid in priority to (and therefore out of the same fund as) all other debts (which were payable out of the company's free assets alone) but only after the costs and expenses of the winding up had been paid or provided for; and (ii) be paid (so far as "the assets" were sufficient to meet them) "forthwith" subject to the retention of sufficient funds to meet such costs and expenses. In this context "the assets" must mean the assets out of which the preferential and other debts both were payable, that is to say the company's free assets. The liquidator was not authorised to retain any part of the assets comprised in a floating charge, which would have to bear the costs and expenses of any receivership, to meet the additional costs of a winding up in which the charge holder did not participate and from which he derived no benefit.

[78] Subsection (5)(b), re-enacting s 2 of the 1897 Amendment Act, preserves the priority of the expenses of the winding up and gives the preferential debts priority over the claims of the charge holder but only in the distribution of "the assets of the company available for payment of general creditors". This expression confirms the priority of the liquidation expenses but only out of the company's free assets, and it is used, not (as Lord Denning seems to have assumed) in contrast to the term "the assets" in subsections (5)(b) and (6), but in contrast to "any property comprised in or subject to that charge."

[79] The decision in Barleycorn was clearly contrary to the understanding of the profession at the time. Lord Denning dismissed the statements to the contrary in all the standard text books (Buckley, Gore-Browne, Palmer, Pennington, Halsbury) as simply erroneous. He preferred instead a comment in the 1938 10th edition of "the little book by Mr Topham on Company Law" which was written for students (see p 475). I think that Lord Denning misunderstood the passage in question. Mr Topham wrote, at p 280, that the preferential payments must be paid before the debenture holders "but not before the costs of liquidation": In re Glyncorrwg Colliery Co Ltd [1926] Ch 951. That was a receivership case; it established that the costs of the receivership (including the cost of realising the property comprised in the charge) had priority to the claims of the charge holder. Mr Topham cannot have meant that the liquidation expenses also had priority over the claims of the charge holder. He was also the joint author of the 1933 15th edition of a standard practitioner's book, Palmer's Company Law, which stated, at p 457 that the costs and expenses of the winding up were payable in priority to all other claims; but that

"this does not give priority over secured creditors of the company except so far as the liquidator's costs are costs of preservation or realisation, of which the secured creditor has had the benefit..."

It seems likely that in his students' handbook Mr Topham used the word "liquidation", not as meaning "winding up", but as meaning "realisation."

[80] I think that Lord Denning may have trapped himself by his own formulation of the question. By describing the case as one which involved a question of priorities, he may have made the unarticulated assumption that the claims in question were payable out of the same

fund in competition with one another. They were not. There were no free assets to be administered in the winding up, and nothing out of which the costs and expenses of the liquidation could be paid. The assets in the liquidator's hands were all subject to a floating charge which had crystallised on the winding up, and subject to the costs of realising and distributing them (which did not include the preparation of a statement of affairs for the Official Receiver) they were payable to the preferential creditors and (had the funds been sufficient) to the bank as holder of the floating charge.

[81] Phillimore LJ said that he found it very difficult to defend the logic which would make the order of priority as between costs and preferential debts dependent upon whether or not there was a floating charge. The same unarticulated assumption is present here. Questions of priority arise only between interests which compete with each other for payment out of the same fund. It would certainly be difficult to defend the logic which made such a question depend upon whether or not there was a floating charge. The significance of the floating charge is, not that it alters priorities for payment out of a single fund, but that it brings a second fund into existence with its own set of priorities.

[82] In my opinion Barleycorn was wrongly decided and should be overruled.

The meaning of "floating charge"

[83] Even before the decision in Barleycorn a possible defect had been revealed in the drafting of the legislation. In In Re Griffin Hotel Co Ltd [1941] Ch. 129, [1940] 4 All ER 324 Bennett J had construed the expression "floating charge" in the relevant statute to mean a charge which was still floating at the date of the winding up. If the charge holder succeeded in appointing a receiver, or the charge automatically crystallised, before the moment at which the company was put into liquidation, the preferential creditors would have no priority. This was corrected in Australia, where the expression "floating charge" was defined to mean a charge which was "a floating charge at the date of its creation". Once a floating charge, always a floating charge for the purpose of the priority of the preferential debts. The Cork Committee thought that this was probably the test in England also, but considered that it would be prudent to add a definition on the lines of the Australian legislation; "Insolvency Law and Practice" (June 1982) (Cmnd 8558) p 356, para 1578; and this was done in the 1986 Act.

[84] Such a change would not have affected the position in Barleycorn, where no receiver was appointed and the charge was still floating at the moment of the winding up. But it does affect the position in the present case, where the receiver was appointed and the charge crystallised long before the date of the winding up order. But for the change in the definition of "floating charge" the preferential debts (let alone the costs and expenses of the winding up) would not have enjoyed priority over the claims of the charge holder under s 40 (which is in fact the relevant Section) or s 175.

[85] The decision in Barleycorn caused no difficulty in the great majority of cases before the 1986 Act, because the floating charge normally extended to the whole or substantially the whole of the company's assets and the receiver was usually appointed and the charge crystallised before the winding up. (In the case of a compulsory liquidation the relevant date was the date on which the winding up order was made and not the date on which the winding up petition was presented: see In re Christonette International Ltd. [1982] 3 All ER 225, [1982] 1 WLR 1245). This may serve to explain why the decision in Barleycorn seems to have escaped the notice of the Cork Committee.

[86] After the 1986 Act, however, the decision acquired greater significance. Its history since has been one in which judges, bound by the decision, have wrestled with the problem of avoiding the absurdities to which it could lead. In MC Bacon Ltd. [1991] Ch. 127, [1990] 3 WLR 646 a liquidator claimed that the costs of an unsuccessful attempt to set a floating charge aside should be paid out of the assets subject to the charge in priority to the claims of the charge holder. But for the decision in Barleycorn the claim could not have got off the ground. A more absurd and unjust outcome could hardly be imagined. The court was able to avoid it only by finding a way to disallow the costs of the action as recoverable expenses of the liquidation.

[87] The Court of Appeal were bound by Barleycorn and were right to apply it. But they went out of their way to endorse it. It is not necessary to deal at length with their reasoning. It is sufficient to say that it is marred by the same misconstruction of the statutory provisions and the same confusion between priority and property as vitiates the decision in Barleycorn itself.

[88] Since there are two distinct funds which have not been pooled, which belong to different parties, which are actually or potentially administered by different office holders and which are subject to different statutory regimes (and with different definitions of preferential debts) there are two different sets of priorities. They are as follows:

1 Assets subject to a floating charge: (Section 40 of the 1986 Act):

(i) the costs of preserving and realising the assets;

(ii) the receiver's remuneration and the proper costs and expenses of the receivership;

(iii) the debts which are preferential in the receivership;

(iv) the principal and interest secured by the floating charge;

(v) the company.

2 The company's free assets: (Section 175 of the 1986 Act):

(i) the costs of preserving and realising the assets;

(ii) the liquidator's remuneration and the proper costs and expenses of the winding up;

(iii) the debts which are preferential in the winding up;

(iv) the charge holder to the extent that the preferential debts have been paid out of assets subject to the floating charge;

(v) the general body of creditors.

[89] Each fund thus bears its own costs of administration, as one might expect; neither is required to bear the costs of administering the other; and in particular the assets comprised in the floating charge are not required to bear the costs and expenses of the winding up as well as those of the receivership.

Conclusion

[90] I would overrule *Barleycorn*, allow the appeal, set aside the orders made by the Court of Appeal, and substitute a declaration that none of the costs and expenses of winding up the company are payable out of the assets subject to the floating charge until the whole of the principal and interest charged thereon have been paid.

Appendix 11—Culpability of Professionals

Brokers and dealers who are involved in a fraud are also investigated. Being an accessory to a serious financial fraud means being guilty to conspiracy to defraud.

It is important to appreciate that the person who has committed the fraud may not be the only person against whom a remedy can be obtained. There may be other people involved in committing the crime.

By way of example, it may be more realistic and cost effective to commence proceedings against any broker or dealer involved in an advanced fee scam.

In the future, it may include certification authorities. Many countries and, notably, the European Union are looking to Certification authorities to verify the identity of e-traders by issuing digital certificates. There therefore may be scope for a claim against a Certification Authority that issues a certificate to a launderer.

Lawyers and accountants who have been involved in setting up any scheme may also be legitimate targets. My firm recently acted for the Claimants in an advanced fee fraud where the Defendants were a British Virgin Islands shell company operated by a Swedish national whom it appears was in jail in Norway for fraud and a UK shell Plc that was run by businessmen based in Pakistan and Birmingham. Neither was an attractive Defendant. However, the case of my clients was that they relied on statements made by the solicitor instructed by the UK shell Plc that their money would be safe. The solicitor's insurers settled out of Court rather that establish whether or not a duty of care existed to my clients in those circumstances.

More controversially, it may also include computer hardware and software companies who have left back doors in their systems which are then accessed by hackers or alternatively where a flaw in their product allows a virus to spread. Indeed, that allegation has specifically been made in respect of the recent Code Red virus. Whilst this is an untested area of the law it does seem that a victim of fraud may have a claim where it is known that launderers can short circuit a computer's security systems simply by accessing these back doors.

However, internet service providers are unlikely to be liable for electronic crimes committed through the services they offer unless they have actual knowledge of the crime. This is the gist behind the European proposals for an electronic commerce directive which also imposes no obligation on them to monitor information transmitted or stored on their network or to actively seek facts or circumstances indicating illegal activity.

Source: SFO

Appendix 12—Directors' Misrepresentation

R v Kirkup, Mitchell, Mason and Chapman [2004]

Five company executives were sentenced today at Leeds Crown Court having pleaded guilty to defrauding business victims of nearly £5 million in a worldwide advance fee fraud conducted through their Anglo American Group venture capital business based in West Yorkshire. They made false promises as to their ability to deliver finance projects mounting to US$24 billion. a

The sentencing details were:-Paul Mitchell (born 27/8/61)—3½ years' imprisonment, Richard Kirkup (born 9/7/44)—3½ years' imprisonment, Angela Mitchell (born 27/12/59)—2 years' imprisonment, Mark Mason (born 11/6/61)—Community service 120 hours, Victoria Chapman (born 22/4/66)—Community service 120 hours .

Anglo American Ventures Ltd was set up in early 1993 to assist busines,Chapman [2004]ses seeking start-up or "seed capital" and development capital. The defendants claimed both for themselves and for the company to have substantial expertise and success in the business of sourcing funding for commercial enterprises and that the company was established in its field. Anglo American advertised its service globally. A fee was required in advance to consider an application for capital. As time went by further fees were required from victims at different stages. However no venture capital was made available to any client within the five year trading period. The reality was that Anglo American neither had the expertise nor the ability to successfully fund or raise finance for projects. Nearly £5 million fee income had been generated for Anglo American. It was an advance fee fraud from the start.

The advertising prompted many thousands of potential applicants to ask for further details. Over 4,000 of them were subsequently sent "Offers of Support" by Anglo American with a fee request ranging between one to ten thousand pounds depending on the scale of the venture required to be evaluated. Collectively these requests would have generated £13 million. Not all took the bait, but about eleven hundred did, sending in over £1½m in application fees alone from 78 countries. Many went on to suffer further and more costly deceptions at later fee paying stages of their applications. Some would proceed as far as joint venture plans requiring greater fees. There were 317 proposed and agreed joint venture plans and 79 paid up plans. Usually expressed in US dollars, they represented projects totalling $24 billion. The reality was that Anglo American only ever managed to connect three clients to nothing more than a bank loan and other financial assistance amounting to around £100,000. This starkly illustrates the scale of the wild promises made by Anglo American.

Paul Mitchell and his wife Angela Mitchell, and Richard Kirkup were founding directors of Anglo American. Mark Mason, became a director at a later date. He knew Paul Mitchell and Richard Kirkup when the three had worked for the same life insurance company. Victoria Chapman had known Angella Mitchell when they both worked at an office interiors company. Chapman joined Anglo American as office manager, later becoming "assistant director". The company also employed staff in more junior positions who are not implicated in the fraud. The principals in the fraud were the Mitchells and Kirkup. Paul Mitchell was its architect. These three defendants were the most highly rewarded.

The original registered address for this imposingly named international finance operation was 9 Moor Knoll Drive, a modest house in East Ardsley, West Yorkshire. It was the home of the Mitchells. However the corporate stationery was modified to show the address as "Unit 9, Moor Knoll Drive". This was to give the impression of trading from offices on a business park. To add to the illusion of a global operation, company letterheads were adorned with the names of foreign cities "Los Angeles-New York-Hong Kong-Johannesburg-Geneva" to suggest offices and connections throughout the world. It was a fiction. There was no global presence.

Anglo American moved to office premises at Langham House, 140-148 Westgate in Wakefield in 1994 and later to a prestige location in Bond Terrace, Wakefield. They also used a Mayfair accommodation address to which potential victims would be invited to conduct business.

Anglo American Group Plc was created as the holding company for "Ventures" and also for a similar operation called Spiredale Ltd, but it was "Ventures" that brought in the bulk of the fees. (The Group Plc was not a stock exchange listed company).

The defendants made false claims about their credentials and the company's operations in their communications with clients. Paul Mitchell styled himself as an investment banker. Angela Mitchell and Richard Kirkup made similar false or inflated claims about their expertise. They projected themselves as top-flight business professionals. The clear intention behind this facade was to convince potential clients that Anglo American was an introducer to loan facilities of some substance and experience. Correspondence would cite claims of a team with over 20 years experience in funding projects world-wide. It was a fiction.

The company website, brochures, advertisements and its corporate video all carried the same illusion. Advertisements were placed in the Wall Street Journal, the European, The Times, the Financial Times and other significant business newspapers. The company website also drew in a lot of the income. The promotional video typifies the intended illusion. It included pictures of a power station with the caption "Location India-Financing a new power station—$150 million" to suggest it was an Anglo American assisted project. The power station neither had any connection with Anglo American; nor was it in India. It was the Drax power station in North Yorkshire.

Other video fictions include a $100 million coal mine in China, a $50 million timeshare and resort complex in Spain, a $27 million manufacturing plant in Southern Africa and a $10 million cellular phone project in Russia.

The Anglo American corporate brochure stated that the company had "successfully contracted joint venture projects totalling in excess of US$ 2 billion." Individual project requirements of up to $500 million were claimed to be deliverable. False career claims featured in the brochure for the Mitchells and for Kirkup. It also included a fabricated attestation from the company's (unidentified) solicitors and a bogus press release announcing a $50 million finance deal for production of edible oils in India, though no details were given for independent verification.

The brochure included a quotation from Shakespeare's play, Julius Caesar, to suggest the corporate ethos;

"There is a tide in the affairs of men, which taken at the flood, leads on to fortune; Omitted, all the voyage of their life is bound in shallows and miseries. On such a full sea we are now afloat; and we must take the current when it serves, or lose our ventures."

With promotional tools and messages such as these, the fraudsters pulled in £4.8 million.

Clients were attracted from across the world. Advance fees were taken for a wide variety of business ventures. One example is a $6 million scheme for four exclusive menswear shops marketing a French designer brand in prestige locations—Covent Garden or Sloane Street in London; Rue St Honore in Paris; Via della Spiga in Milan; Fifth Avenue or Madison Square in New York. Another example was a, $83 million basket of joint ventures through a broker in the Czech Republic. These were for a Rover car dealership, a shopping centre, a health clinic, a leasing business and a golf and hotel complex. Other examples further illustrate the diversity of the aspirant projects:-Tourism projects in Austria; Mineral water production in Italy;Renovation of merchant ships in Greece; Powerboat business in the UK; Stud farms in France, Financial restructuring of a company in Portugal; Tour operator in the USA; and a Ford car dealership in Brazil.

No project seemed to be too big or diverse for them to accept a fee. Their claim was that they had the right contacts for whatever the business.

This case is a classic example of advance fee hurdles; each jump either pulling in additional fees or making the applicants cut their losses and withdraw. Many applicants were referred to organisations listed in a published venture capital handbook who usually advised that that the venture was not practical. This therefore was a fruitless route for the applicants, most of whom had already explored the usual sources of loans. It was hardly the service expected of a supposedly well placed and experienced operation. Anglo American had no special contacts and no influence in the venture capital sector. Of the thousands of clients they attracted, only three received any financial assistance, one of which was a bank loan that could have been acquired through routine banking channels. These "successes" amounted to not much more than £100,000. Conversely, there were many more examples of applicants being passed on to other so-called venture capital introducers in other countries who were known to the defendants and who also sought up-front fees from the applicants.

By the time the business ceased to trade in 1998, £4.8 million in income had been dishonestly obtained over the five-year trading period. Yet, despite the level of revenue, it had few assets. Pre-tax profits were negligible. The defendants rewarded themselves handsomely. They sucked cash out of the business in the form of salaries, dividends and benefits, first class travel, a plush office and high quality motor cars. (Jaguar, Bentley, Porsche, BMW, Lotus and Aston Martin with private number plates AAG—for Anglo American Group, the holding company). When the business traded at a loss in 1997 they still continued to misuse the fee income.

Together, the Mitchels officially gained over £400,000 (plus company benefits and facilities). Kirkup gained over £200,000. Secretly, they shared £1 million siphoned off over the period of trading which they put in an Isle of Man bank account. This was concealed from the auditors, their own accounting staff, the Registrar of Companies and the Inland Revenue. False sets of accounts were filed on behalf of the company. Mason and Chapman were not found to have benefited from the secret £1 million, but they enjoyed good salaries, commissions and cars. The creation of Anglo American was found on one goal. It had been set up and operated from the start as a fraud for the benefit of the Mitchells and Kirkup and later also for Chapman and Mason who enhanced their earnings as turnover increased, knowing it to be a dishonest enterprise.

The Department of Trade & Industry received complaints from victims and commenced an investigation in October 1997. A court order shut down Anglo American in May 1998. The DTI had already alerted the SFO who launched an investigation in March 1998, jointly conducted with officers from the West Yorkshire Police fraud squad. On the 9th and 10th of that month, search warrants were executed at Anglo American's offices and the homes of the Mitchells and Kirkup. As an illustration of the reach of the fraud, investigations were conducted in seventeen jurisdictions by invoking mutual legal assistance arrangements and involving the cooperation of Interpol and many other overseas police forces.

All five defendants were charged in March 2002 with two counts of fraudulent trading in respect of Anglo American Group Plc and its "Ventures" subsidiary. A trial was scheduled for Leeds Crown Court on 26 January 2004, but just ahead of the opening the Mitchells pleaded guilty. The remaining three defendants considered their positions and by 10 February, changed their pleas. Kirkup admitted to the fraudulent trading charge. Chapman and Mason pleaded guilty not to fraudulent trading but to substantive counts of obtaining money by deception added by way of amendment to the indictment. Consequently, no trial accrued.

In passing sentences, HHJ Shaun Spencer QC said, "In terms of an example of greed, this case takes some beating". He commended the SFO and the West Yorkshire Police for the conduct of the investigation and the preparation of the case, citing in particular, officers DS Phil Hirst and DC Steve Butler and SFO case secretary Keith

Source: The Serious Fraud Office.

Appendix 13—Directors Use of Company Funds

Stephen Jupe was sentenced today at Southwark Crown Court to 5 years' imprisonment for defrauding investors and creditors through his £4 million turnover investment scheme in bonded single malt whisky and champagne

Stephen Jupe set up Securitised Syndicated Investments Ltd ("SSI") in 1992. It traded as Marshall Wineries, offering investments to the general public in young single malt scotch whisky to be held in bond until maturity under his label Grandtully Single Malt Whisky. He also marketed investment opportunities in champagne. Jupe was the controller of the business. He devised the marketing strategy, he dealt with the whisky and the champagne suppliers, he hired and instructed the staff and he controlled the finances.

The activities of the company and the director's use of company funds came under DTI scrutiny and the business was closed down in November 1996. Jupe attempted to resurrect the business through the creation of a "phoenix" company using a similar name so as to disguise from suppliers and clients that anything was wrong. Investors and creditors were victims.

Suspected fraud was referred to the Serious Fraud Office. Jupe was charged in 2002 with fraudulent trading contrary to section 458 of the Companies Act 1985 and with using a prohibited company name contrary to section 216(4) of the Insolvency Act 1986. He was tried at Southwark Crown Court commencing 2 February 2004 and was found guilty on 23 April.

Justice Stewart sentenced Jupe to 5 years' imprisonment.

Soursce: SFO

Appendix 14—Disqualification of Directors

(3½ year sentence for Roddam Twiss in $2 million "humanitarian causes" fraud.)

Roddam Twiss was sentenced today at Southwark Crown Court to 3 ½ years' imprisonment for conspiracy to steal 2.2 million US dollars in a high yield investment scheme. He was banned from acting as a company director for 7 years and has been ordered to pay confiscation of some £89,000

Roddam Twiss was chief executive of the Dragon Group which included The Grosvenor Trust, Grosvenor Ventures Inc and Asset Management Associates. The Grosvenor Trust promoted claims of providing assistance for humanitarian causes through exclusive investment schemes with promises of "high profits". Twiss claimed to have the involvement of prominent figures in the City and public life as trustees to administer the Grosvenor Trust. Using his family background to gain introductions and make contacts, Twiss solicited monies from private investors and consortiums that had substantial sums of money at their disposal.

Suspicion arose amongst investors by the summer of 1998 when funds had not yet been transferred to the appropriate investment schemes. Twiss and his associate Coury had instead transferred money to a law firm in France and then to an account set up by Coury and to Twiss' personal account in London. Twiss was estimated to have benefited almost £540,000. (Coury was alleged to have laundered the remainder through Switzerland to the Lebanon where he resides). To avoid suspicion falling on him, Twiss reported Coury to the Metropolitan Police with allegations of fraud.

The suspected fraud was referred to the Serious Fraud Office in 1999. Twiss was charged in June 2001 with theft, conspiracy to defraud and conspiracy to steal. (A warrant was issued for the arrest of Coury). A trial date for Twiss alone was set for September 2002 but was postponed for court administrative reasons. Coury was arrested in Switzerland in early 2003 and there was a further postponement to allow for Twiss and Coury to be tried together. However Coury's health deteriorated whilst in extradition custody in Switzerland and after he was returned to face trial . On 18 December 2003, the SFO took the decision, on medical advice, that Coury could not be tried on health grounds.

The trial of Twiss proceeded at Southwark Crown Court commencing 20 May 2004. He was found guilty on 27 July (See note 1 below).

In passing sentence, the HHJ Wadsworth said that Twiss "had shown no remorse or regret" for his actions and that a 5-year sentence could have applied but he took into account that Twiss though "an able and willing partner" had played a "role second to Coury ". He also took into consideration the time taken for the conclusion of proceedings and Twiss' age (64).

The sentence was 3 ½ years of which half is to be served and the remainder on release under licence. Twiss was also banned from acting as a company director for 7 years and ordered to pay a confiscation order of £89,087.

Appendix 15—Professionals as Fraudsters

(Quantity Surveyor and Chartered Architect)

The principal offender convicted for defrauding a Dorset charitable trust has today had his original three-year prison sentence judged to be unduly lenient and increased to six years. Sentences of two other offenders remain unchanged. In separate proceedings all three offenders in this case have been ordered to pay £1½ million compensation and costs.

At the recommendation of the Serious Fraud Office, the Attorney General referred the sentences of the three offenders in this case to the Court of Appeal as being unduly lenient. The appeal hearing opened today at the Royal Courts of Justice. The appeal judges ruled in favour of the appellant in relation to the offender Guy Pound and his original sentence was quashed and a new sentence handed down. The sentences of Anthony Green and Peter Beard remain unchanged.

Three construction industry professionals were convicted on 16 February 2004 for defrauding the Talbot Village Trust in Dorset of £3 ½ million through **manipulation of building contracts by invoicing for building work not done** and disguising inflated professional fees in the contracts.

Guy Peter Pound, **an architect,** was sentenced on 19 April 2004 to three years' imprisonment. He was described as the dominant conspirator in this fraud who exercised considerable influence over the other conspirators. His original sentence has been quashed and a new sentence of six years' imprisonment has been imposed.

Anthony Erskine Green, **a quantity surveyor,** was sentenced on 26 March 2004 to 9 months' imprisonment suspended for 12 months. Today's judgement was to leave the original sentence stand.

Peter Russell Beard, **a quantity surveyor,** was sentenced on 26 March 2004 to 9 months' imprisonment suspended for 12 months. Today's judgement was to leave the original sentence stand.

Attorney General Lord Goldsmith said, "Major fraud is a serious offence which can have long term impact on its victims. The decision by the Court of Appeal today has given a clear indication that those who orchestrate these offences can expect substantial penalties. Victims, witnesses and the wider public can have confidence that the criminal justice system will impose sentences that reflect the gravity of the offences and their effect on individuals and society."

Court orders made on the defendants to pay compensation to the Talbot Village Trust and to repay costs to the Legal Services Commission amount to around £1½ million. This follows the conclusion of confiscation proceedings against all three defendants heard at Southampton Crown Court. The specific outcomes were that on 9 August 2004, Anthony Green was ordered to pay £168,871 as compensation and Peter Beard to pay £171,584. Each was also ordered to repay £150,000 defence costs. On 4 October 2004, Guy Pound was ordered to pay compensation of £860,280 (or be sentenced to an additional two years' imprisonment in default).

Appendix 16—Solicitors' Fraud in Probate Cases

(Example of Lawyers' dishonesty and Fraud)

Beneficiaries are being swindled out of millions of pounds by trusted advisers. DISHONEST solicitors and legal advisers are plundering the wills of elderly people and swindling the rightful beneficiaries. The Royal National Institute for the Blind (RNIB), which has been a victim of probate fraud, estimates that it costs £150m a year.

Tim Stone, head of legal services at the RNIB, said: "The perpetrators tend to be very skilled and most people are not even aware of it."

Probate fraud is often committed by solicitors and other legal advisers who are appointed to wind up an estate. They have access to all the deceased's property and paperwork.

Probate fraud is a big problem. There is no control over solicitors when they are drawing up a will or administering an estate. The means of deception are varied and frequently ingenious. They include bogus wills, mythical credit-card bills and hidden bank accounts. And the sums involved can be huge. Nicholas Furr and Paul Flint, who ran Legacies (Will & Probate Services) in Brentwood, Essex, "misapplied" more than £4m in funds from the families of the recently deceased. The pair were not solicitors but provided will-writing services and administered estates. Since the crime was discovered the firm has gone bust and only £200,000 has so far been returned. The two men are banned from running a company for 11 years and their case may be taken up by the Serious Fraud Office.

Fiddling the accounts or stealing from the home is extremely easy, as the RNIB knows all too well. When Evelyn Hudson died, her will stated that her estate should be left to the charity. The RNIB duly received the estate accounts from a firm of solicitors, Sparrow & Sparrow, based in Bognor Regis. The accounts showed Hudson had credit-card bills of £14,039 when she died, and outstanding nursing-home charges of £7,943. These would all need to be paid by the estate before the rest of the money could be handed over.

The RNIB was surprised by the scale of the bills because it knew that Hudson was in her eighties when she died. It made some inquiries and discovered that she had never owned any credit cards; nor did she have any outstanding nursing-home bills. The estate administrator who had drawn up the accounts had invented the bills and tried to pocket the £21,982.

In another case, **a solicitor failed to mention the deceased's Swiss bank account worth £34,000. And one lawyer charged £45,000 in fees to wind up an estate when he should have billed for only £3,000.** It is not only solicitors who commit fraud. Neighbours, carers, rogue tradesmen and even family are also guilty. Probate issues hit the headlines earlier this month when (edited 10 Apr 2005) was taken to court by her three stepchildren after they were cut out of their father's will seven weeks before he died.

The transfer of large sums of money or property, or the disappearance of valuable items are cause for alarm.. Other warning signs are the inclusion of someone else's name on a bank account, the sudden involvement of a relative who takes over the management of the person's finances but leaves bills unpaid, or a person who is anxious and confused about his or her finances.

It is particularly easy for someone who has been granted enduring power of attorney (EPA) to commit fraud. EPA is given by an elderly person to a solicitor, family member or friend, and grants the executor complete control over his or her financial affairs and property, either now or in the future.

Source: *Times Newspapers* 2004, July 25.

Appendix 17—More Solicitors as Fraudsters

Twenty two solicitors convicted in legal aid fraud.

Some staff at Robinsons Solicitors, a law firm in Cheltenham, UK, were convicted of defrauding the legal aid system.

The SFO secured ten convictions in 2001, including principal partner Tim Robinson who was sentenced to seven years imprisonment and ordered to pay £½ million as confiscation. In phase 2, twelve other convictions have been secured by the Crown Prosecution Service.

This is about a fraud conducted between March 1989 and January 1995 where 29 members of Robinsons the solicitors' practice were charged with fraud on the legal aid system. Eleven defendants were prosecuted by the Serious Fraud Office, of which ten were convicted and one not proceeded against. The remaining defendants were dealt with by the Crown Prosecution Service.

The conspirators at Robinsons Solicitors systematically defrauded the then Legal Aid Board now the Legal Services Commission, by dishonestly claiming from the legal aid fund for work not in fact done.

Robinsons "the firm" specialised in criminal law, with branches at various times in Cheltenham, Gloucester, Bristol and Swindon. Cheltenham was at all times the headquarters of the firm and from where Tim Robinson, who was the managing partner, controlled the business which he founded in 1972. By 1994 the firm employed around 80 people. The fraudulent operation came to light when one of the fee-earning staff reported the malpractice to the Legal Aid Board. The Gloucestershire Constabulary fraud squad conducted an initial inquiry and in June 1994 a report was made to the SFO and a joint investigation soon followed. As the investigation proceeded, it was decided in 1997 to split the case in two. The SFO concentrated on the 11 conspirators based at the firm's head office in Cheltenham, which included Tim Robinson, and the CPS proceeded against the defendants who operated from other branches of the firm. The Gloucestershire Constabulary was the principal police force involved throughout. Officers from the Avon & Somerset police and the Wiltshire police also contributed to the investigation. The trials took place at Bristol Crown Court, heard by HHJ Smith QC. Counsel representing the SFO were Ian Glen QC, Timothy Spencer and Andrew MacFarlane.

Over a period of years, members of the firm perpetrated a fraud by manipulation of the Legal Aid Board's Green Form claims scheme whereby solicitors applied to the Board for payment for certain legal services they provided to their clients. The Board was systematically defrauded by working methods that were devised by Tim Robinson.

The structure devised was that solicitors within the firm fulfilled the role of advocates at the Magistrates Courts. They also attended at police stations occasionally, but this role was normally undertaken by the firm's law clerks. Thus the solicitors were largely "freed" from administrative functions and had relatively little contact with clients. The vital engines of the firm—and the fraud—were the clerks. It was they who frequently attended at the police stations and communicated with clients and "prepared" cases. The chief clerks were vital participants. They were appointed by Robinson and enjoyed a close relationship with him. They supervised the other clerks and liased with Robinson about the number of chargeable hours the firm's employees were producing.

Each clerk, as a fee earner, would complete a daily time sheet which listed the legal aid files worked on that day together: time spent on attendance at police stations and the completed Green Forms were all recorded. The Green Forms and the Police Station Easy Entry Forms, were attached to the time sheets, all of which were then batched up for submitting to the Legal Aid Board on a daily basis. The Green Forms and Police Station Easy Entry Forms needed to be completed to ensure that the firm would be paid, they included name of the client and the type of advice given. Weekly compilation sheets of the hours worked and Green Forms completed were sent to the firm's partners.

The clerks' basic pay was low; average £10,000. Chief clerks were paid around £15,000. For a 50-hour week the rate was less than £4 per hour, but the overtime rate was high, usually between £15 and £18 per hour. Therefore, overall the clerks' rewards were generous, including company cars, but this did require each clerk to claim vast amounts of chargeable overtime hours. Robinson had decreed that clerks could only claim the overtime rates on Green Form work. With billions of pounds spent on security systems, security software, personnel training and management consultants, implementing fraud policies, with changers upon changes, there is still billions of pounds lost each year in the United Kingdom through fraud, £45 Billion in 2003, by many reports.

Economic analysis of serious financial fraud finds that in general, such frauds occur because of large groups who supply illegal goods and profits and control prices also, competitive lobbying and corruption, easier access to markets. Punishment for fraud should be tougher on those who are more able at avoiding detection and punishment.

Appendix 18—Stop Press

Today there was an important published case decision particularly important to this work. It is the case <u>FEETUM and others v LEVY and others Court of Appeal, 21 Dec 2005.</u>

The appointment of administrative receivers by the holder of a floating charge on a company's property was invalid where the project which the company was involved with did not come under section 72E of the ENTERPRISE ACT 202. The court of Appeal dismissed the appeal of CABVISION LTD, granting Mr Feetum, Mr Marsden, Mr Smith, Mr Sharp and Mr Church, partners of Tower Taxi Technology LLP their request to make the administrators; powers void and invalid. Cabvision Ltd was set up to generate revenue from advertising on small screens installed in taxis. Tower Taxi Technology LLP was later set up by these men to raise investment in the project in order to increase the number of taxis with small screens to 10,000. They hoped to raise £90 million from a bank loan and from subscribers. Because the partners disagreed during the course of business, administrators were appointed but Lord Justice Parker disposed of the argument that *Foss v Harbottle* principle ruled.

The main reason was that the Project had no terms about "Step-in Rights" so no-one was entitled to step-in unless the partners themselves had sought administration. The project did not include step-in rights and so did not fall within except in section 72E Enterprise Act 2002, making the appointment of administrative receivers invalid.

This case is another example of bad drafting in the Enterprise
Act 2002, and has not been addressed by the Company Reform Bill. Some of the UK's legislation is woefully inadequate.

(Another example of bad drafting in the Enterprise Act enables the Office of Fair Trading to serve "STOP NOW" orders on con artists who swindle consumers but excludes businesses from protection from these con artists. Small businesses especially, do not have the resources to conduct background checks on persons or business partners. They often do not have the time to check their correspondence thoroughly and so they get caught by scams on them. Sadly it is these same businesses which do not usually have insurance against fraud perpetrated on them.

978-0-595-38135-7
0-595-38135-9

Printed in the United Kingdom
by Lightning Source UK Ltd.
108816UKS00001BA/3-34